Revisioning the DRE

Revisioning the DRE

DONALD G. EMLER

Religious Education Press
Birmingham, Alabama

Library of Congress Cataloging-in-Publication Data
Emler, Donald G.
  Revisioning the DRE/Donald G. Emler
  Includes bibliographies and index.
  ISBN 0-89135-071-3
  1. Directors of religious education.   I. Title.
BV1531.E45 1989   89-34050
268'.3—dc20   CIP

Religious Education Press, Inc.
5316 Meadow Brook Road
Birmingham, Alabama 35243
10 9 8 7 6 5 4 3 2

Religious Education Press publishes books exclusively in religious edu-cation and in areas closely related to religious education. It is commit-ted to enhancing and professionalizing religious education through the publication of serious, significant, and scholarly works.

PUBLISHER TO THE PROFESSION

To Suzanne
ONE WHO TEACHES BY EXAMPLE AS WELL AS BY PROFESSION

CONTENTS

Preface

This book seeks to create a dialogue between the theory base of religious education and the professional practice of the director of religious education (DRE) in local church settings. It grew from a concern that the academic preparation of professional educators should consider the actual task performance in the local church. I believe that professional roles should inform the academic community and that the academic community should assist in providing the theory base to guide the profession. This dialogue should enhance both the practice and the theory of religious education.

Part I of the book describes the theoretical framework or vision that guides religious education as a unique field. The choice of the generic religious education to describe the field is intentional as the field is broader than Christian religious education or Christian education, both of which indicate a subset of the larger field. Religious education is a blend of social-science perspectives in which organizational development, education, sociology, psychology, administration, and group dynamics are interactive, seeking to provide a holistic education for a learner in the context of religious faith. It includes more than the traditional Sunday school or CCD programs.

Part II explores the specific roles the DRE performs in the local church. These include administrator, program developer, educational consultant, teaching-learning specialist, researcher, diagnostician, evaluator, and faith interpreter. In terms of doing the DRE's regular job, none of these roles is more important than others, although some may be more time-consuming. While the DRE must be capable of using the latest biblical or theological resources in the content of teaching as a teaching-learning expert, the other skills must be developed for effective leadership in the church.

Central to the book is the assumption that the DRE is a professional religious educator who offers a specific body of knowledge to the church. In that professional competence, the DRE is a specialist in contrast to the clergy who are trained to be generalists. The book grew from my own twenty-five years of experience as a certified minister of religious education and service to several churches ranging in size from eighty-three members to nearly 2,000 members. In addition, during the past thirteen years while on the faculty of Centenary College of Louisiana I have maintained my involvement in local church religious education as a regular adult Sunday school teacher and used part of my sabbatical to participate in the children's summer religious education programs of Noel United Methodist Church, Shreveport.

A second assumption is that the church must enable its lay members to become theologically literate in several theological perspectives. There are many theological positions, for example, neo-orthodoxy, fundamentalism, process, liberation, and so forth. Through the religious educational programs of the church the laity must be enabled to understand the basic propositions of these theologies. In addition, mainline Christianity must begin to provide access to a theological perspective that speaks to a scientific understanding of multiple universes in which time and space are relative if it wishes to reduce the exits of its more liberal middle-adult and young-adult members.

A third assumption is that there is a need for more education to be provided to prospective DREs. A public school principal must have both undergraduate and graduate training in the same field. With the diversity of roles related to both the content and the practice of religious education as outlined in the book, the DRE would be well served to have both an undergraduate major in religious education and then a masters in religious education.

This must be a joint adventure on the part of the denominational colleges and the seminaries blending both the content areas and the technical and human relations skills.

Over the years my thinking in these areas has been stimulated by dialogues with collegues in the United Methodist Association of Professors of Christian Education (UMAPCE) and in the Association of Professors and Researchers in Religious Education (APRRE). This stimulation has been at the personal level, through consulting with Allen Moore and Howard Grimes on the academic boundaries of the field, through reading the books by and discussing with Maria Harris and Dorothy Jean Furnish the specific profession of the DRE, and the mentoring of Grant Shockley who has guided many of us in the field.

As I have been writing this material, I am convinced that our institutions shape our identity and our perceptions. I was surprised to learn that few Protestant writers prior to 1975 quoted Roman Catholic authors and visa versa. This is sad as we face many of the same issues and hold many similar values. We are impoverished by failing to learn from each other. Often the separation is due to way that books are advertized in catalogues. Catalogues usually come from specific publishers with only their material highlighted, so that we seldom see what is in a general field. We must accept the challenge to seek out the writings of collegues in the broad field.

I am grateful to James Michael Lee who invited me to write this book based on a paper originally presented to APRRE. As editor he has challenged my thinking as well as my writing in many helpful ways.

I am grateful to Centenary College where students and faculty have challenged and stimulated my ideas. Special appreciation is expressed to Dean Dorothy Gwin for providing a faculty study grant that enabled me to begin serious writing and a later sabbatical to complete the manuscript. I appreciate the assistance of Ella Edwards in the initial stages of research, as well as the feedback from students who used the manuscript and made suggestions for its improvement. The Louisiana Chapter of the Christian Educators Fellowship under the leadership of Doris Marsallis provided opportunity to test the ideas in the manuscript with professionals currently serving in the field. Particular appreciation is expressed to Robert Ed Taylor whose wise companionship has provided encouragement through the years.

My deepest gratitude is expressed to my wife, Suzanne, and my children, Matthew and David. They have been extremely supportive, often encouraging me when I was ready to quit. Suzanne regularly provided me with deeper insights into educational ideas and was patient with my long hours at the computer. David and Matthew represent the emerging church with its questions of meaning in a post-Einstein universe. Because of other children like Matthew and David, I hope this book will contribute to the professional practice of many DREs who serve faithfully and who are seeking a deeper understanding of some of the ways to perform their ministry in religious education.

Part I

Revisioning the Basic Framework

Chapter 1

Vision and Practice — An Interactive Relationship

"No one will live all his life in the world into which he was born, and no one will die in the world in which he worked in his maturity."[1] —Margaret Mead

Both the field of religious education and the professional practice of the director of religious education are in the midst of trying to determine an appropriate vision for the future. Currently there is disunity regarding the primary theoretical approach appropriate to religious education as well as the appropriate institution for the preparation of the future professionals.

The title for the field and of the persons professionally employed in the field is unclear. Should the field be called "religious education" or "Christian education" (or "Jewish or Islamic education")?[2] What does it mean to use the title "Director of Religious/Christian Education" in contrast to "Program Director" or "Coordinator of Lay Ministries," and so forth? At the ecumenical level, the term religious education appears to be most inclusive. The term can be used to refer to a larger number of traditions than the narrower "Christian education."

Are the employed practitioners members of a craft or a profession? The requirements for professional certification are divergent, with different levels of certification and emphasis on educational level in each religious body. There is no uniform job description or evaluation procedure for religious educators employed in a common agency such as the local church of a specific denomination, let alone uniform description across religious lines.

Even the principal location and clientele for the practice of religious education is debated. Traditional clients have been children and youth in Sunday school or CCD programs, in religious private schools, and more recently in adult study groups. Another clientele includes the academic setting in the diversity of a public university, a denominational theological seminary, or a religion department in an undergraduate college. Some suggest the real arena for religious education is the general public, as found in liberation traditions.[3]

Focus on the Professional DRE

This book is about the roles of the professional educator who is employed by a local church. Although a church may give a person it hires almost any label it desires on its letterhead, this book will use the title Director of Religious Education (DRE) to designate the professional nonclergy person charged to lead the local church's educational ministry. The DRE has met the basic qualifications set by the denomination for educational certification at its highest professional level. Religious education will be used as a generic term to describe the arena of ministry served by the professional.

I recognize that the functional roles of the DRE can also apply to the ordained minister of education who also serves as an educational specialist. Notwithstanding, my focus specifically on the DRE is intended to provide a clean and realistic vision of the primary professional. I also recognize that many local churches do not require their educational minister to be a professionally equipped individual and that most churches will have the pattern of one cleric who shares the ministry with the laity of that congregation.

This book will focus on the professional educator rather than on the specific definition and development of the academic field. Allen J. Moore claims that the academic field of religious education is distinct from the profession.[4] He distinguished between the thrust of the seminary and the thrust of the local church. The separation of the academic field from professional practice seems reasonable from the point of view of both theory development and mode of practice. However, Moore's distinction breaks down when one more closely analyzes the work of the religious educator in the local church. This person is a professional precisely because he or she combines a knowledge of basic religious education theory learned in the seminary or graduate school with practical skills to make these theories operative in the here-and-now setting. In this sense the DRE is a more complete religious educator than the professor in the seminary or graduate school. The DRE combines theory and practice, while the religious education professor typically lacks enfleshment in the practical order.

Craft vs. Guild

There is an urgent need to clarify whether the role of the DRE is a craft or a profession. A central issue is the fact that many churches hire their religious educators directly out of the congregation. These persons usually lack requisite professional preparation in religious education. A common description of a craft is that it performs customary duties that are modified by trial and error rather than operating out of a comprehensive theoretical base. This description fits most educational assistants who lack a college or seminary degree in religious education. Sad to say, this description usually fits associate pastors who are assigned religious education duties but have taken few if any professional courses in educational ministry.

A profession, on the other hand, has a body of knowledge or theory that systematically guides practice. The professional, therefore, is a person who consciously grounds practice in theoretical analysis and conclusions. Theory is both descriptive and prescriptive. It both defines the practice and provides workable guidelines for the successful enactment leading the practice. When based on appropriate research, theory enables the profession to predict the outcome of specific actions. Good theory interacts reflectively with practice to create new theory and to expand the theory.[5]

An example in public education would be the contrast of a professional teacher and a teacher's aide. Both persons may be skilled in relating to the students, and may be able to effectively help the student gain skills in reading, mathematics, and so forth. However, the teacher should be able to tell the observer why an action is chosen based on theory and what its predictable outcome is. The aide may be able to perform the activity but is not responsible for the theory base. As a result, the aide operates on a hit-or-miss basis. In order to develop a vision of the profession, then, one needs to have both a theory base and an understanding of that theory.

Historical Background

One way to understand a profession is to be familiar with some of its history. The history of the Protestant director of religious education begins near the start of the twentieth century while the Roman Catholic directors or parish coordinators of education begin their history in the mid-1960s as part of the developments related to Vatican II.

Protestant Historical Background

Conflicts and Changes

In the early part of the twentieth century several factors were emerging both in society and in Protestantism which would change the models of Protestant Christian education. These included technological changes, such as the automobile, lightbulb, telephone, wireless (radio), immigration, temperance crusade, the feminist movement, and the initial migration from the rural to urban areas of America.[6] The Sunday school had been the dominant method of nineteenth-century Protestant Christian education. It was primarily a lay volunteer institution with an evangelistic orientation in a rural society.[7] Following World War I, as society began to migrate en masse to the urban city, the Sunday school lost its support base in the revival movement. Criticism was raised that the Sunday school had become the transmitter of white, middle-class values. Empirical social science investigated the traditional Sunday school and reported its failure to achieve its goal of the character development of its students. The old emphasis on conversion and Bible study was replaced in the mainstream denominational literature with the new focus on nurturing the child.[8]

The Sunday school had modeled itself on the public school. However, at the turn of the century, John Dewey's concepts of progressive education were influencing public education, and through the efforts of William Rainey Harper, president of Chicago University, and George Albert Coe, professor of philosophy of religion at Northwestern University, Dewey's ideas found popularity in the newly formed Religious Education Association. Added to progressive education was the emergence of psychology as a science which was quickly adapted into educational psychology.[9]

Theological Conflict: Modernism vs. Fundamentalism

In the theological arena, the Protestant church was facing a deep split between the modernists and the fundamentalists. During the nineteenth century several factors developed that caused the split. In the early part of the century, geological studies found that the creation story in Genesis was unscientific. In the middle of the century, Charles Darwin (1809-1882) presented his studies in biological evolution.[10] At the same time, American seminaries were discovering the work of German liberal theologians such as Friedrich Schleiermacher (1768-1834) and biblical scholars such as Julius Wellhausen (1844-1918).[11]

As the twentieth century began, three significant broad clusters of Protestantism emerged. These clusters cut across denominational lines. These clusters were: 1) the modernist or liberal clusters; 2) the fundamentalists, some of whom later split off and become the modern evangelical movement; 3) the holiness movement (leading to pentecostal clusters) founded in 1906 at the Azusa Street Mission in Los Angeles. This movement was grounded in nineteenth-century Methodistic-pietism, in pentecostalism (baptism of the Holy Spirit and glossolalia), and in fundamentalist doctrinal principles as central to their identity.[12]

The Response of Fundamentalism

The development of high-level scholarship in both biblical studies and in natural science challenged many conservative Protestants so deeply that these persons sponsored in the late 1800s and early 1900s a series of Bible conferences. The purpose was to refute the liberal biblical scholarship such as Wellhausen's "J, E, D, P, Document Hypothesis" of Genesis, as well as other liberal theological ideas.

The climax came in 1895 at a Bible conference held at Niagara Falls, New York, which formulated the "five points of fundamentalism" which became the normative statement for Protestant evangelicals. Between 1910 and 1915 a series of pamphlets written by Princeton Seminary professors Charles Hodge, B.B. Warfield, and others called *The Fundamentals: A Testimony to the Truth* were published and distributed by two California laymen, Layman and Milton Stewart.[13] In 1910, the Presbyterian Church in the U.S.A. made acceptance of the fundamentals a requirement for ordination.

Reacting to the emerging sophisticated studies in Bible and in natural science, Protestant fundamentalists rejected science and the scientific method as being godless. The fundamentals included the required beliefs in the verbal inspiration and absolute inerrancy of the Bible (since modified to mean only the original documents), the virgin birth and deity (including the miracles) of Jesus Christ, the substitutionary theory of the atonement, the bodily resurrection of Jesus, and the imminent corporeal return of Christ to earth (the second coming). These became the source of the fundamentalist doctrines elaborated in early twentieth-century evangelicalism.

The Modernist/Liberal Response

The liberals or modernists, as the name implies, embraced the new liberal ideas of natural science and biblical scholarship. It was the liberal methods of biblical scholarship and inquiry that gave need for a new kind of professional leader, namely the religious educator. The new content and methodology of religious education needed someone who could teach the local church Sunday school teachers.

The Religious Education Association Is Started

The importance of the progressive educational philosophy can be seen in William Rainey Harper's convening of the first Religious Education Association Convention in 1903.[14] Harper was concerned that there was no correlation of history, literature, and the sciences in religious or moral instruction. Second, Harper took issue with the decision of the Sunday school's International Uniform Lessons that rejected the new biblical scholarship and the new educational psychology. He called for a revision of the Uniform Lesson Series based on consideration of the "stages of mental, moral, and spiritual growth of the individuals." Third, Harper urged that the new methods of psychology and other sciences be applied to the other agencies of religious instruction, such as the home and the day school in order to assist in the "right education of the young in religion and morals." Finally, Harper called for the organization of a new professional group that would improve religious and moral instruction. The new group would use liberal biblical scholarship, educational psychology, and other features of progressive education learning theory.

The people responding to the call in 1903 were primarily seminary or university leaders and paid Sunday school superintendents. Of the 1259 charter members of the REA, none had the title of Director of Religious Education.[15] By 1909 several persons had been employed in large churches with the title.

Liberalism and Early DREs

In the early decades of the profession, religious education directors tended to identify with liberal theology, the social gospel movement, and progressive education. Washington Gladden, a major leader of the social gospel movement, spoke to the 1908 REA convention identifying religious education with character education and with morality education. He proclaimed the urgency of getting people to accept the teachings of Jesus (i.e., the ethics of the Sermon on the Mount) so that "all our troubles, national and international, would soon be at an end." Almost as if he were speaking to an audience today, he stated the public nature of religious education as he proclaimed the nation's need for "education in the principles of social justice."[16]

Early Religious Education Based in Progressive Education

The educational undergirding of the profession during its early years was that of progressive education. In 1930, Harry Munro, professor at Brite (College of the Bible) at Texas Christian University and a leader in the International Council of Religious Education, described the director as "a technically trained religious educator employed by a local church to have general charge of the educational aspects of its total program, and standing beside the minister as a professional member of the church staff."[17] The central arena of the religious educator in this early period was with children and youth, primarily in the form of character education.

Neo-orthodoxy Challenges Liberal Religious Education

The winds of change were blowing, however. These winds would cause the optimism of the liberal educational movement to crash along with the stock market. In 1928 Hugh Hartshorn and Mark May published their findings on character education (*Studies in Deceit*) revealing that people who were active in either the Sunday school or other forms of religious education were not any more moral than those who did not participate. Sunday school attendance could not be legitimately correlated with being moral. The fundamentalists condemned the study, while the liberals cried out for better educational methods.

In a 1934 article in *Religious Education*, "Let Religious Educators Reckon with the Barthians," H. Shelton Smith challenged many liberal theological assumptions with new insights from the Swiss neo-orthodox theologian Karl Barth.[18] Neo-orthodoxy had caused a restructuring of the liberal theological views including overthrowing the liberal view of God as immanent and replacing it with the conservative view that God is transcendent, the renewal of Christology as central, the placement of greater emphasis on the Bible as the word of God in a broad sense, and most importantly a change from viewing humanity as capable of personal renewal to viewing humanity as totally depraved. Sometimes called new-reformation theology, Calvin and Luther indeed had been rediscovered. The domination by the liberals was over.

Religious vs. Christian Education

The theological shift from liberalism to neo-orthodoxy involved the titles for the religious educational professional in the local church. Signifying the transition from the broad educational perspective to a narrower theological perspective was the change in director's title from Director of *Religious* Education to Director of *Christian* Education.[19]

As World War II broke out the battle was intense between the neo-orthodox and old liberal theological positions as the foundation both for Protestant religious education and as the prevailing theology of the educated clergy. By the end of the war, liberalism as an explicit theological position had lost most of the battles, although it continues today as a theological method.[20] As a theological method, liberalism seeks to be open to new truth, weighing evidence for new ideas while still being grounded in a core of Christian belief.[21] Although the religious educators would use progressive educational models, neo-orthodoxy would guide mainstream Protestant theology until the early 1960s. However, evangelical fundamentalism continued to remain the primary theological stance of the laity and indeed for a high percentage of Protestant clergy.

Theology Becomes the Base for Christian Education

In 1950 Randolph Crump Miller stated the clue to the church's educational ministry was theology; consequently, the appropriate title for the profession is *Christian* education.[22] "The purpose of Christian Education is to place God at the center and to bring the individual into the right relationship with God and his fellows within the perspective of the fundamental truths about all of life." Miller's influential slogan was, "Theology in the background: faith and grace in the foreground." Thus the task of Christian education is to discover a relevant theology and then by using the best educational methods derived from theology bring the learner into a right relationship to God.[23]

Miller also raised concern for the role of religious education in the seminary curriculum. He realistically understood it would not be part of the department of theology; however, the discipline needed to be more than a sub-department called Christian education, meaning only the Sunday school.[24] Christian education was more than methods based in an educational bag of tricks. Christian education is related to the comprehensive ministry of the church. Every pastor is called to teach the scriptures to the persons in their charge so that the people may learn the way to spiritual salvation. Therefore, each pastor must be grounded not only in theoretical theology but also be grounded in the practical ministry of communicating the gospel so that its meaning is revealed and experienced within the ongoing community of faith. However, the seminary failed to hear the importance of Christian education as called for by Miller and other theorists such as

D. Campbell Wyckoff and C. Ellis Nelson. While most seminaries had required courses in pastoral psychology, Christian education was dropped as a requirement for basic theological studies and many mainline Protestant seminaries eliminated their master's degree studies in religious education altogether.

At the same time many local church practitioners were working with comprehensive church education programs. The title for the principal religious educational activity at the local church level had changed for mainstream Protestants from Sunday school (identified with nineteenth-century fundamentalism), to church school, which was intended to mean the variety of programs found throughout the church's life. In 1972 C. Ellis Nelson suggested that church education was a more comprehensive term. "The general purpose of (church) education is the same as the purpose of the church, but the particular role of education is to foster deliberate efforts to help persons in the church develop a Christian mentality."[25] Ironically, in the mid-1980s most Protestant churches returned to the Sunday school title.

Nelson also underscored the breakdown of neo-orthodoxy as the theological position undergirding Christian education. He suggested that the role of the religious educator is primarily that of fostering theological inquiry with new interest on adult education rather than the familiar nurturing of children and youth. The new theologies included existential theology, process theology, and liberation theology along with the resurgence of pietism.[26]

Roman Catholic Religious Education

The role of the local church director of religious education in the Roman Catholic tradition is a fairly late development. The reason for this is simple: Until the mid-1960s, religious education was regarded as a primary province of the parochial school. The nonschool CCD program for children attending public schools was regarded as a stepchild of the parochial school at best.

Vatican II Changes Catholic Religious Education

As a result of the Second Vatican Council (1962-1965) all this changed. First, the religious view of Catholicism changed dramatically. The windows were opened up as suggested by Pope John XXIII and fresh air entered. Public education was no longer regarded by Catholics as inherently godless. Parochial schools were no longer on such a high pedestal. Second, many nuns left the convent to seek religious fulfillment in the lay life. Because the nuns heavily subsidized parochial schools by working for extraordinarily low wages, many Catholic schools closed down— parents often could not afford to pay lay teachers in Catholic schools a decent salary. The upshot of all this was the need to develop strong religious education programs which would take place outside parochial schools. The Catholic DRE was born.

Kerygmatic Movement Sets
Religious Education in Liturgy

New perceptions of religious education were emerging on the international scene and these began to influence American Roman Catholic practice. Most of these new perceptions came from Europe. Josef Jungmann, an Austrian Jesuit and theologian at the University of Innsbruck taught a kerygmatic approach to religious education, an approach centered in liturgy and the joyous proclamation of the Good News of salvation history.[27] Johannes Hofinger, a Jesuit from Austria's Tyrol and a devoted student of Jungmann at Innsbruck, popularized Jungmann's views in North America beginning in the late 1950s.[28] The new catechetical movement combined interest in doctrine, biblical study, and liturgics. It also made educational procedure a "handmaid of theology." The centrality of kerygma, the proclamation of salvation history, within the context of liturgy and the life of the Christian witness would find its primary location in the life of the parish worship setting rather than primarily in the parish school.

Reflecting the kerygmatic movement, Gerard Sloyan was a pioneer in American Roman Catholic religious education and liturgical renewal.[29] His articles on catechetics guided the church to new insights on the relationship of content and methods. He opposed the Baltimore Catechism because of its theological and pedagogical inadequacies.[30] His reasons included the failure to use the emerging biblical scholarship in the church and the failure to relate to the life situation of the learners. Sloyan, however, cautioned the church not to substitute Bible history for the real

Christ. He proclaimed that "Christian formation is mostly do-ing."[31]

Religious Education Serves All Age Levels

Vatican II encouraged Catholic parishes to build on new im-ages of family and People of God. Adults expressed new interest in serious religion studies. No longer could education be just a part of the parochial school for children and youth. Mary Perkins Ryan articulated the issue in her controversial book, *Are Parochi-al Schools the Answer?*[32] Those who served in parish religious education programs such as leaders in Confraternity of Christian Doctrine (CCD) recognized the need to enhance religious educa-tion opportunities and curricula across the age levels.

The newly employed parish coordinator of religious education focused on the total program of parish education, serving both families of children in the parish school as well as those who attended public school. Adult religious education courses for par-ents as well as the students preparing for the sacraments were developed, along with a full program of leader training to staff the new courses being offered.

A central feature of this new profession within Catholicism was the new identity of the coordinators or directors of education. In their teaching role about church doctrines, they both identified with the role of theologian, as well as being a friendly critic willing to challenge doctrines that did not resonate with the ex-periences of the people they served. Now a new group of profes-sionals were part of the church outside the official priesthood or a religious order who could offer exposure to the variety of thought in the best educational forms.

Charting a Vision to the Future

Since the late 1960s the trends in religious education have taken several directions. At one level a spirit of ecumenical inter-ests and resourcing has happened among various Protestant de-nominations, and also between Roman Catholics and Protes-tants, National organizations, such as the Religious Education Association and also the Association of Professors and Research-ers in Religious Education, have provided the forum for the exchange of ideas across traditional boundaries. Both Protestants and Roman Catholics at the local church level have sought to clarify what it means to be a professional religious educator. How should the role be related to ordination and/or religious orders? What are the duties of the local church professional educator in contrast to the pastor or the parochial school teacher? What level of training should be required for certification?

Many Theoretical Approaches Inform the Field

At the same time attempts have been to clarify what it means to be a professional religious educator, the field of religious education has been divided into many theoretical approaches. In the most widely accepted delineation of broad theoretical sweeps, Harold Burgess[33] describes four broad approaches that includes the historical "social-cultural approach" based in the pioneer work of early religious education leaders George Albert Coe, Sophia Lyon Fas, and William Clayton Bower. In addition Burgess lists a "traditional theological approach" which seeks to transmit an authoritative salvific message exemplified in evangelical-fundamentalism and conservative Catholicism, a broad "contemporary theological approach" reflecting the work of James Smart, Randolph Crump Miller, Iris Cully, and Gabriel Moran, and "the social science approach" based in the writings of James Michael Lee.

Organizing the representatives differently, Jack Seymour[34] describes five approaches. These include "Religious Instruction" based in the writings of James Michael Lee, "Faith Community," or catechesis using the writings of John Westerhoff, "Spiritual Development" found in the research of James Fowler, "Liberation Approach" represented by Malcolm Warford, and the "Interpretation Approach" illustrated by Thomas Groome. Other theoretical approaches are presented by James Loder[35] rooted in transformation, Gabriel Moran[36] based on revelation broadly considered, and Maria Harris[37] grounded loosely in aesthetics and feminism concerns. Robert Worley[38] finds his theory in organizational development and Mary Elizabeth Moore[39] has proposed a tradition-ing approach in which the historical tradition is reformed by its incarnation in the present group of persons, while simultaneously the present group of persons is transformed by historical tradition. The black experience[40] provides insights into still another broad approach to religious education.

It seems that the proliferation of approaches or theories of religious education is surpassed only by the diversity of theological interpretations. When theological neo-orthodoxy ceased to dominate the seminaries in the late 1960s, the new expressions of existential theology, hermeneutical theology, liberation theology, political theology, feminist theology, process theology, and so forth, began an especially acute competition for adherents.

Actual Job Descriptions vs. Academic Theories

A key concern today is the difference between the religious education theories being discussed both at the seminary/graduate school levels and in professional meetings and the real world of the actual job descriptions of the local church professional educator. Both the practice of the parish religious educator and the expectations of the local church should inform theory. Theory should also guide the general practical field. The *theory* of religious education and the *practice* of religious education in the local church should be interactive; neither should be developed without the other. We are at a time when there is a need for a clear vision of what is the profession of religious education in both Protestant and Catholic settings.

Criteria for an Authentic Vision

How can we evaluate an appropriate vision for the practice of the work of religious education by a director of religious education? Three characteristics of an authentic vision can be given. *First*, the vision should be appropriate to the practice. What are the realistic expectations of local churches as they hire professional religious educators? *Second*, an authentic vision should have the ability to explain, predict, and verify the practice. By their very nature, all professions are founded on theory or a body of knowledge that enables them to make judgments about actions that will bring predicted desired results. Professions have a body of knowledge that serves as their guiding base or vision. It is assumed that the director of religious education seeks to be a professional. *Third*, the vision should enrich the practice of the profession. The vision serves to give a self-identity to its members. It provides a set of ideals that both form a criteria for excellence in action and the goal of future efforts. An authentic vision is one that is open rather than closed. Its nature is to be evolving by intention. It has the power to flow from the practice as well as be corrected by the practice.

The basic problem today in religious education is what is the authentic vision for the field of religious education in general and for the director of religious education in particular. Historically, the options have been primarily in either education or in theology. There are contending groups representing each of these areas today in the academic and professional arenas.

The following chapters will look at potential visions in the theological framework and from the educational framework in order to evaluate their assumptions and insights. The goal is to propose a vision that considers the practice of the profession as its basis.

NOTES

1. Margaret Mead, "Thinking Ahead," *Harvard Business Review* 36 (November-December 1958), p. 34.

2. The titles of chapters describing the profession by Dorothy Jean Furnish, "The Profession of Director or Minister of Christian Education in Protestant Churches" and Maria Harris, "U.S. Directors of Religious Education in Roman Catholic Parishes," in *Changing Patterns of Religious Education,* ed. Marvin J. Taylor (Nashville: Abingdon, 1984) illustrate this contrast.

3. John Elias, "The Three Publics of Religious Educators," *Religious Education* 77:6 (November-December 1982), pp. 615-627.

4. Allen J. Moore, "Religious Education as a Discipline," in *Changing Patterns of Religious Education.*

5. James Michael Lee, "The Authentic Source of Religious Instruction," in *Religious Education and Theology,* ed. Norma H. Thompson (Birmingham, Ala.: Religious Education Press, 1982), pp. 117-119.

6. Clifton E. Olmstead, *History of Religion in the United States* (Englewood Cliffs, N.J.: Prentice-Hall, 1960), pp. 461-465.

7. Robert W. Lynn and Elliott Wright, *The Big Little School,* 2nd ed., (Birmingham, Ala.: Religious Education Press, 1980), pp. 117-145.

8. See Jack L. Seymour, *From Sunday School to Church School:*

Continuities in Protestant Church Education in the United States, 1860-1929 (Washington, D.C.: University Press of America, 1982); Dorothy Jean Furnish, *DRE/DCE—The History of the Profession* (Nashville: Christian Educators Fellowship of the United Methodist Church, 1976).

9. Stephen A. Schmidt, *A History of the Religious Education Association* (Birmingham, Ala.: Religious Education Press, 1983), pp. 11-21.

10. Frederick A. Norwood, *The Development of Modern Christianity* (Nashville: Abingdon, 1956), pp. 196-197.

11. Ibid., pp. 154-155.

12. George M. Marsden, "From Fundamentalism to Evangelicalism: A Historical Analysis," in *The Evangelicals: What They Believe, Who They Are, Where They Are Changing*, ed. David F. Wells and John D. Woodbridge (Nashville: Abingdon, 1975), p. 126.

13. Olmstead, *History of Religion in the United States*, p. 474.

14. "A Call for a Convention to Effect a National Organization for the Improvement of Religious and Moral Education Through the Sunday School and Other Agencies." See Boardman W. Kathan, "William Rainey Harper: Founder of the Religious Education Association," *Religious Education* 78:5-S (September-October 1978), S-12 for full text.

15. Dorothy Jean Furnish, "The Profession of Director or Minister of Christian Education in Protestant Churches," in *Changing Patterns of Religious Education*, p. 19.

16. Washington Gladden, "Bringing All the Moral and Religious Forces into Effective Educational Unity," in *Who Are We? The Quest for a Religious Education*, ed. John H. Westerhoff III (Birmingham, Ala.: Religious Education Press, 1978), p. 29.

17. Harry C. Munro, *The Director of Religious Education* (Philadelphia: Westminster, 1930), p. 16.

18. H. Shelton Smith, "Let Religious Educators Reckon With the Barthians," *Religious Education* 24 (January 1934), pp. 45-51. These ideas were later formalized in his book, *Faith and Nurture* (New York: Scribner, 1941).

19. John Westerhoff III, ed., *Who Are We? The Quest for a Religious Education* (Birmingham, Ala.: Religious Education Press, 1978), p. 97.

20. James C. Logan, *Theology as a Source in Shaping the Church's Educational Work* (Nashville: Board of Discipleship of the United Methodist Church, 1974), p. 22.

21. See L. Harold DeWolf, *The Case for Theology in the Liberal Perspective* (Philadelphia: Westminster, 1959) and John B. Cobb Jr., *Liberal Christianity at the Crossroads* (Philadelphia: Westminster, 1963) for development of the idea of liberalism as a process rather than a set of theological beliefs.

22. Randolph Crump Miller, *The Clue To Christian Education* (New York: Scribner, 1950).

23. Ibid., p. 15.

24. Randolph Crump Miller, "Christian Education as a Theological

Discipline and Method," *Religious Education* 58 (November-December 1953), p. 120.

25. C. Ellis Nelson, "Is Church Education Something Particular?" *Religious Education* 57 (January-February 1972), p. 199.

26. Ibid., p. 204

27. Josef Andreas Jungmann, *Die Frohbotschaft and unsere Glauben-verkundigung* (Regensburg, Deutschland: Pustet, 1936) and Joseph Andreas Jungmann, *Handing on the Faith: A Manual of Catechetics,* trans. and rev. by A. N. Fuerst (New York: Herder and Herder, 1959).

28. Johannes Hofinger, *The Art of Teaching Christian Doctrine: The Good News and Its Proclamation* (Notre Dame, Ind.: University of Notre Dame Press, 1959).

29. Sloyan received his doctorate in general education. Soon after, he turned his attention to religious education. Many of his keenest religious insights came from his attendance at European religious education meetings. An analysis of his writings reveal that most of his articles were written after his attendance at these meetings. These articles usually brought to an American Catholic audience the results of these European conferences.

30. Gerard S. Sloyan, "Roman Catholic Religious Education," in *Religious Education: A Comprehensive Survey*, ed. Marvin J. Taylor (Nashville: Abingdon, 1960), p. 399.

31. Gerard S. Sloyan, "Catechetical Crossroads," *Religious Education* 59 (March-April 1964), pp. 160-161.

32. Mary Perkins Ryan, *Are Parochial Schools the Answer?* (New York: Holt, Rinehart & Winston, 1964).

33. Harold William Burgess, *An Invitation to Religious Education* (Birmingham, Ala.: Religious Education Press, 1975).

34. Jack L. Seymour and Donald E. Miller, *Contemporary Approaches to Christian Education* (Nashville, Abingdon, 1982).

35. James Loder, *The Transforming Moment: Understanding Convictional Experiences* (San Francisco: Harper & Row, 1981).

36. Gabriel Moran, "From Obstacle To Modest Contributer," in *Religious Education and Theology*, pp. 42-70.

37. Maria Harris, "Women and Church Ministries," *P.A.C.E.* (1976) and "Religious Education and the Aesthetic," *Andover Newton Quarterly* 17 (November 1976), pp. 125-132.

38. Robert C. Worley, *A Gathering of Strangers* (Philadelphia: Westminster, 1983).

39. Mary Elizabeth Moore, *Education for Continuity and Change: A New Model for Christian Religious Education* (Nashville: Abingdon, 1983).

40. Olivia Pearl Stokes, "Black Theology: A Challenge to Religious Education," in *Religious Education and Theology.*

Chapter 2

The Theological Framework as One Vision

Theology dominated the literature as the basic framework for religious education for many years. To appreciate the theological vision of religious education, it will be helpful first to look at the nature of theology, then to view global proposals on the way in which theology relates to religious education, and finally to consider a brief historical overview of how theologically oriented religious educators have described the relationship of theology and religious education.

The Nature of Theology

Etymologically, theology is the science of God. Theology can be defined as that science which studies God and God's workings in the world using the Bible (and for Catholics, the official magisterium) as both the point of departure and the norm.

Theology is not the only science which studies the workings of God in this world. Other scientific areas which study God's activities include the psychology of religion, the sociology of religion, religious literature, church history, and the like. None of these sciences or disciplines is theology, nor is properly governed by theology. What makes theology unique as a study of God and God's workings in the world is the fact that theologians use revelation as the supreme norm for testing the validity of their scientific findings. The principal methodological problem in this way of proceeding is that while there is one Bible there are various conflicting theologies of the Bible and its meanings.

While theology is not the only major way of gaining cognitive meaning of God's creative action and humanity's response, it is nonetheless a very important and indeed an indispensable way of learning about God.

Like all other forms of science, theology is a cognitive or reflective activity and not either an affective or a lifestyle activity. Theology is done primarily with the head rather than with the heart. Theology is a systematic intellectual reflection on conduct rather than conduct itself. Technically, theology in itself does not even seek to make people better; rather, theology seeks simply to understand human conduct from the perspective of revelation and its own understanding of Christianity.

Branches of Theology

Biblical theology. Biblical theology is that branch of theology which seeks to explore the sacred text in order to extract theological meaning from it. Thus biblical theology differs from a literary study of the Bible which endeavors to examine the Bible from the point of view of grammar or style.

Historical theology. Historical theology considers from a theological point of view the doctrines of Christianity and the effect of time on their development. Thus historical theology differs from church history which endeavors to examine the continuing ecclesial community from the point of view of strictly historical considerations without rooting those considerations in biblical norms.

Systematic theology. Systematic theology is that examination of the most basic Christian doctrines from the perspective of these doctrines in and of themselves. Systematic theology investigates and elaborates on such topics as salvation, sin, and Christology. Systematic theology also places these doctrines in a mutually interactive system which gives breath and meaning to the individual doctrines. It should be underscored that systematic theology does not prove the truth of Christianity either universally or from a specific denomination's own perspective. Rather, systematic theology seeks to clarify fundamental doctrines of the church, explore assumptions, and to mine deeper the hidden riches of doctrines already manifest or latent.

Practical theology. Practical theology is the attempt to examine, from a theological perspective exclusively, the relationship of theology to here-and-now human activity. Practical theology is intrinsically different from the corporate or individual practice of Christianity. Practical theology is one kind of cognitive reflection on practice; it is not practice.

Religion Contrasted to Theology

Religion and theology are essentially different from one another and should not be confused. Religion is the actual concrete practice of Christianity. Religion is the here-and-now living out of one's existence in faith, hope, and love, all empowered and sustained by God's grace. Theology is one important kind of cognitive reflection on religion. Theology does not generate religion. Theology examines religion and sees how it stands up to theological norms and views. The personally lived nature of religion (as distinct from the objective scientific character of theology) was highlighted by William Temple who wrote that "the heart of Religion is not an opinion about God, such as Philosophy might reach as the conclusion of its argument; it is a personal relation with God."[1]

While the nature and branches of theology are relatively stable because of the basic scientific methods it uses, nonetheless the forms of theological interpretation are in constant flux. It is important for the religious educator to remember that there is not one single theological perspective held by all Christians. Today there are many contending theologies in the Christian domain. Two examples, representing vastly different perspectives and implications are fundamentalism and liberation theologies.

Two Contrasting Examples:
Fundamentalism and Liberation

Fundamentalism, in varying degrees with its nineteenth-century roots, tends to be the largest in size of lay followers. Sometimes called evangelical or conservative theology, fundamentalism places high authority on the literal biblical tradition. God is wholly transcendent to humanity. Human nature is basically corrupt and requires a vicarious, substitutionary atonement by Jesus for atonement of our sins and corrupt human nature. Both salvation and sin are understood in personal terms, namely each individual's private and continuing response to God's initiative. In the final analysis, a human being can do nothing to usher in God's kingdom. The kingdom is in the heavenly sphere and not here on earth.

In contrast, liberation theology originating in twentieth-century culture, such as black theology, feminist theology, or third world theology focuses on the social dimension of sin or evil and views salvation in a broader context of "love, power, and justice for all people"[2] It protests the privatization of the Christian faith and applies the concepts of faith to society as a whole. God's nature is understood in immanent terms. Rather than emphasizing a personal savior, leading the believer to heaven, the role of the Christ is to be a liberator of the oppressed people (the various minorities of women, poor, or non-Anglos). The role of humanity in the kingdom of God is important. The reign of God is not totally dependent on a supernatural force outside of humanity, but rather on people's active free cooperation with God's work.

Theological Foundations for Religious Education

Historically, theologians and theology have been related to the church's religious education work in several different ways.

1. *Theology as the content* to be transmitted. Sometimes this is described as the faith of the community and sometimes, as in religious studies, the academic study of a theological position. The study of the doctrines of the church as traditionally done in catechetical learning would be theology as content. In this model there is a separation of the functions of education and theology. Instructional methods are separate from the considerations of theology. In this view, the goal of instruction is to communicate the content in effective ways.

2. *Theology as the normative authority.* In this position, theology serves as the ultimate and proximate norm both for the content to be taught and for the pedagogical procedures used in teaching. James Smart, an advocate of this dominance of authority in neo-orthodox theology, described the task of theology to

"mount the watchtower and scan its life and faith in all directions, in order to detect the presence of blindness, unbelief, un-
faithfulness, and sin, and give warning."[3] Smart cautioned religious educators from taking "supposedly scientific conclusions
from the secular educator" as they might be either non-Christian
or even anti-Christian assumptions.[4]

3. *A dialogue between education and theology* represents a
third relationship. The theology held by the teacher does exert a
certain influence over which procedures and which content is to
be utilized in religious education. If religion is perceived as character formation, then stories and methods to develop character
will be chosen. If religion is the assent to certain fundamental
beliefs, then the transmission of a specific salvation message will
be the agenda. If it is to develop a relationship to God or to other
human beings, then relational activities and content will be chosen. Yet, the choice of the best method of communicating that
goal will be an educational decision. Education is the resource for
choice of methods while theology is the resource for the goal.

Theology and Religious Education

Early 1900s: Modernism/Liberalism

In the early 1900s, professional religious education was undergirded by classical liberal, i.e., modernist theology. Modernism
accepted the historical-critical methods of biblical studies and the
emerging scientific ideas that included geological and evolutionary theories. Modernism had a high view of human reason and
sought to build a better society through the efforts of Christian
persons.

Philosophical concerns of the early twentieth-century educators included progressive education and educational psychology.
Religious education was a mixture of evangelism and learning so
that *the child* would have sufficient knowledge to make personal
decisions about the Christian faith. The development of Christian character was the goal of this knowledge.[5] The child was the
focus of this period's religious education. In addition, religious
education sought to transform all of society. George Albert Coe,
followed by William Clayton Bower, wrote that the church was to

promote Christian ideals leading to the reconstruction of all of society so it would become the "Democracy of God."[6]

Arthur Bennet, one of the first professors of religious education at the Boston University School of Religious Education set forth the 1920s modernist's arguments against the fundamentalists. "Religion relates life to God. Hence, education is religious when its conceptions, aims, and methods are directed in terms of religious idealism."[7] Bennet, building from Horace Bushnell's view of nurture as the center of religious education, reemphasized the importance of the home as a center for religious nurture. Children caught religion through imitation. While the ideal Christian democracy was undergirded by the institutions of the home, the church, and the public school, the primary responsibilities for creating the Christian way of life were in the home and the church.

The "church school," according to Bennet, was for the purpose of religious education. "The church school should select the materials for its curricula, determine its methods, and choose its teachers with direct reference to the needs of religion. It should accept the findings of scientific pedagogy as valid in related fields of knowledge and at the same time modify or adapt these methods to the nature of its own materials and to the needs of the child."[8]

Modernist theology and its concomitant educational philosophy had a positive image of humanity and society. It assumed that humanity would be able to rationally understand God's revelation in nature and the Bible. Jesus was the example of the ideal human who revealed God's love in action. Through education, people would be able to rationally develop into the moral Christian life. This was possible because God was both an immanent personal God and a transcendent God who was revealed in nature as well as through the church.

Neo-orthodoxy

The Great Depression brought a major reorganization of Protestant theology and religious educational theory. Karl Barth's commentary on *The Epistle To The Romans* published in 1918 became the foundation for the renewal of the church following World War I. The disillusioned leaders could no longer hold the idea of the progress of humanity either individually or culturally that had been a major idea of liberal theology. The classical liberal/modernist theology of the early part of the century was replaced in the seminaries by neo-orthodoxy. A new emphasis on the sovereignty of God, salvation by the act of Christ, revelation and biblical theology would remind the church of the uniqueness of Christianity. Although each representative of neo-orthodoxy, such as Karl Barth, Emil Brunner, Paul Tillich, Reinhold Niebuhr, or Rudolph Bultmann, would use different meanings for the terms, the language was definitely Christian and not general religion.

H. Sheldon Smith signaled the change for religious education in his 1934 article, "Let Religious Educators Reckon with the Bartians."[9] The modernist's concept of the immanence of God was challenged by neo-orthodoxy's insistence on God's transcendent, wholly other nature. The importance of the Bible as the revelation of God's Word in which Christ is revealed was central. Jesus Christ was the revealed Word of God. Now, educational method should find its norm in the Bible both in content and method, not in life situations.

In 1940 Harrison Elliott penned the last major pre-war defense of classical liberal/modernist theology as the foundational framework of religious education. Elliott rejected the radical shift of theology concerning the nature of humanity and God proposed by neo-orthodoxy. He was still certain that the answer to his book's title, *Can Religious Education Be Christian?*[10] was "yes!" However, the answer was actually the last hurrah of the old-line modernists/classical liberals.

Post-World War II: New Leaders

The global events surrounding World War II would call forth a new creative leadership for the future. James Logan, Professor of Systematic Theology at Wesley Theological Seminary, Washington, D.C., described contemporary liberalism as being "identifiable most accurately as a theological method rather than as specific theological content."[11] The term "liberalism" following World War II will refer to a broad spectrum of theologians and educators who are committed to openness in the search for religious truth but are rooted in the dynamics of the Christian biblical and theological traditions. Representatives range from Paul

Tillich who wrote from the perspective of a Christian philosophical theologian to L. Harold DeWolf writing from a more evangelical perspective. Contemporary liberalism emphasizes the importance of experience and reason in the understanding of scripture and tradition. Rather than liberalism being an erosion of conservative Christianity, "it is the Christian gospel that makes us [sic] liberal."[12]

The 1940s was a time of confusion in the field of religious education as the forces moved in different directions. The split of terms and of the foundations was evident among Protestants, Catholics, and Jews. Protestants accepted Lewis Sherrill's thesis that "to reach the deepest understanding of Christian education, whether in history or at the present, one must begin with Christianity itself and proceed thence to education."[13] Roman Catholics still focused their attention on the Catholic parochial school as the central and most complete arena for "religious education." Jewish tradition also used the title "religious education" and of course was not affected by the theological conflicts over neoorthodoxy found in Protestantism.

Theology the Clue to Religious Education

New leadership emerged in liberal Protestantism in the early 1950s, reflecting the change in emphasis from modernist theology to liberal methods for thinking theologically. Randolph Crump Miller at Yale Divinity School became the new theorist leader for Christian education with the publication of his book, *The Clue To Christian Education.* (Paradoxically, Miller and most liberal Protestants who followed him in the next generation, usually used the term "Christian education" much like the conservatives clung to this term. Paradoxically, too, Miller was the editor for twenty years of the journal called *Religious Education.*)

Miller was concerned for the comprehensive educational ministry of the church rather than only one small aspect, i.e., the church school. He began with three psycho-social insights regarding Christian education: 1) The family is the primary religious nurturing agent, 2) the whole life of the congregation teaches instead of just the Sunday school, and 3) children are not miniature adults psychologically. There are stages of development in life.[14]

Miller introduced the slogan, "Theology in the background,

faith and grace in the foreground."[15] According to Miller, "The clue to Christian education is the discovery of a relevant theology which will bridge the gap between content and method, providing the background and perspective of Christian truth by which the best methods and content will be used as tools to bring the learners into a right relationship with the living God who is revealed to us in Jesus Christ, using the guidance of parents and the fellowship of life in the Church as the environment in which Christian nurture will take place.[16] Theology, as understood by Miller, is "truth-about-God-in-relation-to-man."[17] Theology was not the substantive content to be studied but was the means for the task of education.

This was a period of new curriculum developments in almost every denomination. While the various writers debated whether curriculum should be content (Bible) centered or child centered, Miller proclaimed that "the purpose of Christian education is to place God at the center and to bring the individual into the right relationship with God and his fellows within the perspectives of the fundamental Christian truths about all of life."[18]

Christianity was the clear definition of religion for Protestant religious education, liberal as well as conservative. Miller wanted education to become "almost synonymous with evangelism" as both evangelism and education were to confront persons with the claims of the Christian truths so that they "put their trust in God . . . and . . . live as Christ's disciples in the fellowship of the church."[19] Miller used modern empirical theological methods within a moderate liberal theological stance to combine educational methods, theology, and personal living concerns within a Christian environment.

Christian Education as Nurture

Other Protestant writers supported this position. Iris Cully, a student of Miller's, proposed that the whole church is the teacher of Christian education under the term of nurture. Christian education was more than Sunday school teaching and broader than instruction with its variety of methodologies.

Religious education for Cully includes instructional activities, but it goes beyond transmission of knowledge. Education is intellectually oriented, but progresses toward understanding. Religious education involves the student in searching for meaning through the exploration of alternatives. It seeks to enable students to develop a set of attitudes that will be expressed in action in the lifestyle of a Christian. These actions are represented in commitments to justice and peace in daily settings. Religious education also develops the student in terms of appreciation for religious symbols such as ritual, art, and customs.[20]

Nurture Requires a Community

Nurture, for Cully, while having many similarities with education, requires a community. Education may happen individually, in isolation, but nurture always requires another. Religious nurture may happen in the home, church school, or any aspect of the church's life. It is motivated by the recognition that God's love for the parents or teachers is the source for their nurturing love. Nurture happens as the person experiences the life commitments of his or her significant community. Observing the action of a father preparing to teach a Sunday school class, a mother preparing to spend a day in the food pantry, or a youth group being supported by the church for a work camp are nurturing example experiences for youth. Nurturing tells the story of God's love and demonstrates God's love in relationships with others. Religious nurture always has the dimension of God's presence. Commitment to God is the goal of religious nurture. God's spirit functions to bring a commitment in the learner toward those values and appreciations defined in the community's life as important.[21]

New Curriculum Objectives

As post-World War II liberal theology moved to the center of Christian education, two other events took place that shaped the understanding of the framework. New objectives were published and the plans for a new curriculum were developed. In 1952 the National Council of Churches began work on an objective statement. It was completed in 1958. A second committee reported a similar statement for senior high youth.[22] In summary, the objectives described the goal of Christian education in terms of God's revelation, humanity's progressive discovery of the revelation, the role of the Holy Spirit in the Christian life, the importance of the church, and the nature of discipleship as being lived in the world.

The key point is that the objectives were theologically focused rather than methodologically concerned as had been the case with some of the earlier objectives.

Cooperative Curriculum Project

The second development was the creation of the Cooperative Curriculum Project chaired by D. Campbell Wyckoff of Princeton Theological Seminary. The Committee on Uniform Lesson Series of the National Council of Churches through a series of studies sought to create a curriculum design that would be used by the various denominational boards of education in their curriculum development. The denominations were moving toward curriculum revisions based on neo-orthodox and post-World War liberal theology together with denominational emphases.

The Cooperative Curriculum Project Committee, appointed in 1960, had sixteen denominations participating in the project. It incorporated the new developments in educational psychology, biblical scholarship, and the latest theological viewpoints for its comprehensive curriculum plan that was published in 1965.[23] The curriculum plan influenced the participating denominations' curriculum at various levels, but it demonstrated the widespread ecumenical commitments to the theological concerns related to the design of the new curriculum.

In 1960 it was possible to bring a large group of denominations together in an ecumenical project that was based on a common theological understanding such as neo-orthodoxy and post-World War liberal theology. By the end of the decade the outward uniformity was shattered. Women, ethnic minorities, and youth challenged the social agenda of the church (or its lack of an agenda). The former consensus of theology in the seminaries broke down and fractionated into process theology, liberation theology, biblical theology; even fundamentalist/evangelical theology sought to replace neo-orthodoxy as the theology of the mainline churches.

The Theological Framework Today

Practical Theology

The articulation of theology as the central framework is illustrated by Allen Moore's article, "The Recovery of Theological

Nerve," in 1984 which called for "a new critical awareness of the theological task."[24] Moore calls for Christian educators to use practical theology as the framework for Christian education. He describes practical theology as a "hermeneutics of the church-world relationship."[25] Religious knowledge is to be in dialogue with secular knowledge, at the same time religious education is to rediscover and reimage the historical metaphors of Jewish and Christian tradition for spiritual formation. For Moore "the beginning and end of religious education is thinking, talking, and acting 'theologically.' "[26] (Of interest is the fact that Moore is not a theologian but a specialist in the psychology of religion and the social foundation of education.)

The issue becomes which of the many theologies available should be the norm? Moore demonstrates how a practical theological approach based on liberation theology would function.[27] Using secular knowledge and analysis, he cautions the American church on accepting liberation metaphors too easily. Economic injustice is a central concern for both black and feminist liberation theology as well as third world models. Christian education based on liberation theology moves from discussions of doctrines to liberating action in the present world based on belief in "the acts of God the liberator."[28]

Liberation Christian education seeks to reveal the hidden assumptions of the church and society to change values at the societal level rather than the personal level. Prophetic social change requires theological reflection on the nature of God's reign as described in the Christian tradition as well as commitment to God's reign in concrete transformation of those systems that are oppressive in the church and society.

Education in Dialogue with Theology

Several other theological framework theorists view the role of education in a somewhat positive and helpful fashion. Education is in dialogue with theology. Sometimes this hermeneutical approach is labeled "doing theology,"[29] or "the interpretation approach."[30]

The Process of Traditioning

Mary Elizabeth Moore presents a hermeneutic theological approach to Christian education. The key for her is the process of traditioning, "by which the historical tradition is remembered and transformed as the Christian community encounters God and the world in present experience, and as that community is motivated toward the future.[31] The role of the church is not to just pass on a tradition, but to reform society toward the vision of the kingdom of God while it is being transformed itself. Moore applies insights of process theology to her framework. At the intersection where people interact with the tradition in their present life, transformation happens that enlarges the heritage, reforms the person and re-creates society in the direction of the kingdom of God. In the traditioning process the world and even God is influenced.[32]

Theology as the guiding, fundamental framework for Christian education offers both an authority of content as well as a guide for the choice of methods. Some theological positions are considered to be liberal such as liberation, hermeneutic, or process. Many Protestant theological seminaries in the mainstream denominations function from these liberal theological perspectives. The national denominational boards of education also tend to represent liberal traditions. On the other hand, many of the local churches at the lay level function from a more conservative perspective and seek Christian education approaches to fit that mold. These groups want a theological approach that transmits the authoritative, biblically based, salvific message to the learners so that personal conversion takes place. Each competitive, divergent theology implies a set of assumptions related to education. There will be no way for the parish director of education to avoid coming to grips with theology in any framework for religious education.

NOTES

1. William Temple, *Nature, Man and God* (London: Macmillan, 1934), p. 54.

2. Grant Shockley, "Liberation Theology, Black Theology, and Religious Education," in *Foundations for Christian Education in an Era of Change*, ed. Marvin J. Taylor (Nashville: Abingdon Press, 1976), p. 80.

3. James D. Smart, *The Teaching Ministry of the Church* (Philadelphia: Westminster, 1954), pp. 32-33.

4. Ibid.

5. William C. Bower, *Religious Education in the Modern Church* (St. Louis: Bethany, 1929), pp. 34-36.

6. George A. Coe, *A Social Theory of Religious Education* (New York: Scribner, 1919).

7. Arthur Bennet, "What Makes Education Religious?" in *Who Are We: The Quest for a Religious Education,* ed. John Westerhoff III (Birmingham, Ala.: Religious Education Press, 1978), p. 46.

8. Ibid., p. 49.

9. H. Sheldon Smith, "Let Religious Educators Reckon with the Bartians," *Religious Education* 24 (January 1934), pp. 45-51.

10. Harrison S. Elliott, *Can Religious Education Be Christian?* (New York: Macmillan, 1940).

11. James C. Logan, *Theology as a Source in Shaping the Church's Educational Work,* Education Futures, Monograph No. 8 (Nashville: Division of Education, United Methodist Board of Discipleship, 1974), p. 22.

12. John B. Cobb Jr., *Liberal Christianity at the Crossroads* (Philadelphia: Westminster, 1963), p. 10.

13. Lewis J. Sherrill, *The Rise of Christian Education* (New York: Macmillan, 1954), p. 1.

14. Randolph Crump Miller, *The Clue To Christian Education* (New York: Scribner, 1950), p. 7.

15. Ibid.

16. Ibid., p. 15.

17. Ibid., p. 5.

18. Ibid., p. 8.

19. Ibid.

20. Iris V. Cully, "Christian Education: Instruction or Nurture," *Religious Education* 62 (May-June 1967), pp. 225-261.

21. Ibid.

22. *The Objectives of Christian Education: A Study Document* (New York: National Council of Churches, 1958) and *The Objective of Christian Education for Senior High Young People* (New York: National Council of Churches, 1958).

23. Cooperative Curriculum Project, *The Church's Educational Ministry: A Curriculum Plan* (St. Louis: Bethany, 1965).

24. Allen Moore, "The Recovery of Theological Nerve," *Religious Education* 79 (Winter 1984), p. 27.

25. Ibid., p. 28.

26. Ibid., p. 28.

27. Allen Moore, "Liberation and the Future of Christian Education," in Jack L. Seymour et al., *Contemporary Approaches to Christian Education* (Nashville: Abingdon, 1982), pp. 103-122.

28. Ibid., p. 116.

29. Sara Little, "Theology and Religious Education," in *Foundations*

for Christian Education in an Era of Change, p. 32.

30. Jack L. Seymour et al., *Contemporary Approaches to Christian Education* (Nashville: Abingdon, 1982), pp. 123-144.

31. Mary Elizabeth Moore, *Education for Continuity and Change: A New Model for Christian Religious Education* (Nashville: Abingdon, 1983), p. 121.

32. Ibid., p. 122.

Chapter 3

The Educational Vision
as Another Framework

Education, schooling, instruction, and nurture have all been used to describe the ways the church enables its members to acquire the knowledge, attitudes, and lifetime skills that are considered important. As mentioned in the previous chapter, education and theology have had a variety of relationships through the ages. Even when the church has focused its energy on a schooling paradigm, the family has had a special foundational role in the spiritual nurturing of the child.

Various educational philosophies have influenced how the church should organize its educational programs. Idealism, behaviorism, and progressivism have competed through history as major influences. Today, new interest in the social sciences attempts to find ways to bring theology and education into a dialogue that will greatly strengthen the ministry of education. The role of psychology in faith development and the social-science approach to religion teaching are the two prime examples of the emerging concerns.

Biblical Roots
Education has been part of the church from its beginning. Jesus frequently was addressed as "Rabbi," that is, teacher. His earliest followers were called disciples, namely learners. Jesus

taught the disciples face to face in life experiences. We might describe it as clinical education in that each experience was a personal one in which learning took place in a real-life concrete situation. Jesus gave an interpretation of the person's experience as he incarnated (embodied) God's love in action. Jesus' central mission of teaching was the kingdom of God, as he took the prophetic style of interpretation of the Jewish scriptures by applying them to new situations. In rabbinic fashion, Jesus did not teach doctrines but helped the people to experience the presence of God in their personal needs and relationships. The goal was to develop trust in God and to give the people directions on how to live faithfully in service in God's reign. It understood that "faith" or trust which is not operationally expressed in the works of love (discipleship or service) is not full faith.

Teaching and preaching were important in the early church as the faithful responded both to the preaching and teaching of the apostles. James Smart contrasts the roles of preaching and teaching for the early church. Preaching, kerygma, was primarily to call the person to faith from sin. No one is beyond the need for repentance and the need for the transforming gospel is felt by both those inside and outside the church. Teaching, didachē, however, is for those who are within the community of faith as a means that will lead to the believers' growth in grace.[1] Many of the New Testament letters of Paul are examples of didachē/teaching as he taught the young churches regarding specific problems in their congregations.

The Early Church

During its earliest centuries, the church used two primary means of education: the first part of the worship service which was called the Mass of the Catechumens [*Missa catechumenorum*] or the liturgy of the Word and the catechumenate.[2] The first part of the early church's worship included the scripture lessons and exhortations and sermons. Then those who were not baptized were dismissed as they were not eligible to receive communion which formed the second part of the service.

The catechumenate was originally a form of adult education concerned with developing a Christian lifestyle in the probationary Christian in addition to learning the beliefs of the church.[3] It was typically for non-Jewish adult converts, leading to baptism. The socialization of the candidate into the moral framework of the church lasted for a period up to three years as the person participated in the life of the congregation under the supervision of a mentor. By the third century the catechumenate had progressed from primarily being a lay-supervised program to being under the control of the ecclesiastical leaders.

Medieval Schools

The early medieval period had several models of education. In Italy, secular schools taught by lay persons, for lay students, teaching grammar and literature continued throughout the Middle Ages.[4] By 1000 A.D. many towns in Italy had municipal schools to teach basic courses of reading, writing, and math. By the fourteenth century the municipal schools had spread throughout Europe.[5] By the high Middle Ages, from the twelfth century on, secular education enabled a large number of lay persons to read, often better than many country parish priests.[6]

In addition, Christian bishops organized bishops' schools. A small group of boys usually ranging from seven years old through eighteen years old were boarders in the bishop's household. The goal was to educate them so that they would take holy orders when they reached eighteen. In addition song schools were organized in cathedral churches, in monasteries, and in some parish churches. The boys were taught the "elements of the faith, singing, spelling, and a little Latin grammar all in return for their services as choristers."[7] Monastic schools were more limited in their scope and student body and primarily prepared students for their monastic order.

The cathedral schools became centers for both general education as well as preparation for the priesthood, teaching both Greek and Latin literature. The curriculum was based on the traditional seven liberal arts.

The medieval university arose from the collection of teachers and students gathered in a particular place. The spirit of urbanization and the emerging humane spirit created the university rather than the church. Salerno, Bologna, and Paris were early sites for studies in medicine, law, and theology. The early degrees were professional degrees which tended to be entrance requirements for the various guilds as teachers. The basic degree was the Master of Arts, admitting the person to the teaching guild. The titles we use today for doctoral degrees, e.g., M.D. (Medicine Doctor), L.L.D. (Legum Doctor), and S.T.P. (Sanctae Theologiae Professor) described the area of faculty teaching such as medicine, civil law, and theology.[8]

The university was a model of secular education. Religious education at the local parish level was dependent on several other sources. Although the middle and upper classes of society were probably literate, the general lower classes were still illiterate. A major source of education was through the sacramental life of the church, including the rite of penance and absolution. The list of sins which required confession and absolution provided a means of control over both the secular and religious life of the people. The medieval miracle and morality plays based on biblical themes were common forms of storytelling for the community. The visual arts of sculpture, mosaic, painting, and later stained glass became the religious picture book for the people. Bible study was not generally done by parish priests during the Middle Ages, with the exceptions of the early reformers such as the Lollards.

Sixteenth Century:
Reformation and Counter-Reformation

The sixteenth-century Reformation idea of the priesthood of all believers required skills to read the scriptures by all people. When the infallible church was replaced by an infallible book, the necessity of universal religious education became a basic need. Although it was some centuries before the dream was realized in most places of Europe, universal education became the responsibility of the state. The ideal of liberty was encouraged by the culture of the Renaissance; the reformers were influenced by their history and immediate cultural ecology. People needed to know how to read the Bible and to read it in their own language. The result was the translation of scripture into the language of the people.

Martin Luther

Martin Luther's journey to his understanding of justification by faith alone came through the academic study of the Psalms,

Romans, and Galatians. Therefore, religious education would be central for Lutherans. A seminal religious educator, Luther used hymns, children's catechisms, and the sermon as part of his educational system. Luther cannot be properly understood apart from his emphasis in religious education. He even chose his black academic robe for preaching in contrast to the sacramental vestments of the priest. Although he emphasized the reading of scripture and the need for individual relationship with God, Luther was also concerned about his people having a correct view of doctrine. He revived the use of both a long and shorter form of catechism to teach doctrine to his students.

John Calvin

John Calvin, like Luther, used a catechism in his educational reforms in Geneva. For Calvin, the purpose of religious education was to realize the reign of Christ here on earth. The New England pilgrims brought the Calvinistic traditions to their schools as colonialists.

Counter-Reformation

The Roman Catholic Church also revised its concerns for correct doctrine. Consequently, the sixteenth-century Catholic counter-reformation revived the catechism as the primary mode of general education. Liturgical guidance through the confessional and confirmation training were also part of the church's new efforts in deliberate religious education.

Society of Jesus (Jesuits)

Responding creatively to the crisis encountered in the Protestant Reformation, the Society of Jesus (Jesuits) developed schools at the secondary and university level. The society intentionally sought to train future leaders—the children from influential families. The goal was to create loyalty to the Roman Catholic Church. The students lived under a severe discipline of strict rules. Their studies were tightly organized and the methods of instruction were revolutionary in that they combined very high intellectual standards with gentle discipline.

Confraternity of Christian Doctrine

In addition to special all-day schools created by the religious orders, each Catholic parish established a CCD program based on the idea that religion can be most effectively transmitted to children rather than primarily to youth or adults.

American Religious Education

The split between secular and sacred schools is historically an American situation. During the colonial period in New England there was an established "state church" dominating the life of the people, except in Rhode Island. The Calvinist, Puritian tradition dominated in New England which had no tolerance for religious dissenters. However, in the Southern Colonies, the edicts of toleration provided a degree of separation between church and state.

The nineteenth century of American education generally followed the New England model which gave white Protestants control over education. With the widespread adoption of the common school advocated by Horace Mann, American public schools in fact became nondenominational, white Protestant schools. This character of the American public school pervaded until the first World War. This dominance was the principle cause of Roman Catholics being forced to create parish schools in the United States during the nineteenth century.

The public school curriculum was, therefore, heavily religious with biblical material being a large part of the resources. *The New England Primer* taught religion as well as reading. The primer included The Lord's Prayer, The Apostles Creed, William Cotton's Catechism, and the familiar prayer, "Now I lay me down to sleep." As the immigrants from non-Anglo, non-Protestant traditions increased, the accommodation between the church and public education broke down.

The American Protestant Sunday School

The Sunday school movement is a classic example of the schooling model of religious education. At the beginning of the nineteenth century American Protestantism had three centers for religious education: the public school, the family, and the Sunday school. By mid-century, not even Bible reading and opening prayer were universal in public education. Horace Bushnell's *Christian Nurture* was as much a call to reestablish the educational role of the family as it challenged the revivalism of his day. The Sunday school, however, was prepared to be the school of the church.[9]

The Sunday school was ethnocentric. Although it began as a school to train the poor to read and write, it soon evolved into an institution for the teaching of middle-class morality. By 1830, its implied objective was to win and hold the United States for evangelical Protestantism.[10] It defined barbarism as being Roman Catholics and democrats.[11] At first the Sunday school used the camp meeting for the conversion of its members. But by the Civil War, the Sunday school was the prime evangelizing agency. It had become the "nursery of the (Protestant) Church."[12]

Key Features of the Sunday School

Several features enabled the Sunday school to be successful. It was a lay movement. Every local Sunday school was led by lay persons, namely, nonclergy. Lay officers practiced democracy in the Sunday school long before they could in most denominations in the state or national level conferences. The Sunday school's regional and national conventions also gave it a unity that transcended its small town separations. Rewards also were part of the tradition. Presenting perfect attendance pins, Bibles for memorized verses, along with banners and music gave the Sunday school many opportunities to celebrate its achievements.

International/Uniform Curriculum

Following a period of disorganization and competition in the publication of Sunday school curricula, the 1872 American Sunday School Union adopted a single uniform curriculum to be published across denomination lines. The International/Uniform series curriculum selected Bible passages to be studied in every class, at every age level for each Sunday. It selected major passages to be taught around the world on a seven-year cycle. Each week there was a memory verse to be learned by every child, youth, and adult attending.

Teacher Training

To support its teachers, the Sunday school developed an emphasis on teacher training. The Chautauqua Institute became a major form of adult education in the late nineteenth century. Originally, John Vincent, secretary of the Methodist Sunday School Union, and Lewis Miller, a businessman and church layman, conceived the Chautauqua Institute to train Sunday school teachers, but the Chautauqua became a popular general adult education format.

The Chautauqua was a residential summer educational program which combined Bible study with courses in literature, art, music, and other disciplines.[13] The residential assembly grounds of the national center of Chautauqua Institute is located in Upper New York State and still provides a major summer series of programs in the liberal arts, music, library training, and other general studies. The format was copied by many denominations as the model for their summer camping programs.

The program at a Chautauqua Institute typically included a morning general assembly followed by classes on chosen topics during each day. The evening would include a vesper service and a play or a concert. The Sunday school teacher was an important link in the success of the movement, but it became so popular that others began to participate. Eventually, it created a home reading program supporting local reading clubs around the nation through the Chautauqua Literary and Scientific Circle, ("a book of the month club").[14]

A Lay Evangelistic Model

The purpose of the nineteenth-century Protestant Sunday school was evangelistic, namely, to pass on a specific revelational message to prepare the person, usually a child, to receive salvation and to receive God's Holy Spirit. The experience of conversion often happened at the camp meeting or revival, but it was prepared in the Sunday school.

In many communities the Sunday school was the substitute church. Pastors typically served two or more churches and, due to distances between towns or churches, usually preached at each church only once or twice a month. On the alternate Sundays, it was the Sunday school superintendent who led the opening and closing "liturgy." The superintendent often was the town's "minister-in-residence" when the "real minister" lived in the other village.

In addition, the "school of the church" in many of the small hamlets, served as the parallel of the community school providing fellowship for all ages, a sense of identity, and setting the social action agenda of the community through such efforts as prohibition, women's and children's rights in the women's groups, and missionary outreach through designation of the last Sunday of the month as missionary offering day. Even the competitive sports were carried into the Sunday school rally in Bible Baseball competitions, and later in dart leagues and other forms of athletics.

The similarity of the school and the church was intentional. John Vincent, the Methodist bishop who was a driving force in the Sunday school, strongly supported the Sunday school copying the efforts of the day school as a means of improving the quality of religious education. He rightly understood that if the Sunday school appeared to be an educationally weak institution, its influence would diminish in "its power to effect Christian character."[15]

Challenges to the Sunday School

Following the Civil War in the United States, several movements developed that challenged the evangelical thrust of the Sunday school. Biblical scholarship was introduced into seminary studies. Many Protestant clergy began to support the new scriptural data and theories. The conservatives saw this as denying a supernatural Christianity. In addition, new challenges arose from the emerging fields of geology and biology related to traditional biblical interpretations. If one could not literally believe the opening chapter of Genesis, some reasoned, then all of the faith was in danger.

To resist these liberalizing, modernist ideas the classic five fundamentals of the faith appeared. They received wide circulation and by 1910 the Presbyterian Church's General Assembly adopted them as official doctrine. Additional fundamentals have been added through the years. Correct beliefs were a means for receiving the Holy Spirit as well as testing the Spirit.[16]

Today, the Sunday school serves different roles depending on whether it is housed in a traditional "fundamentalist" Protestant congregation or in a "liberal" mainstream Protestant congregation as the "church school." Many of the evangelical ideas still operate in the conservative congregations. In the mainstream groups, the Sunday school became the "church school" and its role became more of nurture than of passing on specific doctrine.

Teaching-Learning Theory and Religious Education

Just as there are diverse theological positions, there are a variety of learning theories. Many of the psychological learning theorists eventually bring forth an educational philosophy. These philosophies range from idealism to behaviorism, from cognitive approaches to stimulus-response approaches, from mental discipline models to environmental, gestalt/problem-solving models. Religious education has not accepted any of the theories as its single overarching theory, and some are rejected outright. Yet, the theories do provide insights about how learning happens and how the teacher can organize the curriculum to better communicate the message intended. Three major categories of theories seem to have been most active in religious education over the years: mental discipline theories, behaviorist or conditioning theories, and gestalt or problem-solving theories.

Mental Discipline Theory

The mental discipline theories have been popular in Christianity from Augustine to modern fundamentalists. They view the learner as sinful, but they assert that if the mind is exercised, it will grow. Memorization of vast amounts of scripture is helpful, even if not understood by the learner. Information that is entered into the memory before it is understood will be brought forth when appropriate in the fullest mature fashion. Therefore, the educator need not worry if learners do understand complex religious ideas. They will use the information when it is time for them.

We also learn goodness by keeping our minds away from bad thoughts. In a Calvinist orientation, people do good because there is goodness in them. That good is cultivated by mental discipline. Mental discipline theories are popular with groups that accept an authoritarian code, either religious or political, and who believe the task of the home and community institutions is to enculturate goodness and discourage all objectionable behavior. If we read good books, hear good sermons, we will be able to harness the evil that is inside us with a good will. Most groups wishing to censor books today operate from this perspective.

Behaviorist Theory

The behaviorist or conditioning theories use stimulus and response sequences that guide behavior or the gathering of knowledge. Conditioning theories have influenced the field of learning more than any other.[17] Conditioning focuses on the specific behavior of the learner. The teacher seeks to create an environment (stimulus) that causes the learner to acquire the desired information and to respond in desired appropriate ways. The learner is essentially passive, reacting rather than initiating learning behaviors. The teacher, who knows the emotional needs and desires of the student, establishes the best conditions for the learning.

The research of E. L. Thorndike, E. R. Gutherie, and B. F. Skinner generated alternate educational models using conditioning. The teacher decides what responses are desired regarding the actions or knowledge of the students. The material is presented directly related to that goal. It is the basic model used when memorization of material or of a particular practice is desired. If the responses are those desired, reward the student through a compliment, a good grade, or a privilege, such as going first in line or receiving a perfect attendance pin. Those responses that are not desired are ignored. In some cases, punishment is administered to extinguish undesirable behavior. This theory is typically used by parents to discipline their offspring and by teachers who endeavor to control learners subtly or forcefully.

Gestalt or Problem-Solving Theory

The third set of learning theories is the gestalt or field theories. Gestalt means the apprehension of the configuration of relationships in a whole rather than individually or in parts. How does a learner perceive his/her situation? What are the motivations, self-concepts, and values that are part of the total experience? The physical, emotional, intellectual, spiritual dimensions of a person's life are all part of his or her cognitive field or gestalt. In any given situation some forces are positive, such as parents' or a friend's approval for this action. Other forces in the same situation may be negative, such as someone who is disliked will be there, a second friend's disapproval, or too much time is involved. Learning happens in the context of others who participate in the overall gestalt. We are influenced even by those not present in the current setting.

Gestalt learning theory emphasizes problem solving. Inquiring for solutions and discovering alternatives are central in the theory. In genuine gestalt learning the learner is active and sets the goals for learning. The Chinese proverb, "I hear I forget; I see I remember; I do I understand," reflects the concept that a student who discovers something him/herself tends to understand and remember the discovery longer.

A teacher using inquiry-based learning procedures would use many open-ended questions and follow each major question with probing questions. Effort is made to help students to learn from each other rather than depend on the leader for the "correct answer."

Discovery or gestalt learning theory builds on ideas by John Dewey. In problem solving, truth has a functional task or pragmatic role. One discovers the truth that works by experimentation.[18] Dewey believed that "all genuine education comes about through experience."[19] Educators have the task of knowing "how to utilize the surroundings, physical and social, that exist so as to extract from them all that they have to contribute to building up experiences that are worthwhile.[20]

Religious education has used and uses today each of these theories of teaching-learning. The task of the creative religious educator is not to lock onto only one learning theory, but to know which theory is most useful in a particular situation. Persons learn through identification as proposed in the mental discipline theory; they also learn through behavior modification and practice; and they learn through problem solving. There is also the awareness that the Christian faith is more than knowledge about God, but involves an inward appropriation of the presence of God. Students identify with the teachings of Jesus through exploring the biblical story. Then they must practice their faith until it becomes an internalized part of their lives, using it to meet the common problems of living so that God's presence is experienced in all of their personal life as well as in society.

Faith Development and Religious Education

There exists another social-science field that has implications for the educational framework. Structural psychology has presented constructs of the person's cognitive, affective, religious, moral, and faith development.

Ronald Goldman: Religious Readiness

Through his research in English schools, Ronald Goldman challenged assumptions about a child's readiness to learn religious concepts.[21] Studying the religious education curriculum and the responses of students from elementary through high school, he concluded that too often religious concepts are presented before children and youth have the maturity to understand them. Consequently many of these younger learners tend to either reject them at a later date as irrelevant or to accept them at an immature simple level.[22] Goldman wants the research data on how children learn religion to play a central role in religion curricula and in curriculum development.

Goldman's study was based in the research of Jean Piaget. A philosophical psychologist, Piaget found that children develop cognitively through a series of interactive changes which are similar to a person's physical development. The child develops from concrete ways of thinking to abstract ways of thinking. A person must be approximately eleven to thirteen before genuine abstract thinking is possible.

Since the cognitive portion of religion depends on abstract language such as spirit, love, and incarnation, religious educators need to be aware of the need for developing incremental experiences. A person may use abstract language at any time, but the use of words may not reflect understanding. Three-year-old Billy was brought to the Mother's Day Out program. His mother told the director that she hoped Billy would learn to share through the activities of the program. Later that morning Billy and another child were fighting over one of the toys. The director told them that they had to share. Billy responded, "I won't share!" The director explained the rules that in "this room we share the toys and take turns." "Oh," cheerfully replied Billy, "I'll take turns, but I won't share."

Moral Development

On the basis of carefully conducted empirical research, Lawrence Kohlberg discovered that the most basic universal moral virtue is justice. He also found that there are six discrete but related developmental states by which persons grow in justice, that is to say, grow morally. For example, Kohlberg found people moved from avoiding punishment as a principle for moral action, to the acceptance of the community's values, to the internalization of humane values for action that transcend a given community. Kohlberg's research was later expanded and challenged by Carol Gilligan. She included a broader base of research subjects than did Kohlberg, notably women. Of special importance to religious educators is that Gilligan's research discovered that an important dimension of moral development in females is that of caring.[23] Kohlberg based his research on the quest for justice as the source of moral value.

Faith Development

James Fowler has applied the work of Piaget to studies of faith development. Faith in Fowler's schema is not necessarily religious. Nor is it to be equated with belief. Faith is cognitive, namely how a person makes sense of life. Faith is described best as a verb. "I faith something to be true." Utilizing the theology of H. Richard Niebuhr and Paul Tillich in his basic psychological model, Fowler explored how a person relates to a transcendent or ultimate environment.[24]

Faith development, like other developmental theories, focuses on how people structure their thoughts about faith rather than the content of the thoughts. Faith development involves the interaction of how we think, our ability to do cognitive role-taking, our moral judgment, our bounds of social awareness, and how we order our world perspective, and finally our competence using intellectual symbols.

In faith development theory a person has to reach a certain chronological age and have comparable life experiences to move from one stage to the next. However, development is not automatic. A person's development can be arrested at any stage. The purpose of a transition into the next stage is that subsequent stages provide a more satisfactory resolution to life's experiences. As Fowler's titles suggest, he has found that most people tend to be arrested in Stage 3, Synthetic-Conventional Faith.

The early stages of faith development, "Intuitive-Projective" and "Mythic-Literal" reflect anthropomorphic ideas of deity, appeal to known authorities for their ideas, and accept religious ideas literally. In these stages, persons have no awareness of conflicts between myths or the authorities who hold these ideas. In the middle stages, "Synthetic-Conventional" and "Individuating-Reflective" persons become aware of multiple levels of symbols and of authorities. Differences are resolved by compartmentalization or by subordination.

In Stage 3, differences in symbolization are resolved when persons compartmentalize symbols. In this stage persons tend to be prejudiced toward other religious groups or the assimilation of everyone into one, e.g., "All Americans are Christians" or "We're all trying to get to the same place."

Stage 4, in Fowler's schema is called "Individuating-Reflective." Young adults in this stage tend to leave home, an event which breaks down the dependence on family approval and creates new centers of authority. Persons in this stage are often critical of the institutional church and take seriously commitments of the church to family, lifestyle, and beliefs. The people in this stage often have a strong urge toward self-fulfillment. Religious symbols are demythologized in this stage. The authority of a system outside of personal reference is often accepted as the way to deal with the polarities of finding one's own answers to life-directing questions.

Stage 5, "Conjunctive Faith," is the period in which the paradoxes of faith are both admitted and unified in both the person's mind and experience. The person chooses a religious commitment while at the same time understands that alternatives also have truth. The person admits and recognizes his or her own prejudices, values, myths, etc. The person seeks to use universal principles of justice rather than the values of his or her own group and accepts the possibility that judgment will go against the group. In this ability to see both sides lies a danger for the stage 5 person as one group as it may be paralyzed into inaction which appears either as complacency or cynical withdrawal.[25] Symbols are remythologized in this stage. The symbol becomes important when it is translated into an idea. For instance, the Christmas story is not debated as history but accepted because it is an important religious description of the incarnation.

Fowler's last stage, "Universalizing Faith," is based on universal human values, and very few reach this stage, even in part of their lives. The person in this stage becomes an incarnation of the kingdom of God, lives in an inclusiveness of community, and has a radical commitment to human justice and love.

Contributions to Religious Education

The major contribution of developmental psychology to learning theory is the description of the stages in the several fields of intellectual, emotional, moral, and spiritual development. It is obvious that some groups will object to the concept of development. To respond situationally and to accept one's own authority for decisions as proposed in Stages 5 and 6 of moral and faith development is not the ideal for extreme fundamentalist groups. It is also impossible to know the exact stage of each person in a congregation without extensive interviews.

DREs, and other religious educators, can use the concepts in planning a comprehensive youth and adult ministry. For instance, it might be helpful for an adult religious educator to be in Stage 5 so that alternatives are explored by the class. Discussion of the multiple meanings of ideas are expressed and encouraged. On the other hand, a person in Stage 3 might be the best choice to be in charge of the "sunshine" or "membership care" committee. Care involves empathy and Stage 3 persons personalize their care. The personalizing of taking supper to a new baby's family is central to Stage 3, while more global concerns are reflected in the higher stages. In the parish's board meeting, a conventional person will center on short-range plans while the Stage 5 person will tend to seek system information or long-range plans.

In terms of deliberate religious education, it is difficult to predict precisely what actions will cause a transition from one stage to the next. A wide variety of experiences that both affirm the person in the current stage as well as experiences that stimulate concerns of the next stage probably will be most helpful in the quest for more mature and complex relationships.

Religious Education and Social-Community Approaches

The social-community approaches are concerned with the social relationships and include insights and frameworks from the areas of sociology, history, government, education, and anthropology. They are concerned with the quality of the congregation's life as a community of the people of God.

Catechesis and Faith Enculturation

John Westerhoff, whose enculturation model is based in social-scientific anthropology, describes the faith enculturation that socializes the person into the tradition of the church as catechesis.[26] Catechesis is concerned about life in the world, but focuses on the life of the Christian community. It is a pastoral function. The paradigms of schooling and traditionally organized teaching are rejected by Westerhoff.[27] Faith enculturation takes place in the context of worship, liturgy, as well as pastoral care and church administration. All of the church's life is part of the larger pastoral ministry of catechesis. The goal of catechesis is to bring the person into relationship with the revelation of God so that the Christian story impacts (converts) the individual's life, the church, and the world.

C. Ellis Nelson proposes another religious education approach which builds on the communal life of the congregation and the way that life socializes the person into the traditions of the community. Nelson presents the thesis "that faith is communicated by a community of believers and that the meaning of faith is developed by its members out of their history, by their interaction with each other and in relation to the events that take place in their lives."[28] Nelson broadens the mission of the church and of educational work to include the larger community in which it lives and the kingdom of God in the whole world, although he limits this to the individual actions of enlightened and inspired individual Christians rather than the whole church.[29]

Christian Religious Education: Thomas Groome

Thomas Groome writes from an educational context. He asserts that when describing the intentional educational work done by the Christian community it should be called "Christian religious education."[30] For Groome, "Christian religious education is a political activity with pilgrims in time that deliberately and intentionally attends with them to the activity of God in our present, to the Story of the Christian faith community, and to the Vision of God's Kingdom, the seeds of which are already among us."[31]

God's present activity in the world is placed in dialogue with the biblical faith tradition of the Christian community. Christian religious education builds on the Christian traditions of the bibli-

cal story and liturgy as a way to see God's action in daily life.
Persons are invited to reflect cognitively on their own story and
the faith's story and then to enter into a hermeneutic dialogue
between their story and "the Story" in a way that the future
leading to God's kingdom is claimed. This vision of God's kingdom is a life that lives by the values of love and justice at the
same time it promotes the kingdom's values.[32] Groome states
clearly that educational activity does not have private consequences, since the individual and the citizen are the same person.
Nor can a Christian's spirituality ever be "private." For Groome,
any spirituality that ignores responsibility for the world is not a
Christian spirituality.[33]

A Social-Scientific Base For Religious Education

James Michael Lee

Probably no scholar in the twentieth century has been more
persistent and more forceful in placing religious education within
the framework of education rather than in the ambit of theology
than James Michael Lee.[34] Lee is acutely aware that the issue of
whether religious education is ultimately a form of education or a
branch of theology has major practical consequences on how
religion teaching will actually be executed.

In attempting to place religion in its proper ecology, Lee does
not start out like almost all other religious educationists who
simply assume or declare a priori that religious education belongs
to theology or education. Instead, what Lee does is to proceed a
posteriori, namely to examine the actual concrete here-and-now
dynamics of the religion teaching act itself and then see whether
educational theory or theological theory adequately explains how
religion teaching actually does work.[35]

The result of Lee's careful empirical analysis of the religion
teaching act is that without a doubt religion teaching is a form of
education and not a branch of theology. The goal of education is
to facilitate desired learning experiences, while the goal of theology is to cognitively examine the workings and nature of God.
What religion teachers do first and foremost is to endeavor to
facilitate desired learning outcomes. All their pedagogical activi-

ties are directed to this goal. Hence religion teaching is a branch of education.[36]

Religious Education a Social Science

Because education is itself a branch of social science, Lee calls his overall way of looking at and interpreting religious education a "social-science approach."[37] By this term it is meant that social-science theory is capable of doing what every adequate theory must necessarily do, namely, to explain why a particular religion teaching practice works or does not work, to predict which religion teaching practice will or will not work, and finally to verify whether or not a learner actually learned what the religion teaching act was designed to teach that person. Because theology deals with realities of a far different kind than the facilitation of learning, theological theory lacks the power to explain why a teaching practice works or fails. Theological theory similarly is unable to predict which teaching practice will work and which will flop. And finally, theological theory is incapable of verifying whether something has been learned or not.[38]

In the theological approach to religious education, the religion teaching act is regarded as nothing more than a messenger boy for theology, namely a means whereby theology was handed over to the learner.[39] The social-science approach gave religious education what it has urgently needed for so long, namely ontic autonomy—a field of study and a field of work in its own right.

Lee's trilogy is devoted to establishing a viable macrotheory for religion teaching. A macrotheory is a sort of grand theory or super theory, that is, a theory which can incorporate theories and laws of lesser scope such as the theory behind one or another specific teaching practice. Pivotal to any workable macrotheory of religion teaching is that it be value-free, namely, that it is capable of explaining, predicting, and verifying every kind of religion teaching act regardless of the specific concrete values which that particular teaching act embodies. Thus a workable macrotheory of religion teaching should be able to explain, verify, and predict the activities of all kinds of religion lessons regardless of whether these lessons are United Methodist lessons, Catholic lessons, Jewish lessons, or the like. Because social science is intrinsically value-free in that it is not inherently tied in with any specific set of religious values, Lee declares that it is possible to erect a macrotheory of religion teaching on a social-science base. This is not possible with a theological approach to religion teaching since each particular theology necessarily is tied to a specified set of religious values.[40]

Precisely because James Michael Lee's social-science approach is essentially educational in nature, it will over and over stress two fundamental points, namely, the holistic nature of the learner and the concrete dynamics of the religion teaching act.

Lee: Holistic Nature of Learner

In terms of the nature of the learner, Lee's educational approach emphasizes holism. By this he means that the learner is an amalgam of four interacting domains: psychomotor, cognitive, affective, and lifestyle. None of these can be eliminated in effective religion teaching. This holistic approach leads Lee to another central point in his approach, namely, that what religion teachers teach is primarily religion rather than theology. Theology is a cognitive science, whereas religion is the name given to the way a person lives his or her life in the real world. Because religion is a human activity and not a form of scientific investigation, all genuine religion teaching must be holistic and emphasize the four domains of human existence, Since lifestyle is the axis, hallmark, and end result of religion, Lee states that religion teaching methods and goals should be lifestyle-based. This is a significant departure from the theological (noneducational) models of religious education which regard religion teaching as primarily a cognitive affair utilizing cognitive methods to achieve cognitive goals.[41]

Lee: Dynamics of Teaching Act

In terms of the concrete dynamics of the religion teaching act, James Michael Lee has, through careful empirical analysis, discovered two major forms of content. The first of these is substantive content, namely the so-called "what" the teacher teaches. The second major form of content Lee calls structural content, the so-called "way" the teacher teaches. Lee adduces research to show that the pedagogical procedures which the religion teacher uses actually teach learners something independent of the substantive content being taught. Thus, if a religion teacher teaches in an unloving manner, the learners will learn an unloving form of religion. Teaching procedures constitute contents in their own right. Often—usually, in fact—structural content will exert a more powerful and more lasting influence on learners than will substantive content. Whereas advocates of the theological approach to religious education have a low regard for teaching procedures, Lee sees teaching procedures as extremely important in the overall work of the religious educator.

Lee's careful attention to the centrality of the actual here-and-now religion teaching act reveals that teaching is a complex series of interactions involving four major variables present in every pedagogical situation: the teacher, the learner, the subject-matter content, and the environment. Teaching, then, is not standing in front of a group of learners and talking. Rather, from the educational perspective, teaching is structuring the pedagogical situation so that each of these four variables interact with one another in such a way as to bring about the desired learning outcome. This structuring is no easy task, and demands knowledge of the science of education together with skills in communication.[42]

In short, Lee's social-science approach to religion teaching combines the structure of science with the heart of religion.

NOTES

1. James D. Smart, *The Teaching Ministry of the Church* (Philadelphia: Westminster, 1954), pp. 19-20.

2. L. Howard Grimes, "Church Education: A Historical Survey and a Look to the Future," *Perkins School of Theology Journal* (Spring 1972), p. 22.

3. James Michael Lee, *The Content of Religious Instruction: A Social Science Approach* (Birmingham, Ala.: Religious Education Press, 1985), pp. 634-637.

4. Frederick B. Artz, *The Mind of the Middle Ages A.D. 200-1500: A Historical Survey* (New York: Knopf, 1958), p. 305.

5. Ibid.

6. Ibid., p. 306.

7. Ibid., p. 305.

8. Carl Stephenson, *Medieval History: Europe from the Second to the Sixteenth Century* (New York: Harper & Brothers, 1951), p. 271.

9. Jack L. Seymour, *From Sunday School to Church School: Continu-*

ities in Protestant Church Education in the United States, 1860-1929 (Washington, D.C.: University Press of America, 1982), p. 25.

10. Robert W. Lynn and Elliott Wright, *The Big Little School: 200 Years of the Sunday School*, 2nd ed. (Birmingham Ala.: Religious Education Press, 1980), p. 40.

11. Ibid., p. 47.

12. Seymour, *From Sunday School to Church School*, p. 37.

13. Malcolm Knowles, ed., *Handbook of Adult Education in the United States* (Washington, D.C.: Adult Education Association of the U.S.A., 1960), p. 15.

14. Lynn and Wright, *The Big Little School*, p. 156.

15. Seymour, *From Sunday School to Church School*, p. 37.

16. David F. Wells and John D. Woodbridge, *The Evangelicals: What They Believe, Who They Are, Where They Are Changing* (Nashville: Abingdon, 1975), p. 30.

17. Robert R. Boehlke, *Theories of Learning in Christian Education* (Philadelphia: Westminster, 1962), p. 75.

18. Arthur W. Munk, *A Synoptic Philosophy of Education* (Nashville: Abingdon, 1965), pp. 51-52.

19. John Dewey, *Experience and Education* (New York: Macmillan, 1938), p. 13.

20. Ibid., p. 35.

21. Ronald Goldman, *Religious Thinking from Childhood to Adolescence* (New York: Seabury, 1964); and *Readiness for Religion* (New York: Seabury, 1965).

22. Goldman, *Religious Thinking from Childhood to Adolescence*, p. 222.

23. Carol Gilligan, *In a Different Voice: Psychological Theory and Women's Development* (Cambridge, Mass.: Harvard University Press, 1982).

24. James W. Fowler, *Stages of Faith: The Psychology of Human Development and the Quest for Meaning* (San Francisco: Harper & Row, 1981), p. 31.

25. Ibid., p. 198. For a fine interdisciplinary examination of Fowler's work, see Craig Dykstra and Sharon Parks, eds., *Faith Development and Fowler* (Birmingham, Ala.: Religious Education Press, 1986).

26. John H. Westerhoff III, *Who Are We: The Quest for a Religious Education* (Birmingham, Ala.: Religious Education Press, 1978), p. 268.

27. John H. Westerhoff III, *Will Our Children Have Faith?* (New York: Seabury, 1976), p. 9.

28. C. Ellis Nelson, *Where Faith Begins* (Atlanta: John Knox, 1967), p. 10.

29. Ibid., p. 201.

30. Thomas Groome, *Christian Religious Education* (San Francisco: Harper & Row, 1980), p. 24.

31. Ibid., p. 25.

32. Ibid., p. 50.

33. Ibid., p. 26.

34. Lee has written a detailed and elaborate trilogy setting forth in scholarly fashion the outline of his approach to religion teaching. The first volume, *The Shape of Religious Instruction* provides the foundational rationale for seeing that religion teaching is a form of education (and, therefore, of social science) and not a form of theology. The second volume of the trilogy, *The Flow of Religious Instruction*, deals exclusively with the structural content of religion teaching. The final volume of the trilogy, *The Content of Religious Instruction*, deals exclusively with the substantive content of religion teaching.

35. James Michael Lee, "The Authentic Source of Religious Instruction," in *Religious Education and Theology*, ed. Norma H. Thompson (Birmingham, Ala.: Religious Education Press, 1971), pp. 100-197.

36. James Michael Lee, *The Shape of Religious Instruction* (Birmingham, Ala.: Religious Education Press, 1971).

37. Social science is not to be confused with social studies or the like. Actually, social science is the name given to the disciplines or field which scientifically examine human interaction from a social and/or behavioral perspective. See Ibid., pp. 133-181.

38. Lee, "The Authentic Source of Religious Instruction," pp. 117-121.

39. Lee, *The Shape of Religious Instruction*, pp. 225-226, 246-248.

40. For discussion of value freedom in religion teaching, see Lee, *The Shape of Religious Instruction*, pp. 142-144, 207-208; James Michael Lee, *The Content of Religious Instruction* (Birmingham, Ala.: Religious Education Press, 1985), pp. 24, 42, 71, 107, 265, 660, 764.

41. Lee, *The Content of Religious Instruction*, especially pp. 608-735.

42. Lee, *The Flow of Religious Instruction*, pp. 230-268.

Chapter 4

The Fruitful Vision

The previous two chapters dealt with rival visions for a theoretical framework for religious education. Each of these two contending visions generate, in turn, various specific religious education procedures and explanations. Each of the two major visions and all the derivative procedures and explanations have audiences and writers in both popular literature and in each denomination's graduate schools and seminaries. As we evaluate the various theories several general assumptions need to be challenged.

Problems with Current Frameworks

Which Theological Base?
In the early twentieth century modern religious education was perceived as a sub-part of progressive education as well as of the liberal theology of that era. By mid-century the professors of Christian/religious education began to describe the field as one located in theology. The organic relationship to education was dropped. Neo-orthodoxy was the dominant theological position, replacing liberalism/modernism. Today, however, there are many theologies in the marketplace competing for acceptance.

This raises the question of the relationship of religious educa-

58

tion to any particular theology. When a theological theory/method loses power and prestige, does the religious educator also automatically lose the basis for authority? (It is also significant to observe that at the same time religious education was moving toward theology to be "protected" by its umbrella, pastoral counseling became the darling of the seminary curriculum.)

Lack of Social-Ethical Involvement

The relationship of religious education tied intrinsically to theology has caused another problem highlighted by Stephen Schmidt in *A History of the Religious Education Association.*[1] Until the 1970s, the global worldwide issues of peace, justice, and other general social concerns had not been addressed to any great extent by religious educators. Local church religious education tended to be ghettoistic by restricting the content it taught to local church concerns and outlooks. Religious education meant Bible study, the Sunday school, or a report of the latest continuing education event the pastor had attended at the seminary. (Because the whole seminary, except for social ethics departments, tended to ignore the larger social issues, religious educators should not be chided for ignoring the world and focusing primarily on church/institutional concerns.) Still, today, even with the church finally responding to societal issues, religious educators do not seem to adequately know how to equip and enable learners to participate in the ministries of peace and justice. The most religious educators seem to know how to do is to tell learners that they should be concerned.

Seminary Models Focus on Pastor-as-Educator

The context of the academic institution tends to determine what is defined as religious education.[2] This may help to understand two main assumptions.

First, since many of the books describing approaches or theories of religious education are written by seminary professors, the major image of their student tends to be the ordained clergyperson. Many of their books reflecting the relationship of ministry to education assume a power base equivalent to the pastor-in-charge. Thus the socialization/enculturation model that is primarily liturgical in practice, as well as the liberation models that depend on the influence of the pastor-in-charge rather than a staff member, are examples of the importance of the pastor/ minister as educator. However, the question arises is this the appropriate image of the *lay* (nonordained) professional religious educator?

Institutional Contexts Define Field Differently

Second, the context of the academic institution often exerts major impact on the goal definition for which the professional preparation of future religious educators is directed. If one can generalize, one can assert that seminaries tend to prepare persons for the preaching (and sacramental) ministry. University graduate departments specializing exclusively in classic nonprofessional academic areas such as theology or religious studies (with only a smattering of religious education courses) tend to prepare their students for teaching in higher education or in high schools which like to emulate higher education. Professional departments in graduate schools such as the department of religious education tend to prepare persons for service as a parish DRE or as a high-school religion teacher. Undergraduate colleges which have ministry and/or religious education offerings (usually Protestant institutions like Centenary College of Louisiana) tend to prepare persons for local church lay professional leadership ministries. In the latter connection, it should be emphasized that although Protestant undergraduate colleges have sometimes been criticized for having career church education courses simply for convenience, these programs typically were inaugurated as a response to the church's request for professionally prepared leadership at a time when many Protestant seminaries were unfortunately phasing out their Master of Religious Education (MRE) degree programs.

Christian Education and Religious Education

In the Introduction to *Changing Patterns of Religious Education* Marvin Taylor outlines the evolution of the use of Christian education and religious education as terms for the field. In the early days of the Religious Education Association, the title "religious" was simply a means of "separating education which had *religious* purposes from general education."³ It was not a specific theological position and could therefore accept persons from all faiths into the movement. However, when Protestant churches became influenced by neo-orthodox theology, the term "religious" became associated with the liberal tradition and was dropped in Protestant circles in favor of Christian education.

Christian Education

Lewis Sherrill opened his philosophy of Christian education by stating, "To reach the deepest understanding of Christian education, whether in history or at present, one must begin with Christianity and proceed thence to education."⁴ This was easily adapted to the familiar nurture model popular in most mainline Protestant churches which view Christian education as the development of persons through the love and nurture of the community to know and accept God's love. In addition to the nurture model, two contrasting examples of Christian education popular today include Christian education as practiced by Fundamentalist Protestants and the catechesis approach popular in the Roman Catholic church.

Christian Education: Protestant Fundamentalist Example

Protestant Fundamentalism (and to a large extent, Evangelicalism) is grounded in the exclusive authority of a divinely, verbally inspired Bible. Christian education for Fundamentalism is to proclaim and bring others to the worldview set forth in the Bible. Carl Henry, an Evangelical, declares that a major task in Christian education is to expose "the rationalistic prejudices of our time"⁵ which includes both natural and biological science and many social concerns such as sexual equality. Pluralism is rejected as there is only one correct answer based in the "Fundamentals." An open quest for truth is thus limited to the definition of the particular theological perspective.

Fundamentalist Christian education is larger in scope than the Sunday school. Christian education for Fundamentalists happens in women's groups, men's fellowships, youth clubs, day care, midweek prayer and study groups, and in families. Every member of the Christian fellowship is called "to be the visual embodiment of the church's technical program of Christian education."⁶ The curriculum of the Sunday school is a key part of Fundamentalist Christian education as it contains the specific content necessary for the "born again evangelism model" of children and youth. Curriculum, according to Henry, should be prepared by those who reject "the thought systems of secular education and who recognize the imperative of disciplining and indoctrinating."[7]

Catechesis in Roman Catholic Christian Education

With respect both to exclusivity and to socialization, the Christian education model of Fundamentalist Protestants is strikingly similar to the catechesis model of Roman Catholics. Just as Fundamentalist and Evangelical Protestants reject the term religious education because it is too broad and insufficiently specific (the only education which is genuinely religious is Christian education), so does the official Roman Catholic church reject the term religious education as being too broad and insufficiently specific (the only education which is genuinely religious is that which is directed by Catholic bishops). Catechesis is "that branch of religious education whose foundations, goals, content, personnel, and legitimacy are authoritatively determined by and are politically controlled by the official Roman Catholic *ecclesiasticum*."[8]

Catechesis is an official form of pastoral ministry, a term which in Roman Catholic parlance means an activity formally controlled by the Catholic hierarchy.[9] Formal Catholic documents on catechesis stress that catechesis uses a wide variety of teaching procedures, is conducted in a wide variety of school and nonschool settings, and is given to persons of all ages—but always under the control of the hierarchy. As a pastoral function, catechesis is: 1) always rooted in the ecology of officially approved Catholic theology, and never in the ecology of education, and 2) always targeted at socialization, namely handing on of that kind of Catholicism and developing those correct attitudes and beliefs which will somehow bring about a lifestyle which embodies the learners lived commitment to Catholicism.[10]

Among leading Catholic religious education experts there is considerable disagreement about whether catechesis is the best way to facilitate Catholicism in learners, to say nothing about developing religious pluralism among teachers and students. As a general rule, conservative Catholic religious education experts (almost always with strong formal ties to the institutional church, e.g., clergymen or persons in the employ of the institutional church) favor catechesis as the Catholic desideratum. Among this group are leaders like Berard Marthaler, Michael Warren, and Robert Levis. In contrast, nonconservative religious education experts prefer the term and the reality of religious education to catechesis, suggesting that catechesis is possibly indoctrination and is otherwise insufficiently religious, pluralistic, and human. Among this group are leaders like James Michael Lee, Gabriel Moran, Maria Harris, and Thomas Groome—to name just a few.

Practical Theology

Possibly because they were stung by well-documented charges of theological imperialism brought against their position by religious education scholars such as James Michael Lee,[11] some of the more open-minded proponents of the Christian education and catechetical vision have shifted from a stance of theology absolutely dominating education to a position in which theology dialogues with education. In this dialogue, however, theology still retains proximate and ultimate control over the process and result of the dialogue—and to this extent the dialogue is not really a genuine dialogue at all, at least from the perspective of education.

This new approach is rooted in practical theology, namely that Christian education and catechesis are branches of practical theology.

> Practical theology is critical and constructive reflection within a living community about experience and interaction, involving a correlation of the Christian story and other perspectives, leading to an interpretation of meaning and value, and resulting in everyday guidelines and skills for the formation of persons and communities.[12]

While education has tools to bring to the Christian education/catechetical process, theology still remains unquestionably the dominant member of the dialogue. Theology is the proximate and ultimate norm for all questions raised in the dialogue. Theology is the sole norm for the truth of the Christian story. And theology sets the limits and contours for the dialogue of secular (educational) and theological knowledge.[13]

Thus we can see that the aim in stressing the terms and the

realities of Christian education and catechesis as very distinct
from the term and the reality of religious education has consistently been to highlight the domination of theology over education. In this view, education is nothing more than a tool for the
theological perspective, a tool fashioned from raw material by
theological hands and used for theological purposes. Education
serves as the process to transmit a tradition, and also to reflect
and to transform the person in light of this tradition.[14] This
practical process is far lower than theology since it is only a
vehicle for assisting theology in attaining its ends. Education is far
different from reflection on the Christian tradition itself (theology).

Religious Education

The major counter-perspective to theology as the ultimate base
and norm for religious education is education. The term religious
education is not just an idle term used for convenience; rather the
term religious education suggests and indeed denotes a far fuller
meaning. Religious education grounded in education does not
lose its understanding of the faith community which it serves.
Religious education rooted in education realizes that theological
reflection on practice (practical theology) is far different from the
practice itself. If theological reflection were to equal practice,
then, as James Michael Lee argues, every practice ranging from
teaching to medicine to sports would become practical theology
when some person theologizes about teaching or medicine or
sports. If Christian education or catechesis or religious education
were indeed a branch of practical theology, then the skilled practical theologian would thereby automatically be a skilled teacher, a
skilled physician, or a skilled sportsperson—something which
Lee argues is obviously ridiculous.[15]

Pluralistic Approaches to Truth

And again, unlike the terms Christian education and catechesis
which are unabashedly confessional, the term religious education
suggests the intrinsic pluralism of the enterprise. Religious education, because of both of the words in this term encompasses a
plurality of vision. The premise is that there is not only one
approach to truth, but many.[16] Education is broader than any of

its parts, such as schooling. And education in its finest form is the opposite of indoctrination. Although formal settings such as the Sunday school and the CCD constitute major aspects of the contemporary context for religious education, these institutions are only one part of the larger paradigm of religious education.[17] Gabriel Moran points to the new direction for religious education in the context of religious pluralism. He declares that the "hegemony of theology over education programs in Christian circles is one of the obstacles to the emergence of religious education."[18]

Religious Education Risks Critical Questions

Moran challenges theology for its history of blocking religious education from asking questions.[19] Based in its officially approved doctrines of revelation, theology has labeled certain questions as blasphemy or "off-limits." Religious education is willing to raise questions both about the content of theology and the structure of the religious life. Religious education sees theology as being informative about values and choices of methods, but it also believes that there are options in both.

Fully recognizing that religious education is not located only in the classroom, Moran insightfully contrasts the role of education to preaching for a commitment to a position: "A classroom is not primarily a place to sing praises to God but for the critical examination of conflicting texts and competing interpretations."[20] Charles Melchert also notes the problems of theology's dominance over religious education. The theoretical base of religious education has "been little more than providing a theological rationale for the place of education in church activities," rather than using empirical research for understanding education or religion.[21]

Religious education can utilize the insights of the social sciences (Moran) or it can have its roots in social science (Lee). For instance, in faith development theory the higher stages see life as paradoxical. Conflicting values are accepted as paradoxical, yet in dialogue. The authority of the person is valued over dependence on the authority of either another person or an external set of beliefs or laws. The ability to take the perspective of the other person, without either being prejudiced or absorbing it into one's own position is described as maturity.

Ecumenical and Global Perspectives

Religious education provides for an ecumenical dialogue. In the past there has been the tendency to equate faith with certain creedal statements. In religious education, religious faith is recognized as being separate from belief. Education is not limited to cognitive, intellectual matters. It relates to the whole person. Alfred North Whitehead stated that "life in all its manifestations" is the content of education.[22] "Education is the guidance of the individual toward a comprehension of the art of life; and by the art of life I mean the most complete achievement of varied activity expressing the potentialities of that living creature in the face of its actual environment."[23] The affective and spiritual domains of a person's life are as important as the intellectual. Relationships between persons and between humanity and God are also part of the process.

Religious education looks for universal religious experiences. There is a cosmopolitan ideal in religious education in terms of authority and in belief. Because authority in mature education is personal rather than located in the institution, many churches are threatened. In commentary, what the faith developmentalists call maturity at Stage 5, many Protestant Fundamentalists call "secular-humanism."

Religious education seeks to help the person identify with the global community, at the same time becoming more aware and to identify with the richness of one's own tradition. This is a paradox which religious education sees as necessary for dialogue between traditions. "Religious education has, or ought to have, a twofold goal: 1) understanding one's own religious tradition, so that one can live by the richest resources of that tradition; and 2) understanding to whatever degree possible the religious life of other people."[24] Religious education provides opportunities for students to develop a life of faith. Concerns for the mythic vision which holds the community together, the narration of the biblical story and the church's history as well as the vision of a just shalom, and the examination of personal and social ethics are all part of the content of religious education.

In religious education the teacher owns the tradition of the story as a personal affirmation and offers it as an invitation to students to join in that pilgrimage. The student is free to accept or reject the story and the vision because the invitation is not indoctrination. Yet it is more than a simple secular discussion about religion. The faith commitment of the teacher is acknowledged as valid, while the student is free to accept it, to raise questions about it, to reinterpret it in light of personal experience, or to reject it.

Cultural Challenges and Religious Education

A Future-Oriented Society

Alvin Toffler has described civilization as having three waves.[25] The preindustrial-wave religious education was characterized by the centrality of the family, the neighborhood, and the church. In the second industrial wave, education was moved to the Sunday school or the parochial school. Now in the third wave, we have moved into an information and media society. The changes in communication, science, and human values have caused the growth of knowledge to exponentially change currently every three years. Can the church, which has based its Christian education and its catechesis on a print-oriented curriculum grounded in second-wave models of education and theology, be able to move into a third-wave vision of education and learning?[26] The vision must relate to the practice of the professional educator as well as relate to the broad field of religious education in ways that will enable the professional to predict and/or explain the practice of religious education.

Baby-Boomers and the Church

Our theological views have also reflected first or second wave models. Today, there is interest in the group of young adults called "baby-boomers," born between 1945-1965. They are important to all of society because they are the trend setters. The group sets the values for society based on their sheer numbers if for no other reason. Yet, in general, the church has been ineffective in relating to this group.

One significant characteristic of this group is its relative affluence. Its members are among the best educated in history. Another characteristic is its strong emphasis on individualism. The

group has been called the "me-generation." Based on the psychology of affluence, the group tends to have a sense of entitlement,
i.e., I deserve more of everything.

There is some evidence that the younger members of this
group are beginning to return to the churches today. It is sometimes suggested that many are attending conservative churches
because they are more effective in expressing the demands of the
Christian religion. And because they stress lived Christianity in
contrast to the intellectual Christianity of the liberal churches,
how can the church relate to this group meaningfully today? How
can the church proclaim its mission as caring for others in a
world of hurt and hungry people to a group that is characterized
by a Me-ism attitude?

Several approaches are part of the *popular* answer, but are
flawed. These popular answers call the church to be concerned
about the double meanings in preaching and teaching. For instance, popular folk religion tells the young adult, "Pull yourself
by your own bootstraps. Be a Winner!" Commercial religion,
daily heard on the TV announces, "Be a winner, reach out in
gusto . . . don't be a loser!" The TV evangelist preaches "I got
saved and look how much God rewarded me . . . a lake front
condo, a better job, etc. Even mainstream Calvinistic neo-orthodoxy says, "There are the saved and the damned. Of course I'm
saved." All say, "Me-first."

Meaning of Faith in a Post-Einstein Universe

The research shows that those denominations whose members
come from the affluent and educated have declined the most.
The research also indicates that rather than returning to old
traditional values, the gap is widening in terms of cultural pluralism.[27]

The question for the church is, can a new theology that is
based in contemporary understandings of culture and science, as
well as theology and biblical interpretation, be part of the tradition? James Fowler cautioned that the opposite of faith was not
doubt, but the inability to image any transcendent reality.[28] What
does it mean to have faith or to trust God in a post-Einstein
defined universe?

One helpful theological vision is process theology, blending the insights of evolutionary science, philosophy, and theology.[29] The nature of God in process thought is di-polar formed around two poles: 1) the transcendent, abstract essence of God such as everlasting, always acting in love, creator, and 2) the immanent nature which is experienced as persuasive love in which God shares our joys and sorrows and is affected by our actions.[30] God has an aim/desire for the universe which is to create opportunities for the fullness of life. Human beings are to live in ways that our fullness of life brings abundance to all. In this way true community is experienced and God's reign is more realized. For this reason, process theology is concerned with the oppressed and for any situations where human life is denied its fullest potential. Finally, because of the interrelationship of all of nature, process theology is concerned with ecology so that no part of creation is exploited or defiled.

Any theological vision which seeks to effectively influence a significant block of this highly educated baby-boomer generation must be able to authentically interact with science and technology. This theological perspective must affirm creation in terms of ecology, personal new creations, and the creation of those experiences that express humanity's great artistic endeavors. The theology must be able to dialogue with the artist as well as the scientist in this creative, life-affirming perspective. In addition, a spirituality that unites body and soul imagery while participating in movements of justice and liberation is necessary to balance concerns for personal spirituality with concrete actions to incarnate God's love in the world.[31]

Two Basic Conclusions

This chapter, like the two preceding it, has examined the two competing macro-perspectives for 1) theology versus education as the prime perspective of education in the churches, and 2) religious education versus Christian education/catechesis as the proper name and reality of what the churches are doing educationally. As a result of this analysis, two conclusions emerge pretty clearly—conclusions which form the fundamental basis for the rest of this book.

This first conclusion is that the prime framework of religious education (and, curiously enough, even of Christian education and catechesis) is education. Education specifies how the activity is done, and activity by its nature revolves around the way it is performed. (Activity is simply a name given to the way a reality is active.) Because education is a branch of social science, it will therefore draw on all the other social sciences in fulfilling its mission. Theology is a part of religious education to the degree it is relevant, operative, and important in a particular religious education activity.

The second conclusion is that the proper name and reality of what the church does (or should do) educationally is religious education and not either Christian education or catechesis. Education, like religion, is an open system. Religious education allows learners to personally form their faith in the context of an evolutionary universe in which all answers are not closed but open, just as God is not closed but open. Since the universe, humanity, and God are seen as dynamic realities in process theology, the religious educator will draw on a plurality of Christian and non-Christian theologies and seek answers in heuristic ways.[32]

The Vision for the Religious Educator

If the job of the director of the church's educational activities is ever to become a profession, if it is ever to become truly effective, then this career must be grounded in religious education—that is, in education rather than in theology, and in religious education rather than in Christian education or catechesis. As we will see in the remainder of this book, religious education as education and as religion has enormously direct and immediate practical consequences for the basic workaday tasks of the director in the church's educational activities. Calling the career religious education is not logic chopping or linguistic superfluity; rather, it is the sustenance and the empowerment of one's everyday activity.

The Vision Defined

Religious education involves the deliberate and ongoing planned efforts of the faith community through individual projects, group activities, and organizational concerns to enable persons to develop their Christian faith and to enable both groups and individuals to respond as people of God with ministries in the world. It involves helping the people know the community's Story and how they might live faithfully in the prophetic kingdom of God in ministry. It should be noted that theology, biblical scholarship, church history, social ethics, and other traditional religious subjects are not ignored in this religious education model. The DRE and each teacher must be able to discuss the story, the ideals and values of the Christian faith, as well as be a witness to her/his own relationship to God.

The mature objective of religious education is more than the accumulating of knowledge about religious stories. The learner gains the ability to analyze principles and relationships so that new patterns of acting in the world may be synthesized or created from the knowledge of the basic story. Both the content and the ways of being in ministry are evaluated by the learner. In the same way, mature religious education also seeks to enable the learner to identify, accept, and be committed to appropriate values so that the student is characterized by a value system that has been personally developed in dialogue with the community's story. This is not something that children can complete. It is too abstract and complex. It is nurtured over a lifetime. Therefore, religious education is lifelong.

Religious education is concerned with developing the whole person as a creation of God so that life might be lived in its most abundant sense. Religious education is comprehensive in its relationship to the whole person, meeting psychological, leisure, relational, and other general life needs, as well as spiritual needs. These planned activities may be called religious education either in the narrowest sense because they are sponsored/authorized by the church or because their content is "religious," or in the broader sense concerning one's relationship to God.

Religious education's focus is broader than individualized salvation or leadership in the local institutional church. A major part of religious education is helping people live their discipleship in the world. The content of religious education includes both the biblical/historical story as well as reflection on social ethics and how to analyze and meet contemporary human needs in daily living.

Religious education concerns more than personal religion. It happens in the context of the community of faith. The church is not a closed system. It is affected by the external environment and its own internal organizational goals.[33] The emerging awareness of the contributions of organizational development or systems theory can aid in the design of support systems and in understanding how the various components of a church's educational ministry are interrelated.[34]

Advantages of Religious Education Framework

The framework of education, building on the contributions of the social sciences such as the perspective of organizational development, provide the best basis for the vision of religious education as well as the framework for the DRE's preparation and ministry. There are several advantages for the choice of education as the framework.

Moves Toward Upper Level Faith Development Stages

First, religious education meets the criteria of the higher stages of faith development. Religious education should be capable of creating experiences to assist persons to reach the appropriate stage of development. Any model that requires acceptance of certain theological positions a priori will be incapable of meeting the openness of heuristic faith.

Global Perspective

A second advantage is that religious education tends to emphasize living in the global perspective rather than individualized salvation. What does it mean to recognize all people as God's creation? It is concerned with discipleship and faithful living in the context of daily living. Spiritual formation is one aspect of religious education, but the goal is not fixated at the formation event. Rather, seeking for a satisfactory means for the ministry of every Christian in daily circumstances becomes central. This is more evident if process theology contributes in its own way to the perspective, as a person's decisions have cosmic importance.

Matches the Professional Duties of the DRE

Support for this position of religious education as the overarching model is also found in the professional concerns of the DRE.

The tasks listed in the various advertisements of positions available for DREs indicate the need for educational skills in working with children, youth, and adults. Few positions for local church professional educators call for regular preaching duties, and the high majority are concerned with adult leadership training of local members so that they can perform their ministry. Locke Bowman calls for directors who have skills in assisting lay teachers to teach better and to effectively administer the educational program (i.e., the church school).[35]

The new title that many directors and coordinators are using today is "program director" or "director of program ministries." The skills of organizational development, program development, working with groups such as planning committees, motivating persons to be in ministry, and enabling people to find centers for the use of their talents are helping skills visioned in religious education.

In the past, the church has held the belief that individuals shape institutions. In this view, if the church could save enough people, the world would be transformed into the kingdom of heaven. However, organizational studies indicate that institutions have an identity-forming process of their own that is generally more powerful than any individual. Hence, although professors of Christian education may wish to train professionals who are primarily skilled theologians, who can reflect on the nature of ministry and become teaching theologians in residence, it is not the real world in which their graduates practice. The local church says, "We want someone who can help us creatively do our educational ministry. We need someone who will be willing to work effectively with our youth, and adult workers with youth, to increase their commitments to values taught by the church." The local church transforms the person into the role of specialist in education, not theology. It is the nature of the job which seeks its appropriate roots.

Religious education is concerned with the faith and the discipleship of the individual Christian, the life and mission of the church, and the witness of the people of God in ministry in the world. The vision of religious education challenges the tradition of grounding the field in theology. The educational vision offers the opportunity to integrate many of the perspectives of the field as it enables the complex interaction of persons, the institutional church, and the world to be in process toward the shalom of God.

NOTES

1. Stephen Schmidt, *A History of the Religious Education Association* (Birmingham, Ala.: Religious Education Press, 1983), pp. 173-175.

2. Allen J. Moore, "Religious Education as a Discipline," in *Changing Patterns of Religious Education,* ed. Marvin J. Taylor (Nashville: Abingdon, 1984), pp. 91-95.

3. Marvin J. Taylor, ed., *Changing Patterns of Religious Education* (Nashville: Abingdon, 1984), p. 7.

4. Lewis J. Sherrill, *The Rise of Christian Education* (New York: Macmillan, 1944), p. 1.

5. Carl Henry, "Restoring the Whole Word for the Whole Community," in *The Religious Education We Need,* ed. James Michael Lee (Birmingham, Ala.: Religious Education Press, 1977), p. 66.

6. Ibid., p. 61.

7. Ibid., p. 68.

8. James Michael Lee, "The Authentic Source of Religious Education," in *Religious Education and Theology,* ed. Norma H. Thompson (Birmingham, Ala.: Religious Education Press, 1982), p. 191.

9. James Michael Lee, "Catechesis Sometimes, Religious Instruction Always," in *Does the Church Really Want Religious Education?,* ed. Marlene Mayr (Birmingham, Ala.: Religious Education Press, 1988), pp. 32-66.

10. Michael Warren, "Catechesis: An Enriching Category for Religious Education," *Religious Education* 76 (March-April 1981), pp. 115-127; Berard L. Marthaler, "Socialization as a Model for Catechesis," in *Foundations of Religious Education,* ed. Padraic O'Hare (New York: Paulist, 1978), pp. 64-92.

11. James Michael Lee, *The Shape of Religious Instruction* (Birmingham, Ala.: Religious Education Press, 1971), pp. 242-243; James Michael Lee, "The Authentic Source of Religious Instruction," in *Religious Education and Theology,* pp. 146-156.

12. James N. Poling and Donald E. Miller, *Foundations for a Practical Theology of Ministry* (Nashville: Abingdon, 1985), p. 62.

13. Donald E. Miller and Jack L. Seymour, "The Future of Christian Education," in *Contemporary Approaches to Christian Education,* ed. Jack L. Seymour et al. (Nashville: Abingdon, 1982), p. 162.

14. Mary Elizabeth Moore, *Education for Continuity and Change: A New Model for Christian Religious Education* (Nashville: Abingdon, 1983), p. 121. For another examination of the dynamic but fruitful tension between tradition and prophetism, see Mary C. Boys, "Access to

Traditions and Transformations," in *Tradition and Transformation in Religious Education,* ed. Padraic O'Hare (Birmingham, Ala.: Religious Education Press, 1979), pp. 9-34.

15. Lee, *The Shape of Religious Instruction,* pp. 239-243.

16. On this point see Norma H. Thompson, ed., *Religious Pluralism and Religious Education* (Birmingham, Ala.: Religious Education Press, 1988).

17. This point is a recurring theme running through almost all of the chapters in D. Campbell Wyckoff, ed., *Renewing the Sunday School and the CCD* (Birmingham, Ala.: Religious Education Press, 1986).

18. Gabriel Moran, "From Obstacle to Modest Contributor: Theology in Religious Education," in *Religious Education and Theology,* ed. Norma H. Thompson (Birmingham, Ala.: Religious Education Press, 1982), p. 43.

19. Ibid. p. 59.

20. Ibid. p. 47.

21. Charles Melchert, "Theory in Religious Education" in *Foundations for Christian Education in an Era of Change,* ed. Marvin J. Taylor (Nashville: Abingdon, 1976), p. 21.

22. Alfred North Whitehead, *The Aims of Education* (New York: Macmillan, 1929), p. 7.

23. Ibid., p. 29.

24. Gabriel Moran, *Interplay: A Theology of Religion and Education* (Winona: St. Mary's Press, 1981), p. 37.

25. Alvin Toffler, *The Third Wave* (New York: Morrow, 1980).

26. Ronald A. Sarno, *Using Media in Religious Education* (Birmingham, Ala.: Religious Education Press, 1987), pp. 41-166.

27. R. T. Gribbon, *30 Year Olds and the Church: Ministry with the Baby Boom Generation* (Washington, D.C.: Mount St. Alban, 1981), p. 1.

28. James Fowler, *Stages of Faith: The Psychology of Human Development and the Quest for Meaning* (San Francisco: Harper & Row, 1981), p. 31.

29. Gloria Durka, "Modeling Religious Education for the Future," in *The Religious Education We Need: Toward the Renewal of Christian Education,* ed. James Michael Lee (Birmingham, Ala.: Religious Education Press, 1977), p. 97.

30. John B. Cobb Jr. and David R. Griffin, *Process Theology: An Introductory Exposition* (Philadelphia: Westminster, 1976), p. 48.

31. This dialogue can be illustrated in two resources from radically different perspectives. Matthew Fox, *Original Blessing: A Primer in Creation Spirituality* (Santa Fe: Bear, 1983), presents a spirituality based in creation/incarnation theology which rejects the traditional Fall/Redemption theology which undergirds many of the present theological positions. Donald R. Strombeck, *The Reason for Science* (Davis, Calif.: Stonegate, 1987), writing from the more traditional, albeit liberal, theo-

logical perspectives, presents one example of how the dialogue between science and religion can be developed.

32. Durka, "Modeling Religious Education for the Future," p. 98.

33. See Robert C. Worley, *A Gathering of Strangers: Understanding the Life of Your Church* (Philadelphia, Westminster, 1983).

34. For a careful interfacing of religious education with systems theory see Timothy Arthur Lines, *Systemic Religious Education* (Birmingham, Ala.: Religious Education Press, 1987).

35. Locke E. Bowman Jr., "Analysis and Assessment: The General Protestant Sunday School," in *Renewing the Sunday School and the CCD,* ed. D. Campbell Wyckoff (Birmingham, Ala.: Religious Education Press, 1985), p. 95.

Part II

Revisioning the Profession

Chapter 5

Functional Roles and Skills of the DRE

Is the DRE a member of a craft or a profession? Many persons are employed by churches without academic training and appear to perform assigned duties efficiently. They have often been trained in workshops or just have a general interest in the field. These persons tend to reflect a craft model. Another group is represented by those prepared at the undergraduate college level with majors in religious education. Although not accepted for certification by some denominations, these graduates function with a basic knowledge of theory and professional identity. Since World War II, a graduate degree has been required to receive certification as a Director of Religious Education in many denominations. Historically, the DRE with the master's level academic preparation has assumed a professional identity, although not always meeting the full sociological criteria for being called a professional.

The academic preparation for professional religious educators has not been based on the results of carefully researched assessments of the needs of the church or of the tasks performed by the religious educator related to the religious education ministry. The primary factor for requiring DREs to pursue professional preparation has been related to the process of credentialing or certification.[1] While professional preservice preparation has been mandated by the certification procedures, little attention has been given to continuing in-service professional education or to the lifelong learning needs of the DRE.

During the early history of the Protestant DRE, the religious educator's identity was primarily that of a pedagogical specialist.[2] Ordination was not a major goal for these religious educators. Following World War II, a new trend developed that sought to identify the DRE as a theologian. Part of this move was based on the emerging theological emphasis in the seminary. Another part of this switch in emphasis was grounded in the idea that if the DRE was able to think theologically, staff relationships with pastors could be improved.[3]

For a variety of political reasons, a large number of Protestant seminaries by the end of the 1960s had dropped the familiar Master of Religious/Christian Education degree and only offered the generalist Master of Divinity degree. Consequently—or con-comitantly—the seminary began to focus on the ordained clergy-person as educator rather than on the professional religious edu-cator as the parish's educational specialist. Today there is confusion on whether the DRE should be ordained or continue as a lay professional. Many Protestant female students who for-merly had studied religious education now seek ordination as pastors, viewing religious education as unacceptable because it had been classically identified as "women's work." Employment equality also became an issue for religious education directors. The same issues that face women employed in secular positions of salary and job security face those employed as religious educa-tion directors. In some denominations such as the United Meth-odists and the Presbyterians these political-economic issues have become focused in the push for the ordination of lay profession-als as deacons as means of obtaining access to employment rights.

The DRE as Religious Education Specialist

There is an urgent need for the DRE to reclaim the vision of professional identity as religious educational specialist in the Protestant churches. Many of the arguments presented by the early pioneers are still relevant. Henry Cope, General Secretary of the Religious Education Association from 1907-1923 cautioned against the assistant/associate minister model. "This is the day of specialization; the pastor is a specialist in his (her) field and should not dishonor it by expecting that one trained in another field can lightly step in and do his (her) particular work."[4]

Maria Harris contrasts the work of the director of education with the work of the ordained clergy.[5] Clergy are officials of the institution and as members of the ecclesiastical community are spokespersons for the church. The DRE is not an ecclesiastical officer of the church and indeed has enough apartness from the institution to be able to raise the necessary questions to bring the church into dialogue with the key ideas, values, and attitudes of its time.

Harris and James Michael Lee appear to equate the term ministry with clergy or with clergy-dominated activities. Protestants (and many Catholics), in contrast, define ministry as broader than the ecclesiastical officials. Ministry involves the traditions of caring in the fellowship, service in the world, and the spirituality of the people.

The DRE Is a Professional

Sometimes criticism is raised that the DRE should not be a professional but just be someone who gets along with people. To this criticism the following response must be given. To be a professional is to raise the practice of religious education above uninformed hunches. A professional educator will not chase a new fad technique or program because it is popular. To be a professional means that one can refer to theoretical principles and to relevant empirical research so as to adequately evaluate situations and ideas and be able to choose alternatives rather than blindly repeat previous actions. The nonprofessional educator lacks the theoretical research and background that makes possible this kind of effective evaluation.

Professional competence is different from professional*ism*. To be a competent professional indicates that religious education requires more than amateur skills. The professional educator must possess a body of knowledge about religious education that is beyond his or her own individual personal experience. A professional will know the content of religious education per se as well as general biblical and theological knowledge. In addition, a professional will have acquired the concrete repertoire of skills in order to successfully teach religion to someone else. A professional will also be able to teach these pedagogical skills to other incoming religious educators. Professional competence is subject to review and change according to the needs of the profession. All in all, there are definite theoretical and skill standards that should be expected of all members of the profession.

Functional Leaders Use Legitimate Power

Power is the ability to get things done. The DRE needs power to enable the educational work of the church to be brought to its fullest potential. The generalist clergy are beginning to recognize that a specialist is not one who seeks to gain political control of the church's organization. When the traditional model of management-staff organization is applied to the church, it is clear that the DRE is not a line officer, i.e., second or third in the chain of command. A more creative way to visualize church-staff relationships is seen in effective companies today. This is called functional leadership. It is possible for a person with technical competence and knowledge in an area to be a process authority over that area rather than a senior command officer. The DRE is a functional leader who facilitates, resources, and enables the other members of the church to effectively perform their educational tasks. The DRE serves as a vital linkage between and among the church's capabilities, the community's resources, and the ministries of the members of the parish.

Justice Issues and the Professional

The need for greater professionalization of the DRE is related to the issue of justice. There is no doubt that women who serve as religious educators often feel powerless, both as persons and in their position. The advantage of the DRE accepting the image of a professional specialist in religious education is the establishment of a power base for ministry. Power has often been a fearful word for the religious educator, but it is important. Women DREs have often faced the limitation of power and have been forced to pretend they were less educated or capable than the male clergy. The power of the religious educator is always that of a staff person, not a line officer. Yet the DRE must have a source of power that provides access to information and resources that enable the laity to accomplish their ministry. This requires that the female DRE image herself as a professional.

To be a professional DRE it is necessary to regularly read scholarly research in religious education itself, as well as in those biblical and theological areas related to religious education. To be a professional DRE is also to accept responsibilities as leaders in professional and local organizations. There must be the claiming of identity as a professional religious educator by each DRE in order to enhance the status of all religious educators, regardless of whether these persons are teachers or administrators. The establishment of networks for intellectual and professional support in addition to sharing the latest program is critical for the development of this professional identity.

The DRE Is a Specialized Ministry

The professional identity of the DRE blends several elements. At the daily work, public level, there is the ability to perform certain professional tasks and skills. At a second, personal level, there is the recognition that the DRE enters the specialized ministry of the church in answer to a call from God. Each biblical prophet described a personal call from daily activities to become a spokesperson for God in the midst of the community's life. To be a professional DRE means that one possesses the academic qualifications (grounded in social science and education), has the practical experiences, has responded to the call of God, and has been validated by the church to be involved in a crucial ministry of the church.[6] This call to a specialized ministry helps distinguish between the general ministry of all Christians and the specific ministry of certain employed church professionals such as clergy and DREs.

Summary

To describe the work of the DRE involves several levels of consideration. There is 1) the professional identity, 2) the framework for the specific field of activity, and 3) the foundations for the specific work of the DRE. The DRE is a professional who has responded to a spiritual experience with God which has been validated by the church and is in a specialized ministry of the church. The specialized ministry is in the field of religious education in which the framework is education rather than religion or theology. The foundation of the professional practice of the DRE in the local church is in social studies, including education, administration, organizational development, sociology, structural psychology, and counseling.

The Roles of the DRE

In order to meet the vision of religious education for the future, it is necessary to establish an ongoing dialogue between the practice of religious education in the local church by the DRE and the theories and training that undergird the practice. It is necessary to understand the typical duties that are fulfilled by the DRE in the local church in performing the ministry of education. It is also necessary to consider the vision of religious education so that the practice and the vision can be in dialogue to create effective preparation and support for the professional DRE.

Duties of the DRE

The duties of the DRE can be observed in many listings of job openings. These include the broad categories of working with the Sunday school in terms of curriculum resourcing, leadership training of teachers and other church leaders, supervising lay leadership, selecting and recruiting leaders, and coordinating the age-level ministries through activities such as teaching or advising leaders, and general counseling of youth and others. A 1976 study of how DREs spend their professional time found that working with the Sunday church school (26.5 percent), youth fellowships (14.0 percent), leadership training (13.3 percent), and teaching (7.5 percent) were the top specific activities mentioned.[7]

Additional insights can be gleaned from an expansive vision for religious education. Vision generates goals, and vice versa. A key goal of religious education involves helping people live their discipleship in the world. Duties such as creating programs to reflect on social needs in light of the biblical story and to gain the necessary skills to be in ministry in the world should, therefore, be part of the professional religious educator's duties.

Functional Roles

More helpful than a random list of duties in the development of a professional set of qualifications for a DRE is an understanding of what functional roles the DRE actually does perform. Functional roles are the larger categories in describing what the professional does in performing specific duties.

Dorothy Jean Furnish lists four functional roles of the DRE: program development and coordination, leader development, advocacy, and modeling shared leadership in a multiple staff.[8] Stephen Nevin listed three major roles: theological resource person, master teacher, and organizer or manager.[9] William Case included the roles of educator, organizer, and administrator and supervisor. Helping all to be committed to fulfilling the mission of the church in the world is the central concern of all the functional roles.[10] Maria Harris describes functional roles as activities. The roles she identifies in youth ministry can easily be posited for religious education all across the board. These roles include the activities of didachē/teaching, leiturgia/prayer, koinonia/communion, kerygma/advocacy, and diakonia/troublemaking.[11]

Directors of religious education need to be able to create opportunities which build on content traditionally taught in our programs. These opportunities are concretized through activities using procedures that provide for the greatest human development of persons under values proclaimed by the church seeking to be faithful. Central to any true functional definition of religious education is the DRE's responsibility of creating opportunities for discipleship in the larger world.

It appears that there are several major functional roles that are expected of every DRE. The roles of program administrator and program developer appear basic to every DRE position regardless of whether the person serves as a youth director or across the lifespan. In addition the DRE serves as an educational consultant serving as a resourcer and a facilitator at the level of organizational development. The role of learning specialist has been a familiar one for religious educators. Curriculum planning and materials development when prepared resources are not available have been strengths of the profession. Actual classroom leadership, especially with children and youth groups are also traditional roles of the learning specialist. Teacher preservice and inservice education is a role rightly associated with the DRE.

The DRE must begin to accept responsibility for the diagnosing of real and felt educational needs of the parishioners. If genuine empowerment of parishioners is to occur, it is absolutely necessary to move the development of educational programs from the latest bag of gimmicks to programs which are based on both adequate theory and solid research. The DRE must be able to research the needs of the people and of the organizational church. The purpose of the avid consumption of theory and research is not to create meta-level theory, but to discover what is workable here-and-now for the DRE's own people. Related to the roles of diagnostician and researcher is evaluator. The value of a religious education program must be considered as well as whether the resources are being used in the best possible way.

The DRE enters into his or her profession in response to a vocational call. The DRE is responsible to be an interpreter of the Christian faith. Through professional training, the DRE possesses an adequate background in theology and biblical studies. The DRE is an interpreter of the ancient story and the contemporary currents of theology to the people.

Finally, in working with the various age levels, the DRE serves as a counselor. This is in the tradition of a vocational or educational counselor rather than a psychological therapist. Much of the counseling of a DRE is done in the context of the other functions or activities performed by the religious educator. Thus the DRE should be conversant with the latest research in the psychology of religious counseling.

Skills of an Effective DRE

Robert Katz described three fundamental skills of an effective administrator that cut across personality traits and job descriptions.[12] These skills tend to operate at different levels of organizational responsibility. Each skill is important individually; yet there is also a sense in which they are all interrelated so that they are seldom found in isolation. The three skills in hierarchical order are 1) technical skills, 2) human skills, 3) conceptual skills. While the skills are related to general business administration they are also basic to the functioning of the DRE.

Technical Skills

Technical skills involve the ability to use the specialized procedures, methods, and techniques that are basic to a specific profession. They are usually developed in the preparation phase of a person's career. Technical skills include proficiency in the various procedures that characterize the special field of religious education. Technical skills for the DRE would include the ability to prepare a brochure for a program, to outline a curriculum study, to speak clearly and comfortably before a group, and so forth. Being able to use a computer for word processing or to retrieve data are other illustrations of technical skills. Since DREs often work with committees or organizations, they must possess the basic technical skill of chairing a meeting using general parliamentary procedure. Today, the DRE must develop technical skills in helping persons to prepare and to function in their discipleship in the world as the people of God.

Human Skills

Human skills involve the ability of the DRE to work with people at the individual level and with people in groups in building a cooperative effort in the church. Human skills require that the DRE be aware of his or her own values, perceptions, attitudes, and assumptions. The DRE must be able to support the growth of individuals through relationships that are supportive and trusting. The art of negotiation is part of the human relationship skills in which the DRE both influences and is influenced by others.

The Personal Touch

Being sensitive to the feelings of other persons rather than focusing only on the subject-matter content of the messages is essential in human skills. An example will illustrate this point. A mother brought her three-year-old child to Sunday school for the first time. Seeking out the DRE, the mother stated that her child was above average in ability. She felt the child should be placed in the K-4 class so that he would be challenged intellectually. The DRE in wisdom quickly and gently replied that she understood the mother's concern. "That's a real problem. We have a number of above average children in our Sunday school and have adjusted our classes to accommodate their special abilities." The mother was relieved and her child is happily in the three-year-old nursery.

The DRE needs to be able to use a variety of resources in

human relations skills. Recently a group of religious educators at a professional workshop listed areas of their work that they disliked. High on the list was using the telephone. Yet the telephone is one of the valued human resources in urbanized society. The telephone company's slogan, "Reach out and touch someone," combines the idea of high tech and high touch. It is significant that many elderly spend several hours on the telephone each day visiting with friends, just keeping in touch. Skills in using the telephone to relate to a parishioner's human needs, to recruit persons for various church activities, or to provide information will become increasingly valuable for the DREs. The ability to call someone and make that person feel significant should be a skill sought by religious educators. Many effective DREs write notes of recognition to different persons each week. Both the writing of simple notes and using the telephone successfully are ways in which the religious educator can effectively utilize human skills.

Human skills also relate to working with groups to enhance community, self-understanding, general communication, and conflict resolution. To create collaborative methods of working as a team in groups is a basic skill for every DRE. Empirical research today shows that effective leaders work to build a shared responsibility among the participants of the work team. A sense of interdependence among participants is found in excellent organizations.[13] Passing ideas through the pastor, the education committee, or the church board requires attention to the dynamics of power and individual relationships.

Empathy Is Basic

Advanced skills in human relations involve the ability to accept the values, attitudes, and assumptions of others without trying to make them conform to one's own perceptions. These skills are used when recruiting persons during the interviewing process, when reflecting feelings and ideas in group settings and in counseling sessions, and when leading discussions. The ability to empathize is a skill that will develop sensitivity to the needs of the world and will motivate parishioners to want to work in one or another of the church's missional thrusts.

Human relation skills tend to require maturity and robust life experiences for their fullest development. An actual situation may illustrate the need for maturity based on how two staff members handled a particular conflict situation. Two clergy were newly appointed to a church. The former senior clergyman had been the founding pastor of that church. Soon after arrival, the young minister of education faced serious opposition from one of the groups in the church. This group attempted to thwart all the minister of education's attempts to modify the educational program or youth program, regardless of the merit of his endeavors. The young clergyman felt the opposition as personal. The wise pastor, however, recognized the human dynamics underlying the whole situation. The opposition group was displacing hostility against the former minister who had left the church due to a divorce situation. These people felt hurt and responded in blind anger toward a minister. However, the senior pastor functions as a symbol of the faith. On the other hand, the young minister of education did not have this psychological protection and could be the focus of their striking out in frustration. The pastor took responsibility in the situation, identified the forces causing the conflict for the group to see what was happening to them, and enabled the church to come together again in a cooperative total-church ministry. Knowing how to handle delicate human relations takes maturity and sensitive communication.

Conceptual Skills

The third skill needed by the DRE is conceptual. The ability to see the overview, to conceptualize the whole organization is the skill needed by senior members of the program staff, such as the DRE. To conceptualize the whole includes the ability to diagnose, synthesize, question, visualize interrelationships, and mentally explore future possibilities. It involves the skill of strategic long-range planning for the organization.[14] This is the skill that is limited in the experience of most DREs. Understanding how the overall religious education program fits into the larger life of the church is part of this skill, while at the same time, for example, understanding how religious education programs for children constitute one part of the church's total-life religious educational ministry.

Conceptual skills are related to the problem-anticipation and problem-solving abilities in that the DRE must develop skill in diagnosing the actual problem rather than focusing only on symptoms. In the church, to conceptualize the whole while seeing the parts requires the ability to integrate and synthesize the social, economic, political, historical, and psychological concerns of the community as well as being able to reflect theologically and religiously on the setting.

The effectiveness of the church in the future will depend to a large part on whether its leadership can conceptualize the changes in society and their impact on the life of the church. For instance, what is the mission of the church? If it is to save souls for a heavenly existence, what religious education activities are needed? If it is equipping persons for a shared ministry in the world in the name of Christ, then what training do the people need? How one identifies the mission may determine the means to accomplish its task.

A key part of the skill of conceptualizing is the ability to construct a vision and to articulate that vision for the community. In business settings, the exciting managers are not those who are the great problem solvers but those who have a vision of what the organization should become in light of the changing culture and who can organize their staff around that vision.

When churches are growing in a new suburban community, conceptual questions often are unasked. However, when the economy shifts, or when the initial church membership peak is reached, the ability of the leadership to conceptualize makes the difference between a church that continues to be effective or one that becomes stagnant or declines. What happens when a neighborhood changes from young families to middle-aged couples? What is the meaning for the church's mission in terms of where the people will be willing to serve both institutionally and in the community as people of God with ministries? The ability to accurately define conceptually both membership needs and the related religious education needs associated with these issues makes a significant difference in the church's ability to cope with the environmental changes.

Conceptual Skills and the DRE

Historically, it has been the pastor who has had the responsibility for conceptualizing the church's program and description of mission. It has often been observed that in the very large churches the pastor does not have to know how to do religious education but be able to vision how religious education fits into the total mission of the church as well as to recruit skilled subordinates to perform the technical aspects of religious education.

Today the professional religious educator joins in that responsibility of providing vision. For instance, a DRE does not need to be technically skilled in preschool education to supervise a day care program but does need to understand how the dynamics of that program fit into the larger description of religious education in that church. As the DRE moves into the wider definition of organizational development as an arena for religious education, the ability to do conceptual thinking and conceptual planning is increasingly important.

Many directors have chosen to use a title reflecting responsibility for the entire gamut of the church's mission. When this is a true description of the position, conceptual skills are absolutely necessary for the DRE. The administration of a religious educational program in a large church makes it impossible for the DRE to perform every technical activity. Administration in such a setting requires the DRE to build a cooperative unit of other persons working at various levels in the organization of the church. The DRE must be able to conceptualize, at least for herself/himself, how the various parts, programs, and activities harmoniously work together toward a common goal of the church.

The development of conceptual skills also requires life experiences to mature. Mentors are often helpful when the superior is willing to genuinely coach the DRE on problem definition and problem solving in the church. It may also be the result of working in many areas of the church's life and mission. For this to be shared between the pastor and the DRE in the local church, frequent staff meetings and communications that truly share information are required.

Enabling Skills

A fourth general skill required by the DRE as a professional is that of enabler. In his presidential inaugural address at Garrett Evangelical Theological Seminary, Merlyn Northfelt described the importance of both knowing the substantive content of biblical/theological studies as well as being able to help others to study the Bible and theology. But then, like Paul, he lifted up the most important skill of all: "I refer now to the skill of enabler, of helping a congregation to read the signs of the times, understand the powers at work in the world, and then go with such a congregation supported by faith and informed by Word and Sacrament into the world as God's ambassadors."[15]

Enabling Laity To Be People of God in the World

The DRE's task is to equip all the people of God so that they are enabled to perform their religious mission.[16] In the past the church has focused only on the training of its institutional officers and teachers. These leaders often became solely responsible for the success or failure of the church's program. However, there is a basic problem observed by many adult educators. Most adults do not know how to participate responsibly in the groups to which they belong. Elton Trueblood described enablement as the ministry of encouragement. He called for genuine professionals who had been successfully taught the skill of liberating the resources or human power in other persons.[17] The DRE as an enabler must help laity to participate responsibly both as the gathered congregation and as the scattered church in mission.

During undergraduate and graduate professional training the DRE should focus on technical skills and human relation skills. Human relation skills enhance the DRE's ministry as she/he works with groups and with individuals in the church. Human skills are necessary to help church groups to be efficient in decision making, in conflict resolution, and in the nurturance of each member. As the DRE matures and advances in the responsibilities of the church's leadership, greater emphasis will be placed on being able to conceptualize the total mission of the church and guiding its vision. Overarching all of the functional roles is the central skill of actually enabling the laity to perform their roles as the people of God with ministries in the world.

NOTES

1. Gloria Durka, "Preparing for the Profession," in *Parish Religious Education*, ed. Maria Harris (New York: Paulist, 1978), p. 174.

2. Dorothy Jean Furnish, *DRE/DCE—The History of A Profession* (Nashville: Christian Educators Fellowship, 1976), p. 77.

3. Ibid., p. 84

4. Henry F. Cope, "Directors of Religious Education in Churches," *Religious Education* 10 (October 1915), p. 444.

5. Maria Harris, "U.S. Directors of Religious Education in Roman Catholic Parishes," in *Changing Patterns of Religious Education*, ed. Marvin J. Taylor (Nashville: Abingdon, 1984), p. 215. Harris, like James Michael Lee, sharply differentiates the two discrete functions of ministry and education. See James Michael Lee, "CCD Renewal," in *Renewing the Sunday School and the CCD*, ed. D. Campbell Wyckoff (Birmingham, Ala.: Religious Education Press, 1986), pp. 234-235.

6. There appears to be a reluctance on the part of several Roman Catholic writers to use ministry as a description for anyone except ordained clergy. Protestants, on the other hand, are in a major educational effort to describe the "ministry of all Christians" as descriptive of the laity based on "ordination" by one's baptism into the service of Christ. It is my suspicion that the hesitancy on the part of some thoughtful Roman Catholic experts to use the term may be based on the fact that women may not be ordained in that tradition; this factor, of course, is not an issue in mainstream Protestantism. Ironically, Maria Harris states that the priestly role contains "notions dear to most DREs," namely, the concept of the priesthood of all believers and being "stewards of the mysteries of God" (1 Corinthians 4:1). Maria Harris, "U.S. Directors of Religious Education in Roman Catholic Parishes," pp. 216-217. Few Protestants would use the term priest to describe the DRE.

7. Furnish, *DRE/DCE*, p. 154.

8. Dorothy Jean Furnish, "The Profession of Director or Minister of Christian Education in Protestant Churches," in *Changing Patterns of Religious Education*, p. 200.

9. Stephen Nevin, "Parish Coordinator: Evaluating Task and Roles," *The Living Light* (Spring 1972), pp. 48-56.

10. William F. Case, "The Director of Religious Education," in *Religious Education*, ed. Marvin J. Taylor (Nashville: Abingdon, 1960), p. 260.

11. Maria Harris, *Portrait of Youth Ministry* (New York: Paulist, 1981).

12. Robert L. Katz, "Skills of an Effective Administrator," *Harvard Business Review* (January-February 1955), pp. 33-42. These skills first organized in this fashion by Katz have been mentioned in almost every business management text since the late 1950s.

13. David L. Bradford and Allan R. Chohen, *Managing for Excellence: The Guide to Developing High Performance in Contemporary Organizations* (New York: Wiley, 1984), p. 71.

14. The importance of strategic planning and the human resource

staff perspective is developed in Charles Fombrun, Noel M. Tichy, and Mary Anne Devanna, *Strategic Human Resource Management* (New York: Wiley, 1984)

15. Merlyn W. Northfelt, "A More Excellent Way," *The Garrett Bulletin* 60 (March 1971), p. 5.

16. Intergenerational religious education, involving as it does the shared activities of persons at different phases of the lifecycle, is one way in which all the people of God can be empowered to perform their religious mission. See James W. White, *Intergenerational Religious Education* (Birmingham, Ala.: Religious Education Press, 1988).

17. Elton Trueblood, *The Future of the Christian Churches* (New York: Harper & Row, 1971), p. 30.

Chapter 6

The DRE as Administrator and Program Developer

Administration and program development are major tasks for the DRE. Regardless of whether the DRE focuses on an age level or on the broad general program of the church the two tasks of administration and program development are central functions of a professional DRE that enable the other specific roles such as youth counseling, teaching in the CCD program, or special teacher training events to happen in a productive manner.

The modern DRE, like the seventeenth-century German-American colonist, can easily recite the poem, "My hat has three corners, three corners has my hat, and if it does not have three corners, it wouldn't be my hat" to describe how administration and program development work in tandem with the other functions of a professional. As a metaphor for the roles of a DRE each corner represents one of the many functions of the DRE. The crown of the hat that unifies the corners, represents administration and program development. Thus administration and program development are intertwined like parts of a single hat, yet each point has a different emphasis.

In the past, DREs (and pastors) have tended to place administration on their list of things they particularly dislike about their jobs. Religious administration has been confused with industrial management or, even worse, with a "I have to do every little detail" attitude. Principles of administration which were initiated in industry and which were targeted in the production of goods have often been uncritically brought into the church with unsatisfactory results.

The opposite attitude to the industrial model mentioned in the previous paragraph is sometimes characterized by the satirical comment, that "too often the church is running the best rural program in the city." Many fundamental principles of administration are based on effective management in the nonreligious or "secular" society. Notwithstanding, there are some principles of administration which are grounded in values that provide greater religious integrity and awareness of social change than others.[1]

Administration Theory

New images guide contemporary administration theory. The old concepts of management that focused on controlling and bureaucracy are not functional for the DRE. The new image of administration that is appropriate for the vision of the DRE is leadership. Leadership begins with a commitment to a vision or value, such as allegiance to the Shalom of God. Leadership seeks to build relationships, freeing others to participate, sharing authority and responsibility, and persuading others to join in the pursuit of the vision of God's reign. It is concerned with assisting groups and persons to effectively achieve their objectives.[2]

A professional DRE needs to understand contemporary administration theory and practice so that the church may function at its greatest potential. Effective administration of the church's educational program creates opportunities for lay persons to learn and to perform their ministry as the people of God. In broad terms, the administration of the religious education program in the local church tends to focus on the institution's needs while the program development responsibilities tend to focus on the needs of the participants and programs.

The DRE as an Administrator

The DRE is responsible for the administration of the educational program of the church. As a member of a staff, the DRE generally reports to the pastor, coordinating the program within the context of the total church's mission. Some common duties of the DRE related to administration are related to planning, organizing, leading, controlling, and assessing progress. These are found in most typical job descriptions for a DRE.

When performing those duties that relate to general administration of the church's educational work, the DRE is concerned with a variety of needs relating to the internal operation of the church. When functioning as an administrator, the DRE should utilize those conceptual skills which integrate religion teaching with the whole organization and the total ministry of the church.

Defining Religious Education Policy and Goals

As an administrator the DRE *defines the policies, philosophy and goals of the religious education endeavor* in ways that are congruent with the general policies of the whole denomination and the local church. This is best done in collaboration with a variety of committees, but it is often done prescriptively by the staff.

The philosophy and goals of a particular church guide choices on what programs and ministries should be developed. The choice of which age groups will receive special attention, as well as whether certain types of programs may be appropriately offered by a particular church, are part of that church's policies. The DRE helps the various committees to choose which groups to serve and in creating programs for those groups. These decisions will determine how resources will be allocated. For instance, what programs should be developed for the youth from Bible study to sex education to math tutoring are administrative decisions. Or another example, a downtown church decides its major mission will be from 7:00 A.M. to 7:00 P.M. in order to mesh with the weekday activities of downtown employees while having only a minimum weekend program. This decision, based on the character of the population of the church's ambit, limits the traditional programs in child and youth religious education. However, this selfsame decision redirects the local church's religious education endeavor to such activities as day care for employees and adult learning.

The DRE must keep informed about legal regulations pertaining to the educational programs sponsored by the church. These regulations guide policy and personnel decisions. There are many legal requirements that must be observed, such as fire and safety regulations, license procedures for day care, and economic regulations for staff.

Though the past twenty years have witnessed a growth in independent churches within Protestantism, nonetheless most Protestant local churches and all Catholic local churches are formally affiliated with one or another denomination. Indeed, many people join a local church's membership because this local church is Catholic or Presbyterian or United Methodist or such. It is a professional responsibility of the DRE to maintain a relationship to that denominational tradition. This may involve providing programs sponsored by the denomination, using denominationally published curricula resources in different types of events, and participating in denominational activities outside of the particular local church.

The DRE auspiciously works in close collaboration with committees and task-groups to enable the goals of the local church to be shared by a larger number of people. These groups may be formally elected groups or informal groups such as a task force of teachers working on a specific item. The value of collaboration in policy planning and goal setting is related to the commitment level of the members. People are more willing to cooperate in programs they have personally helped to design. In the process of setting goals in a group, parishioners also learn how to handle their own problems through the use of various models.

Another benefit the process of collaboration may uncover is a wide variety of unmet needs or unmet concerns unrecognized by either the DRE or the people. Some organizational goals in large multiple-staff churches are developed by the professional staff. These are then shared with the lay leadership for approval. One of the leadership qualities which effective DREs must have is the ability to vision what the church should be doing, and how the educational program is an integral part of the total mission of the church. However, it is important that the congregational members participate in modifying and approving these goals and policies so that the parishioners will have a higher level of ownership of them.

Administration of Program Budget

The DRE as an administrator *determines budget needs* in collaboration with various committees and staff for the total educational enterprise. The budget requests are then submitted to the appropriate staff and finance committee for actual fund raising. A key function of the DRE is the ability to describe how each budget item supports the overall mission of the local program, together with the specific priorities in the religious education area. It is especially helpful if the DRE provides some religious and even theological justification for the budget requests so that committees in particular and the whole church can tie in the budget requests with the basic mission of the local church. Being able to vision the larger church's mission and pull the pieces together is part of the task of the DRE as an administrator.

The DRE needs to be able to make reasonable estimates of the cost of programs based on previous experiences. Budget development, unfortunately, is all too often based in gamesmanship. To inflate budget requests as a hedge against fiscal cuts at a later date is poor administration and poor stewardship. To maintain integrity, inflated budget requests is a practice that the church must avoid. A more appropriate method involves setting goals and priorities to base the development of each specific program. This also provides a criteria for program evaluation.

When a budget for the religious education program has been established by the church, the DRE is responsible for supervising the accounting procedures related to the educational program. Monitoring the general financial health of the whole church and the specific expenses of the religious education program will enable the DRE to keep each department supervised within the adopted budget. Emergencies happen in every institution, but there is no excuse for any department to overspend its basic program budget when reasonable supervision is provided. Each church will have its own method of requesting funds, but the DRE must have the authority to guide those expenses and to indicate when money may be available.

Purchasing and Managing Religious Education Equipment
Throughout the process of long-range planning, the DRE will recommend to appropriate committees and then guide the purchase of major equipment approved in the budget related to the overall religious education program. These items often are fairly expensive and need to be placed within the context of need, projected use, and ongoing maintenance. The coordination of the

library budget is often assigned administratively to the DRE. The library provides print and other media resources for the religious education activity and often serves as the distribution center for equipment. Supervision of the library staff would then become part of the DRE's responsibility.

Supervision of Paid Staff

Most DREs work in large churches bringing responsibility for recruiting, training, and developing paid staff members related to the religious education endeavor. Typically these persons are support staff such as secretaries, Sunday nursery workers, and librarians. In many settings the DRE may also be responsible for program-level workers, such as children or youth directors or day care center directors. As a personnel administrator, the DRE must enable the staff persons to have the necessary resources to do their duties as well as opportunities for continued training and development. The DRE is responsible for the representation of his or her staff in staff review and employment concerns with the local church's general personnel and finance committees. One key role of the DRE related to both paid and volunteer staff is the constructive management of conflict in the church generally and in the religious education program specifically. The DRE must know and be able to use principles of creative conflict resolution when appropriate to enhance interpersonal and intergroup cooperation.

In a related financial role, the DRE should be prepared to suggest items or needs which can ideally be funded by special gifts or memorials from parishioners. These items are funded outside the regular budget process and can greatly enhance the religious education program. Without a preprepared "wish-list" many important items are often unfunded and therefore are unavailable for use in the church's religious education program.

Interprets Religious Educational Policy and Goals

Interpreting the goals and policies of the church's religious education work to pastor and parishioners represents a signal opportunity for the DRE to enhance the whole ministry of the church. The DRE interprets the objectives of the religious education program to those inside the church, such as parents or various administrative committees, as well as those outside the church such as prospective members or community groups. The DRE seeks to significantly raise the awareness of the religious education program and its goals in the consciousness of all members of the church. The DRE, as an administrator, facilitates the dissemination of the publicity of programs through traditional church sources and through appropriate mass media in the community.

Research Responsibilities

The DRE also has the task as an administrator to *suggest topics of research needed for promoting new methods, new programs, and new approaches* to institutional and personal needs. This research relates to the needs of the local church served by the DRE. Sometimes these are in the form of pilot projects involving a small group. At other times a certain class can try a specific new pedagogical method within its regular format to evaluate its value. Some of the research will have importance for other churches, but most of the research is focused on the specific local church. Further, much of this research will be of the variety commonly known as "action research."

Computers and Administration

The computer will become increasingly important to effective administration for the DRE. We live in what has been called an information age. Many DREs and clergy have resisted working with computers, calling them a fad. Like the photostat copier, the impact of the computer on culture has long passed the fad stage. Business and global governments now organize their information systems based on computer technology. Computer literacy will be as basic for the DRE as biblical literacy.[3]

In addition to word processing, the computer can assist the administrative duties of the DRE in many areas by making information easily available and by doing repetitive tasks efficiently. The DRE can make multiple uses of the same data by requesting print-outs in different formats. A membership list of the whole congregation now can generate separate lists of age groups, participation levels, or geographical living areas. Direct mail letters can be personalized. Library resources, curriculum resources, or special speaker resources can be catalogued and indexed to be shared with different groups in the parish. The computer can track key dates about members ranging from attendance and pledge payments to birthdays or baptismal anniversary dates.[4]

Artistic creations for newsletters, posters, or statistical presentations can be programed on the computer. An emerging area in church communications is data-sharing through telecommunications. By using a computer with a telephone modem, a local DRE can communicate with regional and national denominational offices for copies of resources, use a national data base for references, or electronic mail. These uses are in addition to the future developments in educational software which are only now beginning.[5] The ability to use the computer to develop the information needed to make decisions as well as for instructional purposes will soon be critical for the DRE.

The DRE as Program Developer

While administration is concerned with the needs related to the operation of the church, comprehensive program development focuses on the needs of parishioners and then seeks to create and implement religious education strategies to achieve instructional objectives based on those needs. Program development is part of the overall religious education work of the church. It is contrasted to classroom curriculum planning which is the planning and implementation of specific teaching/learning experiences. A DRE will plan both at the institutional level and for specific sessions, but like the tri-cornered hat, these are different (though interrelated) points of emphasis.

Program Development Areas

The general areas of program development include 1) the preliminary activities of diagnosis, long-range curriculum planning, and overall goal setting for the religious education enterprise; 2) program design; 3) program implementation; and 4) evaluation and recycling decisions. These general areas tend to correspond to significant blocks of time in the sequence of the comprehensive development procedure. Each general area has specific tasks which, when fulfilled in these time blocks, enable program developers to move successfully to the next area.[6]

Many churches hold an annual planning retreat in which the broad scope of the comprehensive educational program would be developed. The DRE is responsible for the coordination of the general areas of program development, working with committees, teachers, and other staff persons to complete the total process according to the policies and goals for the religious education program of the church.

One helpful footnote in program planning: While policy decisions count both "yes" and "no" votes in committees, only count "yes" votes of people interested in a program decision. If enough people wish a program to make it viable with available funding, then the planning task is to enable them to do it. An example is if a member wished to prepare a monthly television log to inform parents of quality programs to be scheduled and suggest some questions for family discussion, then the church only needs one vote for it to pass, the one who will prepare the resource.

A Model for Program Development

Figure 1 summarizes a procedure for comprehensive program development. The model describes the steps involved in developing the total religious education program that includes creation of short-term special workshops, special programs to meet the variety of needs and interests expressed at each age level, in addition to integrating ongoing regular programs of the church such as CCD or the Sunday school and youth fellowships.

The order of fulfilling the specific tasks in each area or stage of program development may vary, but movement is best facilitated by completing the tasks in the previous stage. Often several tasks are performed simultaneously. For example, in the design stage, the leadership team may be involved in reconciling objectives at the same time as evaluation activities are being planned. All of the tasks within the procedure will eventually need to be accomplished for planning, developing, and implementing a smoothly administrated program. In Figure 1, the solid lines indicate direct movement from one area to another, while the broken lines indicate a feedback loop.

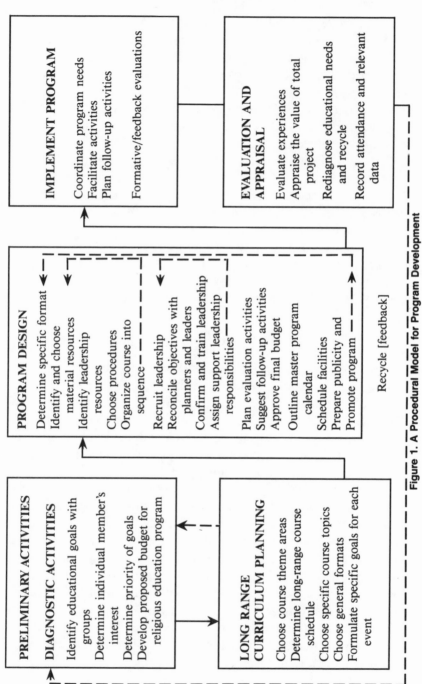

Figure 1. A Procedural Model for Program Development

Diagnostic Activities

The DRE works with a wide variety of groups in the church to develop the comprehensive religious education program. The initial task in program development is to identify the educational needs and interests of persons, groups, and even the entire church as an organization.[7] The most effective diagnosis tends to be done collaboratively with groups because such collaboration creates commitment of the people to the goals. Resources for determining the needs and interests of the people include suggestions from the denominational offices and publications, suggestions from all sorts of church members, and the professional observation by the DRE and his/her staff. In developing a comprehensive religious education program for the church, learning needs and activities for each age group of the church as well as intergenerational activities are identified. Programs for special populations such as singles, older adults, families, and so on, are developed in the comprehensive plan. Ideally, every age level should be involved in each of the major tasks of the church's educational mission.

The DRE is responsible for creating the climate for cooperative planning that enables the members to discover and define their own learning needs related to their discipleship. The DRE is also responsible for developing programatic formats to meet these goals. The diagnostic process that evaluates the long-range goals of the church and confirms and guides the annual planning requires the DRE to be perceptive to unarticulated needs and goals that surface throughout the year. By providing structure and data in a creative manner, the DRE assists planning groups to accept responsibility for planning and commitment for participation in the religious education work of the church.

The DRE guides the preparation of the budget for the religious education program. The budget is based on the priorities of the goals chosen by the responsible committees of the church and, as appropriate, by the religious educators themselves. The DRE must conceptualize how the various programs fit into the comprehensive ministry so that as many needs as possible are accommodated in the final plans. Realistically, the budget sets the priorities of the church and should be seen in this light. The budget sets the level at which the religious education enterprise will have the necessary resources to develop the desired plans. The approval of the budget is one way in which the larger community accepts the proposed goals for religious education.

Long-range Curriculum Planning

The church must plan to develop a comprehensive ministry. Long-range curriculum plans enable the church to have direction for its religious education mission based on its goals of ministry. Long-range plans enable the church to schedule programs when speakers may be available, or to prepare advanced courses for certain topics of interest. Since people enjoy different styles of teaching/learning, long-range planning can schedule all sorts of educational experiences ranging from experiential courses to lecture type presentations.

Comprehensive program planning in religious education is more than considering the CCD or Sunday school curriculum resources. What does the church want to have happen to a person who participates in its religious education program for ten years? What kinds of learnings, skills, and service opportunities does a person who has been a member of the church for five or ten years need for effective discipleship in the world? What kinds of experiences are needed to enable a person to be at the desired level of biblical knowledge and commitment to Christian service? Growth as a Christian does not happen automatically. It happens because the church adheres to the difficult discipline of long-range curriculum planning.

The DRE assists both individuals and groups to plan programs and activities that develop Christian faith. A comprehensive religious education program consists of opportunities to hear and respond to the gospel story and vision, to integrate the Evangel into one's own personal life, to reflect on the great social-ethical concerns of the day, and to devise ways to meet the community's missional needs. The DRE also helps the faith community respond as people of God with ministries in the world. Religious education sees God's activity both within the church and in the world where the people participate in the ministries of love and justice.

A comprehensive religious education program endeavors to

plan for the whole person's needs. These needs are diverse, and include spiritual needs, friendship needs, personal growth needs, and so on. The DRE has the task of helping the responsible church committees to conceptualize how the various parts of the religious educational ministry including the Sunday school, special missions programs, youth fellowships, day care, service projects, and the host of other activities merge together to fashion a comprehensive curriculum.

A wide variety of program options must be created in the church in order that one might actually be helpful to a significant number of persons. In business ventures, it is estimated that only one in every twenty ideas will actually result in success.[8] In order to increase the probability of something succeeding in helping people be involved in discipleship activities the church must create many options and be willing to risk the fact that a lot of these will fail.

Program Design

Determine Specific Formats

To provide for the different learning styles of persons, a wide variety of formats should be an integral part of the planning. Such formats may include large-group events such as a conference or lecture series, small-group activities such as a discussion or workshop model, and independent learning projects that might consist of a reading program or a computer-assisted program. Some parishioners find learning in experiential formats comfortable and enjoyable while other members of the congregation prefer more formal traditional types of formats.

Choose Resources

The DRE works with planning committees or teachers to identify and choose the material and human resources that best meet the objectives planned for the religious education program. The procedures of teaching-learning are guided by the choice of the format. The choice of procedures is interrelated with the choice of leadership. A desired leader may communicate more dynamically using one type of pedagogical method rather than another.

The choice of teaching methods should be guided by the objectives for the instructional event. For example, discussion may provide information about a subject, but if the pedagogical objective seeks to help the participants to do something, a demonstration with practice would be more educationally helpful. In special events that involve several leaders, when the initial choices of resources and leadership are made, the proposed program can be organized into a sequence that describes which speaker will be invited to open a series or what topics should be part of the morning session and which part of the afternoon session, and so forth.

Recruit and Train Leaders

Effective recruitment of leaders requires the successful deployment of the human relations skills of the DRE (or anyone else performing the task). Personal contact at the time of invitation with prospective leaders helps to reconcile expectations so there is a clear understanding and agreement about the goals and program design on the part of the various participants. This also provides opportunities for prospective leaders to suggest alternatives to the planning committee. Plans for orientation of leaders or more elaborate training should be shared when inviting persons to accept leadership.

Every program has both primary leaders as well as support personnel. The responsibilities of the support personnel include roles such as panel moderators, conveners of small groups, registrars, ushers, and so on. The needs of the support personnel within the total program are identified by the planning team. Each person should know when his/her responsibility begins and will be completed, for example, the dates the Sunday school teachers begin their duties and how they will serve, or when the hospitality committee is the have the coffee available for a morning break.

Plan for Evaluation Activities

Another part of comprehensive program development is identifying the criteria for evaluation of the religious education program as a whole as well as each teaching/learning event in particular. Evaluation considers the value of the projects attempted and the efficiency of their enactment. The primary criteria for evaluation are based in the educational goals and objectives of the program and/or event considering both the quality of the event and the positive rate of change caused by the educational program.[9]

Part of planning includes preparation for evaluation. How will the evaluation data be gathered? At what point in the program or series will adjustments be intentionally made? Evaluations should be scheduled at regular intervals such as quarterly or semi-annually for ongoing events. Plans for evaluations during and at the conclusion of short-term events should also be prepared during the design stage. There should be channels for formative feedback[10] (*during* the meeting so that alternatives or adjustments can be formed in the process). The longer the learning experience, the greater the need for feedback.[11] A summative evaluation considers the value of the overall effort and the final results of learning, critiquing the ways the program was developed to guide the planning team for future educational opportunities.

Prepare Budget and Planning Calendar

Several general tasks need to be performed during the design stage of program development, especially for short-term events. It is often helpful to prepare, in advance, follow-up activities or suggestions that can be announced to the participants. At this point in the planning process, the final proposed budget can be realistically determined knowing the expenses of any special leaders and other resource costs. A master calendar for the comprehensive education program and for the administrative duties related to each event should be completed. This enables facilities to be scheduled at appropriate points in the year. A full outline of the comprehensive religious education design including ongoing programs such as the Sunday school or CCD and youth programs, as well as short-term, special events should be part of the master calendar developed by the planners of the religious education enterprise.

Prepare Publicity and Promote Program

The concluding activity of program design is the preparation of publicity and promotion for both ongoing and special programs.

To promote major events, several types of publicity, such as news-letters, phone calls, brochures, or direct mail, are necessary to insure adequate attendance. Maximum results are achieved when publicity is directed to a specific audience. For best results use four or five different types of publicity over a period of several weeks. More programs fail to achieve the desired attendance because the plans for promotion have not been developed than because they are uninteresting. The DRE may assist in the design of the publicity material and often coordinates its dissemination through church mailings, recommending selective lists of target audiences and sending copies to the public media.

Implementation and Evaluation

When a comprehensive religious education program is de-signed, the major responsibilities pass to those who actually teach, lead, or coordinate the sessions and events. In the church these are usually lay persons. During the implementation stage, the DRE becomes the enabler for others to perform their accept-ed tasks. In reality, the DRE is usually responsible for coordinat-ing last minute needs related to the programs. Checking to see that food-service schedules are in place, making sure groups that outgrow their assigned rooms find new facilities, and insuring that the requested equipment has been delivered, and in general to guarantee as far as possible that valuable time is not wasted and that the momentum of a program is maintained.

While ongoing programs such as the Sunday school, CCD, and youth fellowships do not receive the intensive planning that some special events do, all religious education programs need to be thorough in their planning and in their evaluations. Regular channels for feedback need to be developed for the ongoing pro-grams related both to specific weekly programs and to the overall state of the group. The DRE should have a schedule to meet with leaders, such as teachers, coordinators, and officers, to determine levels of goals to be reached with the groups, additional needs, and other relevant information. Evaluations should be received from both participants and from leaders. Attitudes about support services often affect how the content is perceived. Reports on the substantive content, structural content (teaching procedures), material resources, and leadership personnel and facilities should be received from all participants.

Relevant data should be reported to the leadership team, summarized for the general religious education committee, and filed by the DRE for future reference. Personal items related to volunteer staff should not be retained in church files due to legal restrictions. Special events sponsored by the ongoing groups require the same planning procedures used for special events held by the church. For example, the youth ice cream social or children's vacation Bible school, or the annual Sunday school fair need careful planning and records for future leaders. The DRE should maintain records, both print and visual, on program activities in the church. These become the data source for the annual evaluation report by the religious education program to the local church.

Support from the DRE

Part of the DRE's task is to help the whole church articulate its objectives for its entire mission and then assist the church conceptualize how the various parts of its comprehensive program ministry merge together to help persons develop their Christian faith and to respond as people of God with various ministries in the world.

The DRE provides continuous support to groups through administrative services. Staff time and services assist the program planning of all groups in the church. Guiding planners to appropriate church committees for assistance, scheduling, suggesting leadership, sharing ideas for special events, and being an archive of records are resources the DRE can provide to any group. The DRE should be a principal energizer and, after the pastor, possibly *the* principal energizer of the whole parish.

The DRE works in collaboration with a wide variety of planning groups in the local church. The ability to conceptualize how each program moves the parish toward the broad goals of developing the Christian faith and serving as the people of God in ministry will create opportunities at various levels of learning.

The DRE as program developer should devise a well-organized system for developing potential leaders and resource personnel.

Large churches must constantly be inviting and developing potential lay leadership to staff the ongoing religious education programs and to meet emerging ministry possibilities in the world served by the church.

Effective recruitment programs are based on attracting persons to work in an appropriate capacity in the religious education program. DREs should use persons' strengths to motivate them to top performance. The DRE must listen to members to learn their skills and motivating interests. Tom Peters and associates describe case after case where excellent organizations were marked by the leader's trusting that the people could do the needed tasks and by providing the resources for the people to accomplish the desired goal.[12] This is one of the human relations skills that the DRE uses in program development. This model of invitation and motivation also requires that needs and objectives be clearly defined with flexibility for the laity to create their responses. The DRE must orient potential leaders to the objectives and desired methods of proposed programs as a means of reconciling expectations of planners and leaders.

Creative organizations find that working with the strengths of each person provides willing workers who have a commitment to the goals of the institution.[13] To continue to build on the strengths of the lay leadership team, the DRE must encourage both volunteers and the professional staff to participate vigorously and willingly in various in-service continuing educational opportunities.

The DRE must guide the entire parish to fulfill the vision and the specific objectives of religious education. Programs must be created to enable all parishioners to grow in their religious faith. In addition, attention must be given to devising programs that enable people to relate to the key social-ethical issues of life in such a way as to help these individuals make personal decisions about the issues and to enable them to become involved as appropriate. In the past the church has primarily provided religious education programs to enrich the personal faith of members. Today the DRE as program developer must give special attention to helping parishioners live out their ministry in the larger community. This is a new area of program development for most churches, and will require intentional effort from both the DRE and the ordained clergy if the church is to be faithful to its vocation in Christ.

As program developer, the DRE must constantly be alert to possible new religious educational programs that are needed to develop the ministry of the church. In addition, current programs may need to be redesigned to meet emerging needs of the congregation. By working with the goals of the congregation, the DRE will anticipate the needs of the congregation through long-range planning and development.

NOTES

1. For example see, Peter F. Drucker, "Part III, The Non-Profit Sector," in *The Changing World of the Executive* (New York: Times Books, 1982), pp. 107-142 or Robert Worley, *A Gathering of Strangers* (Philadelphia: Westminster, 1983).

2. See David A. Bickimer, *Christ The Placenta* (Birmingham, Ala.: Religious Education Press, 1983), Paul S. Goodman and Associates, *Designing Effective Work Groups* (San Francisco: Jossey-Bass, 1986), and Barbara Kellerman, *Leadership: Multidisciplinary Perspectives* (Englewood Cliffs, N.J.: Prentice-Hall, 1984).

3. See Kenneth Bedell, *Computers: New Opportunities for Personalized Ministry in the Church* (Valley Forge, Pa.: Judson, 1981) and Peter A. McWilliams, *The Personal Computer Book* (New York: Ballantine, 1983).

4. For ideas on word processing see Lawrence Press, *Low Cost Word Processing* (New York: Addison-Wesley, 1983). For many other ideas on using the personal computer in church administration see Kenneth Beddell, *Using Personal Computers in the Church* (Valley Forge, Pa.: Judson, 1982). Many companies sell integrated packages to churches which do the suggested administrative activities. Check with other users prior to investing in expensive programs.

5. E.V. Clemans, *Using Computers in Religious Education* (Nashville: Abingdon, 1985), describes ideas specifically for church education while David G. Gueulette, ed., *Microcomputers for Adult Learning: Potentials and Perils* (Chicago: Follett, 1982), describes ways (and cautions) to use computers for general educational applications.

6. See Cyril O. Houle, *The Design of Education* (San Francisco: Jossey-Bass, 1972) and Malcolm S. Knowles, *The Modern Practice of Adult Education: Andragogy versus Pedagogy* (New York: Association Press, 1976), for examples of program development in education.

7. In organizational development, the whole organization and select-

ed groups are the targets for intervention and centers for education rather than individuals.

8. Thomas J. Peters and Robert H. Waterman, *In Search of Excellence: Lessons from America's Best-run Companies* (New York: Warner, 1982), p. 209.

9. Timothy A. Lines, *Systemic Religious Education* (Birmingham, Ala.: Religious Education Press, 1987), p. 147.

10. The terms "formative" and "summative" to describe evaluation types that happened during a course to improve the teaching/learning event and at the end of a program to determine value of outcomes were originally used by Michael Scriven, "The Methodology of Evaluation," in *Perspectives of Curriculum Evaluation*, ed. R. W. Tyler (New York: Rand McNally, 1967), pp. 39-83.

11. James Michael Lee, *The Flow of Religious Instruction: A Social Science Approach* (Birmingham, Ala.: Religious Education Press, 1973), p. 199. Lee describes feedback as a system in which "each of the variables involved in the instructional act interacts with the other variables in a closed loop fashion so that the effects which any single variable has on the next linked variable in the behavioral chain eventually return to the original variable to modify, reinforce, or enhance it."

12. See Peters and Waterman, *In Search of Excellence* and Thomas J. Peters and Nancy Austin, *A Passion For Excellence: The Leadership Difference* (New York: Random House, 1985).

13. Drucker, *The Changing World of the Executive*, p. 116.

Chapter 7

The DRE as Educational Consultant

The director of religious education serves as a consultant to the church's educational activity. Using human relations skills, the DRE endeavors to personally influence the organizational church, small groups, and persons needing assistance to solve a problem. Consultation is a helping process focusing on the solution of a problem that requires among other things, the development of trust in personal relationships.[1] This trust is necessary for the acceptance of the ideas and resources suggested by the DRE in consulting with groups or persons.

Consultants may be either from an organization (internal) or from the outside. The DRE usually functions as a member of the church's organization and hence is an internal consultant. A consultant links knowledge and resources from many fields related to concerns of the organization or of groups who request it. Anton Dekom defines an internal consultant as one who "views himself as a professional who assumes personal responsibility for the quality of his advice and its appropriateness to the problems facing his client."[2] The effectiveness of a consultant is found in the thoroughness of that person's research on the problem, her/his sound advice, and whether the implementations of the recommendations have been productive.[3]

As a consultant, the DRE links the church with a wide variety of information resources to enable the organization to solve its

115

own problems. Consultants work with others in a collaborative style with the focus on problem solving.[4] The problem-solving approach helps persons and organizations to mobilize and use available resources to solve their own problems. The DRE gains competence for functioning in the consultative role by steeping himself/herself in the fields of organizational development and human resource development.[5]

The consultant role of a DRE is different from a counselor or a supervisor. Consultation is concerned with an organizational or work-related problem rather than with a personal problem.[6] The consultation role has often been associated with organizational development as its emphasis on the total life and well-being of the organization. Consultants link new ideas, values, attitudes, or skills to the organization's concerns.[7] Consulting is different from supervision, because consultation jointly seeks alternatives for the organization.

Consultation requires skills in communications. The ability to listen to the needs of people and to interpret information presented at both the verbal and nonverbal levels is necessary.[8] Diagnostic skills for the identification of real problems that are not just symptoms, problem-solving skills that include the ability to gather and analyze information, and conflict-management skills are all essential resources for the consultant role. Effective consultants have been described as "bright, analytical, perceptive of key issues, diplomatic, articulate, skilled in writing, broadly experienced in business, hard working, temperamentally suited to a staff role, and expert in their specializations."[9]

As a consultant, the DRE will serve the pastor, committees, and individual religion teachers, to name just three. Although the DRE is a staff person, nonetheless, the higher that this position is perceived by the congregation, the greater the level of influence and acceptance of ideas. This fact requires that the DRE have a self-perception as a professional and also that the church recognize the professional status of the DRE. Organizational titles, office location, and committee responsibilities create perceptions that can facilitate the consultation tasks. Titles can either open access to groups or limit the access. The scope of authority of a program director is obviously different from a children's worker. Although two persons may hold similar academic degrees, organizational titles often give more authority and acceptance to one over the other.

The consultant is also a linker of resources, related both to religious education and to general church life. Like a business, a parish is constantly seeking new programs and new ways of doing things. Cultural changes, economic changes, theological changes, religious changes, or curriculum changes all have some impact on the church. Some are helpful while some are fads. When linking the parish to these innovations, the DRE should seek to determine as early as possible those that will have a positive influence on the church.[10] These then become part of the resources of the DRE consultant.

The DRE as an educational consultant is concerned both about the substantive content of the religious education program and the human processes within the total organizational structures of the church. In addition to concern for what is taught in any specific educational event, the religious education consultant is concerned with the human processes in the church as an organization, such as communication, group problem-solving and decision-making functions, and intergroup cooperation and competition.[11] Sometimes the consultative role is a brief one where the consultant using expert knowledge suggests a solution for a specific problem. In other cases the focus is on long-term mutual diagnosis and development of resources to facilitate the organization's ability to create skills necessary for improved problem solving.[12]

There are many sub-roles of the consultant that have direct relationship to the regular duties of the DRE. The tasks may range from simply raising questions for the group's reflection to gathering data so as to identify alternative actions or resources for a group, to developing a training program for the group, to becoming an advocate for a specific action or policy.[13] Paul Lawrence and Jay Lorsch give practical advice to the DRE when acting in the organizational consultant role: To "achieve more sophisticated solutions for organizational issues," the role of the DRE must be viewed "as that of an educator and a diagnostician, as well as a consultant. That is, [the DRE] will need to be able to develop techniques for identifying organizational problems and analyzing their causes. [The DRE] will have to be able to educate [church staff] and other organizational members in the use of concepts to conduct diagnosis and to plan action. Finally, [the DRE] will have to act as a consultant in providing . . . action proposals for the [staff] to consider."[14]

Four key roles of the educational consultant appropriate for the DRE are suggested by human resource developer, Leonard Nadler.[15] These roles are advocate, teaching-learning expert, stimulator, and change agent. Like other roles of the DRE they are often interdependent and not always discrete. The educational consultant serves both as a resource person and as an enabler or facilitator.

The Educational Consultant as an Advocate

Originally advocate was a legal term to describe a lawyer who speaks on behalf of someone. This is related to the term counselor which is also a legal advisor. The word "counselor" is based on the root word that means to consult or to give advice. An advocate may also champion or speak for a cause, an idea, or a product. In the advocate role, the DRE will sometimes promote a certain program for the general well-being of the church or the educational enterprise. At other times the advocate will speak for groups that are unable to represent themselves in the ecclesiastical setting. The DRE often serves as the advocate-representative for children or youth in administrative meetings of the parish.

The advocate role may seem to be in conflict with the consultant model that says the DRE only *helps* other persons to solve problems. In reality, the DRE has a set of values and opinions related to education and to the broad ministry of the church. Furthermore, the DRE must encourage the church to be faithful to the highest values represented in biblical studies and theological thought and in religious practice. There are contending goals and means found in every organization. The professional knowledge and values of the DRE should contribute significantly to the choices of the church.

Sometimes the advocate role consisting of a simple recommendation for the adoption of a certain set of curriculum resources is recommended because the DRE believes "set A" is stronger due to its biblical or theological interpretations than "set B" or it best meets the educational objectives of the local church in more creative ways. The advocate seeks to persuade either the pastor or a committee to accept a specific recommendation based on the perspective of what the DRE believes to be best for the situation. To be an advocate requires that the DRE carefully does his/her homework to know alternatives. Each recommendation has both strengths and limitations. The DRE should know all sides before advocating a plan of action. Successful advocates anticipate potential points of resistance to any proposal so that additional information is prepared to fully inform the people.

Advocates Speak on Behalf of Others

A crucial obligation of the advocate is to speak to institutions on behalf of persons or groups unable to fully represent themselves due to lack of power or exclusion from decision-making positions.[16] Children, youth, and older adults are often represented by the DRE in administrative settings such as board or vestry committee meetings, or staff. Sometimes the advocate role consists in the DRE speaking for the youth and children directly; at other times it consists in helping youth to speak in their own voice, such as being sure they are represented on various committees. Maria Harris lists several requirements for the DRE to be an effective advocate for youth.[17] One significant requirement is the ability to listen to the youth so that the DRE can interpret the issue from the student's perspective.

Advocates Seek Access to Ideas for All

Several areas appear obvious as concerns for the DRE to function as an advocate. Access to knowledge, even if perceived by adults as controversial, is a right of young people. Recently a group of adults debated whether to permit a youth program on apartheid because it might be seen as controversial among some church members. Youth have a right to discuss controversial topics in the parish so that they can apply the Christian values to their decisions. Students need the variety of sources of information that are available from the values discussions in the youth fellowship and the academic discussions in the public school.

An advocate must expect to face controversy. This is a key reason for doing careful background research on points of possible resistance. For example, sex education for children and youth, together with concerns for human sexuality are high on the agenda for the DRE to advocate. Although likely to create some conflict, to advocate the availability of sex education both in the public school and in the local church is the key task of anyone working with youth. Recently a group of ecumenical youth workers were challenged to serve as youth advocates and encourage a local community's school board to develop sex education in the city's schools when it was opposed by some of the ultraconservative groups in the community.

To transmit religious values regarding sex, love, and sexuality (awareness of sexual stereotypes, and so on) is an important task of the church. The benefits of such an advocacy are many.[18] Youth have an opportunity to share and clarify values and attitudes toward sex, love, and sexuality, all in a Christian context. The vocabulary of sex and sexuality can be clarified and raised to new levels of Christian meaning. Parents can be included in a study which sometimes opens discussion opportunities between parent and offspring. In churches where children are baptized, the church covenants with parents to assist in the nurture of the child. A parish program of sex education for youth provides parents with resources to nurture children in special areas. Finally, the advocacy of human sexuality studies that helps to eliminate male/female sex-role stereotypes that limit persons from reaching their full potential as human beings and affirms God's creation as male and female.

Some other areas for the advocacy of making ideas available might include the need for drug education, especially in elementary schools, or peace and justice studies in public high schools in order to raise consciousness of how unquestioned systems limit learning (often history courses in public schools place heavy stress on wars and battles rather than human achievements).[19] Sometimes the advocacy for children's rights in court, protection, medical services for teenagers, or economic rights of youth may be less controversial but are examples of where the DRE may be called to be an active witness in the prophetic mission of the church to the broader community.

While the advocate role is complex, still it boils down to the DRE working to persuade people to accept the DRE's vision for the church's educational mission in the parish and in the world.

The DRE should not recommend a course of action just because everyone else is doing it, but because it represents the best model of religious education and concern. Any course of action which the DRE advocates ought to reflect the same criteria for quality as the other activities of the church with respect to meeting the needs and potentials of the persons involved.

The Educational Consultant as Teaching-Learning Expert

The DRE is an expert in the teaching-learning processes. Again, it is very important for the DRE to have a self-perception of being a professional as well as the formal recognition of the institutional church in the form of being certified or licensed as a DRE. The expert role requires the DREs to have knowledge about education considerably beyond their experience level, elevating their expertise "above the status of an art."[20]

"What do you do with the child who misbehaves?" This statement exemplifies an educational problem. How should the DRE answer the religion teacher or parent who inquires about that problem? "What is a good resource that we should be using for our class? We want your opinion, your expert advice on this." Or again, "What ways can we present ideas to our youth class that will be effective and interesting?" The DRE as a teaching-learning expert is not seeking to sell or persuade either persons or organizations to always follow one or another specific recommendation. Often the expert provides the group or teacher or pastor with alternative choices for teaching-learning action.

The DRE must actively collect research data in the fields of religious education, general education, and organizational development. By engaging in ongoing continuous professional updating through personal research and through contact with other professional educators, the DRE will be current in both the theory and practice of the various fields which go to make up religious education. While the DRE does not need to quote educational theory or research in making responses to teachers or the pastor, still the DRE must know the theory and be able to reflect on the implications of it for the given situation. The theory should inform the specific advice given.

The need for the DRE to be an expert in teaching-learning at the technical level is revealed in an informal survey of clergy in one annual conference.[21] In this survey, 257 Protestant clergy were asked to check off areas they believed were expected areas of competency for clergy. Only 15 of these 257 clergy (6 percent) marked competence in conducting educational workshops and only 2 of the 257 clergy (less than 1 percent) indicated competence in the area of group work and the Sunday school. This informal survey accentuates what most persons probably know, namely, that technical professional expertise of the DRE in the educational process is urgently needed in the church.

Another of the galaxy of the teaching-learning expert functions of the DRE consists in responding to the religious education questions and concerns raised by the pastor or by various groups in the church. This function is a cooperative one, not a competitive one. Human revelation skills are always deployed cooperatively. Effective experts have the ability to communicate in a style that is understood by the people without dependence on technical jargon. The expert must also have the confidence of the people seeking assistance.

Yet another expert function of the DRE is that of being a resource person either to the pastor or different church groups on organizational development and how teaching-learning relates to the needs of groups in the larger organization. Helping parish officers and leaders learn how to lead their committees, and facilitating groups to work together, and to do problem solving are all part of the expert function.

The Educational Consultant as Stimulator

As a teaching-learning expert, the DRE functions in reaction to inquiries. The consultant may take a more proactive function when that individual becomes a stimulator. A stimulator raises issues for the church's leaders to consider as they chart the direction of the church's educational work.

The stimulator does not seek to give answers, rather the role facilitates the church leaders in exploring general topics and directions. The task of the stimulator is to help others to ask the right questions, to explore the possible avenues, and to help them consider alternatives. One of the first duties of a DRE is to help the church to rethink and redefine its basic goals or objectives and to develop a specific, concrete plan to achieve them.[22] Working with the church's educational committee, the stimulator helps this group consider questions such as: What do we want the children to learn by the time they complete the sixth grade or high school? By what specific knowledge and set of attitudes do we want them to be characterized? Why do we have a youth ministry? What do we want to have happen to children as a result of participating in either vacation church school or children's choir? If you choose one or another religion curriculum, what problems should you anticipate? What should be the focus of the adult religious education program? What are our performance objectives for our work with older adults?

The questions for stimulation are not classroom types of questions. Indeed, the stimulator's questions serve to guide the church's leadership and the religious education staff in the kinds of questions they need to ask to accomplish their mission. These are questions that help the various church groups plan effectively.

The stimulator role is difficult because many persons, including DREs, tend to find it easier to give answers than guide others in the quest for answers. The DRE needs to be professionally prepared in a multidisciplinary approach so that resources from the various social sciences of education, sociology, psychology, business, as well as from biblical studies, theology, and pastoral work can give depth and insight to the stimulation interaction.[23] Sometimes giving expert information or advice is the appropriate model for consultation; there are other times when the consultant is most helpful through facilitating the church leaders to answer their own questions through the DRE's stimulation.

The Educational Consultant as a Change Agent

Institutions and individuals are involved in the process of change whether it is conscious or unconscious. Alvin Toffler proposed the idea that the issue is not the *fact of change* but the quantum acceleration of the *pace of change* that creates the feeling of *future shock*.[24] When I was in graduate school in the early 1970s we were told that our degrees would be out of date in five years. Today, it is estimated that information "doubles every five and a half years" and that soon, because of information systems, "data will double every twenty months."[25] Society has gone from a first wave of technology based on agriculture through the industrial second wave to a third wave based on information.[26] Margaret Mead wrote, "The most vivid truth of the new age [is that] no one will live all his life in the world into which he was born, and one will die in the world in which he worked in his maturity."[27] Change will happen automatically. New assumptions are rapidly emerging about information, science, education, religion, family life, values, and the basic meaning of life; consequently, a prime issue for the church is whether the changes will be anticipated, planned, and understood or if the church will be left out of the cultural changes.

The DRE has one of the greatest opportunities to lead the local church in anticipating and accepting changes and innovations. An innovation may be a concept (for example, the approach to church organization or learning centers), an attitude (for example, an attitude toward sexism or clericalism, or homosexuality), a tool with accompanying skills (for example, operating an overhead projector or a computer), or several of these combined. The innovations just mentioned are innovations when they are introduced to a church or individual that had not incorporated the innovation before in its work.[28] "An innovation is not necessarily a new invention" but represents a change in the way the person or group functions.[29] As a change agent, the DRE is concerned with the process of change, helping church leaders to diagnose needs and potentials, and to plan for change.[30] Skills in the behavioral sciences such as education are very important because the change agent usually works with groups. The change agent links the church and its members with innovations in order to influence decisions and to enable acceptance of the alternate value or method of operation.

Functions of the Change Agent

Innovator. In linking the church with the resources for change the DRE serves several functions. Sometimes the DRE is an *innovator.* An innovator initiates new ideas and/or procedures into an organization. This role involves a fair amount of risk. Persons who do a lot of innovation in the church tend to have support groups that are usually outside the institutional church.

The innovator function is on the cutting edge of the church; it consists in bringing bold fresh ideas and strategies into the church at the earliest possible moment.

Communicator. Another role of the DRE as change agent is that of *communicator.* This role tends to legitimize the proposed changes. The change agent must have many contacts with outside groups that are related to religious education, organizational life, personnel, resource development, sociology, and psychology.

Evaluator of innovations. The DRE must also be able to *evaluate innovations* to determine how they will succeed and what will be their importance in the future. The decision on when to buy the first computer is an example. Should the church wait for lower prices and an enhanced model or should a current model be purchased where the staff can learn how to use computers and then later buy a newer expanded model? Many early adapter churches have used computers for several years, but many others resisted in their purchase, not so much on the basis of cost, but on the basis of personal feelings of the staff. Asking the right questions which help church leaders dispel fears of adopting new ideas is part of the DRE's repertoire of communication skills.

The DRE, of course, recognizes that not every invention is valuable for every organization, even if money is available. Sometimes the DRE must play the devil's advocate and ask tough, searching questions about the implications of a new practice or curriculum. Raising important, critical questions to think through issues related to the acceptance of a new method for teaching the Bible, or a new style of spiritual counseling, or initiating a new approach to adult religious education—these are examples of one of the roles of the DRE as change agent. In fulfilling all these different roles, the DRE often will experience a basic conflict between creative new ventures which unsettle existing programs on the one hand and maintaining the program on the other hand.

Regardless of whether the change agent in religious education is a staff member or an outside consultant, the problem-solving tasks required to effectively create change in organizations are similar. These tasks include identifying the real problem through diagnostic activities, collecting relevant data on the specific problem, describing potential resources for change, and communicating alternatives to church leaders. Efforts to bring about needed change may also identify potential directions that the church may wish to pursue for an expanded religious education program. Again the linkage with emerging ideas, potential resources, and alternatives becomes a process function of the DRE's leadership.

Characteristics of Effective Change Agents

Some generalizations have been discovered about effective change agents and innovators. Effective change agents tend to have a relatively high social status, are well-educated, have high communication skills, are usually cosmopolitan in their sources of information, and exert opinion leadership.[31] Effective change agents tend to be early adopters of innovations, possess greater mobility than later adopters, and work in larger-sized organizations. This allows them to have more specialization than is the case with generalists.[32]

Consultants Work from a Scientific Understanding

As a consultant, the DRE must possess a scientific understanding of human behavior. Common-sense hunches about human behavior are not enough. Professional training in group dynamics is necessary to understand the dynamic process of change.[33] To understand how groups work, to be able to diagnose what is happening in a group interaction, to see points of resistance, and to know how to work around them so that doors are kept open rather than causing defensiveness—all these are a part of the repertoire of the DRE as educational consultant. A knowledge of a group's process seems to be a point which many clergy fear. Reuel Howe observed that "most clergymen are afraid of groups, preferring encounter with individuals."[34] The DRE who is professionally trained in group skills can assist clergy in developing a more confident attitude toward group work. The awareness of the values held by the people and the knowledge of which people in the community and church have real power are also keys to effective intervention.

The DRE as an educational consultant seeks to link the church with the wide variety of resources including personnel, organizations, procedures, and values—all of which improve the church's capacity in decision making and communicating the Christian gospel. The DRE as a consultant must know how adults learn, understand how they are motivated, and possess the skills in designing experiences that will enable the adult to deal with the ambiguities of life and to grapple with the consequences of choice with integrity.

The DRE has one of the greatest opportunities to lead the local church in accepting change and innovations. The DRE is both a teacher and an administrator, an advantage that a public school counterpart lacks. This mixture creates an interesting dilemma for the DRE. Research indicates that "teachers and school personnel most directly concerned with pupil control have a high resistance to proposed educational changes."[35] On the other hand, research evidence also suggests that innovation happens when a highly placed educational official serves as "the primary change agent," providing strong, positive, and dynamic leadership."[36] Surely a DRE is a highly placed educational official in the church.

Change Agents Need Support Groups

Any lasting change in the overall religious education program usually requires the support of key leaders in the parish. Change is best accomplished when the key church leaders are integrally involved in its developments.[37] Change also needs the cooperation of those most affected by the change.[38] Attitudes and long-established practices change very slowly. The more that people are involved in charting the direction of a change, the greater their willingness to live into the change.

An advantage of working in a multiple-staff situation is that the DRE is usually given a greater latitude to experiment with new ideas and programs. In such settings, the pastor tends to be primarily concerned with the traditions of the church. Due to his/her leadership training, the DRE serves as the diffuser of innovations and of basic types of resources throughout the church from pastor to religion teachers committees and so on. The DRE needs to know how to lead in change without alienating his/her support system such as the pastor or a lay committee. Sometimes the conflict is with those who believe that religious education is nothing more than basically moralistic, seeking to make children good. Other times it is with the clergy who are dedicated to a gospel based in liberation or feminist theology while the parishioners live in a different theological perspective.[39] Skill in leading without leaving the people is the challenge of the DRE.

Finally, to be effective over the long haul, the DRE must be a member of several professional organizations in order to have regular access to the activities, evaluations, and innovations of other professionals in the related fields. To be a successful consultant, the DRE does not necessarily have to be inventive but must be able to determine personal goals and to be skillful in arranging resources to meet a variety of situations and then be able to communicate those to others. Due to the unique nature of the Christian witness by example, the DRE must also use himself/ herself as a role model, not only for the faith, but for handling change in one's personal life.

NOTES

1. Richard Beckhard, *The Leader Looks at the Consultative Process* (Washington, D.C.: Leadership Resources, 1965).

2. Anton K. Dekom, *The Internal Consultant* (New York: American Management Association, 1969), p. 5.

3. Ibid.

4. Kenneth J. Albert, *How to be Your Own Management Consultant* (New York: McGraw-Hill, 1978), pp. 2-3.

5. Herman Holtz, *How to Succeed as an Independent Consultant* (New York: Wiley, 1983), p. 2. Holtz provides a comprehensive guide for a new consultant. See also Milan Kubr, ed., *Management Consulting: A Guide to the Profession* (Geneva: International Labour Office, 1976), for additional information and guidance on professional consulting.

6. Gordon Lippitt and Ronald Lippitt, *The Consulting Process in Action* (La Jolla, Calif.: University Associates, 1978), p. 1.

7. June Gallessick, *The Profession and Practice of Consultation* (San Francisco: Jossey-Bass, 1982), p. 6.

8. Ibid., p. 68.

9. Dekom, *The Internal Consultant,* p. 14.

10. Albert, *How to be Your Own Management Consultant,* p. 90.

11. Edgar H. Schein, *Process Consultation: Its Role in Organization Development* (Reading, Mass.: Addison-Wesley, 1969), p. 13.

12. Newton Margulies and John Wallace, *Organizational Change: Techniques and Applications* (Glenview, Ill.: Scott, Foresman, 1973), p. 140.

13. Lippitt and Lippitt, *The Consulting Process in Action,* p. 30.

14. Paul R. Lawrence and Jay W. Lorsch, *Developing Organizations: Diagnosis and Action* (Reading, Mass.: Addison-Wesley, 1969), p. 95.

15. Leonard Nadler, *Developing Human Resources* (Austin: Learning Concepts, 1979), p. 235.

16. Dorothy Jean Furnish, "The Profession of Director or Minister of Christian Education in Protestant Churches," in *Changing Patterns of Religious Education,* ed. Marvin J. Taylor (Nashville: Abingdon, 1984), p. 201.

17. Maria Harris, *Portrait of Youth Ministry* (New York: Paulist, 1981), p. 143.

18. Ibid., pp. 144-147.

19. James Botkin, Mahdi Elmandjra, and Mircea Malitza, *No Limits to Learning: Bridging the Human Gap* (New York: Pergamon, 1979), p. 55.

20. Gloria Durka, "Modeling Religious Education" in *The Religious Education We Need,* ed. James Michael Lee (Birmingham, Ala.: Religious Education Press, 1977), p. 103.

21. Marion John Braden, Survey Report of United Methodist Clergy in the Louisiana Conference, 1988.

22. Allen W. Graves, "Administration of the Religious Education Program," in *Foundations for Christian Education in an Era of Change,* ed. Marvin J. Taylor (New York: Abingdon, 1976), p. 108.

23. Lippitt and Lippitt, *The Consulting Process in Action,* p. 105.

24. Alvin Toffler, *Future Shock* (New York: Random House, 1970).

25. John Naisbitt, *Megatrends: Ten New Directions Transforming Our Lives* (New York: Warner, 1982), p. 24.

26. Alvin Toffler, *The Third Wave* (New York: Morrow, 1980).

27. Margaret Mead, "Thinking Ahead," in *Selected Educational Heresies,* ed. Willam F. O'Neill (Glenview, Ill.: Scott, Foresman, 1969), p. 368.

28. Harbans S. Bohla, *Innovation Research and Theory,* paper prepared for the Conference on Strategies for Educational Change, November 8-10, 1965, sponsored by the School of Education, The Ohio State University and the U.S. Office of Education, USOE Contract Number OE-5-10-307, Washington D.C., p. 5.

29. Ibid.

30. Nadler, *Developing Human Resources,* p. 245.

31. Evert M. Rogers and F. Floyd Shoemaker, *Communication of Innovations* (New York: Free Press, 1971), p. 241.

32. Ibid., p. 186.

33. Jeanne Watson Lippitt and Bruce Westley, *The Dynamics of Planned Change* (New York: Harcourt, Brace and World, 1958), p. 289.

34. Reuel Howe, "Training for a Time of Change," *Christian Century* (April 22, 1970), p. 479.

35. Donald J. Willower and Ronald G. Jones, "When Pupil Control

Becomes an Institutional Theme," *Phi Delta Kappa* 45 (November 1963), pp. 107-109.

36. Don D. Bushnell et al, *Proceedings of the Conference on the Implementation of Educational Innovations* (Interim Report) (Systems Development Corporation, Santa Monica, Calif., 1964), p. 29.

37. Margulies and Wallace, *Organizational Change: Techniques and Applications,* p. 155.

38. Ibid., p. 156.

39. Robert L. Wilson, and William Willimon, *The Seven Churches of Methodism* (Durham, N.C.: The J. M. Ormond Center for Research, Planning and Development, Duke University, 1985), p. 5.

Chapter 8

The DRE as a Learning Specialist

The DRE is first and foremost a teaching-learning specialist. This central fact is probably the most important image for the DRE, although it is often neglected. As a lay career person, the DRE is neither a preacher/priest nor a professional therapist.

The functions of a teaching-learning specialist are in some ways related to the functions of the general program developer. Additionally, the tasks of the DRE as a teaching-learning specialist involves media development in which resources are created or adapted by the DRE and classroom teaching which includes direct interaction by sharing ideas, attitudes, and information with others so that meanings of faith are made available that enable a relationship with God to be developed and the discipleship of service is experienced.

Theory Base Essential to DRE as Teacher

The DRE is the vertuoso teacher of the church, modeling the best teaching behavior in each class taught. The DRE must be skilled in the art of teaching. There is a correlation between what the DRE believes to be the purpose of religious education and the choices of teaching-learning strategies. John Miller and Wayne Seller present three major orientations that link curriculum practices with the philosophical, psychological, and social contexts that shape them.[1]

Transmission Model

The first orientation is the transmission model which views the purpose of education to transmit facts, skills, and values to students. Underpinned by behaviorist psychology, the teacher carefully breaks down the content to be learned in blocks that can be controlled for specific responses.

Transaction Model

The second orientation is the transaction model. The student is seen as rational and capable of problem solving. With a high concern for cognitive problem solving, the model objects to education as rote learning and seeks a curriculum to develop students' intellectual abilities. Its roots are in the pragmatism of the progressive education method of John Dewey and the cognitive developmental theories of Jean Piaget and Lawrence Kohlberg.

Transformation Model

The transformation model is the third orientation. Personal and social change are the visions of the model that seeks to promote a transpersonal orientation in which there is a harmony with the environment and ascribes a spiritual dimension to the environment. This metaorientation defines human nature as basically good, at least capable, and emphasizes the interrelatedness of the teacher, learner, and curriculum. These orientations have their advocates among various religious education theorists.

Curriculum Models and Religious Education

The transmission approach is the traditional one in religious education and is advocated by almost all those theorists who assert that the foundation of religious education is theology rather than education. Thus, for example, Johannes Hofinger argues strongly that religious education is the transmission by the teacher to the student, a transmission which insures that sound theological doctrine and ecclesiastically approved views will be given to the students in as unadulterated a manner as possible.[2]

Sara Little represents the transaction approach. Thus she stresses the importance of "understanding and being able to use models or approaches with clear purposes and strategies that give a basis for choice, and therefore for drawing on appropriate knowledge and skills to develop teaching activities."[3] Avoiding any erroneous dichotomy between teaching content versus teaching persons, Little suggests that process of teaching is geared to "help persons understand so that they [can] determine the meaning of a subject for themselves."[4] Leon McKenzie is also committed to a participative style of teaching-learning, and describes the purpose of teaching as "to make meaning available by announcing the Good News . . . by serving the people in their own needs . . . and by forming community."[5]

The transformational approach might be represented by two different groups of religious education theorists. The first is that of the liberationists. This group, such as represented by Daniel Schipani,[6] sees global social problems as the primary focus of religious education curricula. A secular model with relevance for religious education is that proposed by James Botkin and his associates. This viewpoint uses the concept of participation learning which is related to global social problems in ways which are transformational.[7] The second major form of the transformational approach is that taken by Mary Elizabeth Moore. Influenced heavily by both process philosophy and process theology, Moore states that persons are formed and transformed as they receive historical tradition and as they move into the future to change the world. Persons are both influenced and transformed by both the world and God, and in turn are themselves actively influencing and transforming both the world and God.[8]

A holistic approach which subsumes all the various curricular approaches and instructional procedures is that taken by James Michael Lee. Throughout his voluminous writings, Lee has consistently stated that any adequate theory of teaching and any adequate theory of curriculum must of necessity be such as to embrace any and all specific teaching procedures and curricular programs.[9] Conversant as he is with both the empirical research and the theoretical writings on the nature and dynamics of curriculum and teaching, Lee asserts that differential learning outcomes require differential curricular modes and differential teaching procedures. Lee notes that one of the most frequent errors made by uninformed teachers and curriculum builders in religious education is "the fallacy of only one teaching method" and "the fallacy of only one curricular plan," respectively. Empirical research has shown over and over again that no one teaching procedure works equally well for all learners or for all kinds of desired learning outcomes. For example, teaching for affective outcomes demands a curriculum and a set of teaching procedures which are quite different from teaching for cognitive outcomes. Furthermore, the successful facilitation of various kinds of affective outcome requires a different set of teaching procedures and a different kind of curricular spin. Or again, learners of different age levels require different kinds of curricular plans. And again, the culture and the personalities of learners are major determinants of the kind of curriculum and teaching procedure which will work effectively. In some cultures and for some types of learners, participatory learning simply will not work, while in contrasting cultures participatory teaching procedures and curricula constitute especially effective instructional devices.[10]

It should be added that while almost all of the proponents of one or the other curricular approaches and teaching patterns do not go into specific pedagogical ways in which their ideas can be concretely enacted, Lee always directly ties in his theoretical concepts with specific empirically proven teaching practices which enflesh the theories and laws he is advancing.

Multidimensions and Multifacets of Curriculum

In her/his role as teaching-learning specialist, the DRE focuses on the subject-matter content to be learned, the appropriate sequence for its presentation, and the variety of settings in which teaching takes place. Together these three form curriculum design.

The settings for religious education in the congregation are multidimensional. In most churches the greatest number of opportunities may be the school-type settings such as the Sunday school or CCD, pastor-led Bible studies, vacation Bible schools, computer-aided instruction, and so forth. Liturgical/sacramental settings, often led by the pastor, are a second setting type. These settings include activities such as parental preparation for a child's baptism or a youth's confirmation, or premarriage counseling, e.g., a Pre-Cana Conference. A third group of settings prepare church members for service to the church's community such as teacher training, church officer training, usher training, or lay eucharist minister training. Preparing persons to live their discipleship in the world in service might be represented in work camps or in a family education program teaching for world peace. Finally, there are social-relational settings such as youth fellowships, Women of the Church meetings, and camping.

The religious education curriculum of the church is more than the Sunday school literature or CCD textbooks. The religious education curriculum includes written and unwritten resources for every facet of the religious education program. It includes print and audio or visual resources, together with human resources. The whole life of the church's membership becomes part of the religious education curriculum as the intentional facilitation of cognitive, affective, and lifestyle outcomes are communicated through planned processes and procedures as well as through nonverbal and even unconscious means.

The church's religious education curriculum is broader than any set of specific programs. Religious education includes planned programs, but it also includes many unscheduled "person-to-person dialogues," such as an individual's personal reflection on the faith that transforms the nature of the community.[11] The church's religious curriculum is always growing (or should be) as new courses and activities are developed.

The functions of the DRE as teaching-learning specialist build on the church's long-range educational goals as well as the educational needs and interests of the members of the church. The function of teaching-learning specialist has several subroles: long-range curriculum building, short-term (e.g., annual) curriculum design; specific program planning and class session preparation; resource materials and media development; and teacher/leader of specific events.

Long-range Curriculum Planning

Long-range curriculum planning enables the church to be responsible stewards of the congregation's resources. Long-range curriculum design is the best method to create a comprehensive, intentional ministry for the church. Long-range plans are usually for two to four years. A long-range plan serves as a guide and is flexible because new opportunities or needs can be inserted or plans deleted as necessary.

The development of a comprehensive religious education program requires intentional long-range planning by the responsible groups. Such planning usually involves the professional staff of the church (pastor, DRE, and where appropriate the music director), the parish council that plans general ministries, the education committee, and age-level councils. Effective curriculum building requires the involvement of the laity in an appropriate fashion. All the groups and persons mentioned in this paragraph may be responsible in one way or another for the initiation of ideas, program implementation, evaluation, or any sub-part of a religious education activity.

Creative planning requires planners who are creative. And creative planners are those with established conditions which are conclusive to creative activity. The DRE who listens for new ideas at professional meetings, who looks for different approaches in professional reading, and who keeps the new ideas in some organized fashion is the DRE most likely to be creative in the planning process. Creativity takes preparation. DREs who allow others to develop ideas without demanding approval from their church/superiors are the DREs who tend to stimulate creativity in planning groups.

Curriculum Based in Parish-level Goals and Objectives

A basic approach to a comprehensive curricular design begins by using the goals and objectives for the religious education program that have been set by the representative parish committees, usually guided by the DRE. In most parishes the various parish committees and councils are guided by a curriculum design process formulated by the DRE to determine the educational needs of each part of the congregation's life.

Although the professional literature is not always consistent, typically a goal is defined as a broad purpose, while an objective is a specific purpose. A goal generates a wide variety of specific objectives which fall within the ambit of the goal. A goal is usually linked to vision, while an objective is linked to a specific performance or outcome.[12] In a sense, then, an objective is a specific concretization of a broad goal. The selection of resources and strategies for teaching-learning flow directly from goals and objectives. The curricular design is completed through the implementation of the programs, and through the evaluation of results.

The vision of religious education provides a guide for effective goal-setting out of which a long-range curriculum model can be developed. Religious education uses a variety of learning formats to enable persons to develop their Christian faith and to respond as people of God with ministries in the world. Religious education is lifelong and is concerned with developing the whole person as a creation of God. Religious education is concerned with the faith and discipleship of the individual Christian, the life and mission of the church, and the witness of the people of God in ministry in the world.

The use of the sub-parts of the vision serves as a guide for developing specific activities to create a comprehensive program. The DRE is responsible for helping the local congregation formulate and articulate its general educational goals as well as specific objectives for each age group. The value of an articulated objective is that those churches who have consciously developed an objective statement to guide their program development are more likely to be growing parishes.

Comprehensive Curriculum
Includes All Teaching-Learning Opportunities

Comprehensive religious education models reach beyond traditional educational settings associated solely with the Sunday school or the CCD, the Sunday youth fellowship, the parochial school, and the like. Notwithstanding, it is a well-documented truism that a vital Sunday school or CCD program is a crucial key to a successful comprehensive religious education program.[13] The Sunday school and the CCD, therefore, should reflect a comprehensive design as well as be a microcosm of the total life of a church.

Traditionally, many DREs tended to view the Sunday school or the CCD as the primary place of religious education activity. Actually, these two school programs represent only a small part of the total curricular concerns for the DRE. Even when combined with the variety of activities associated with youth ministry, less than one-half of the typical Protestant DRE's professional time is related to these areas.[14] Consequently, the DRE ought to be responsible for the creation and implementation of a wide variety of religious education opportunities taking place in the church for all sorts of different groups.

Through the various committees and councils, the DRE facilitates the creation of learning opportunities for all age groups. If the church is to be more than a marginal institution, it must take seriously learning across the age span. Margaret Mead has written that limiting education to children is appropriate only for a primitive society.[15]

In contrast to this focus on children, it is predicted that by the year 2000, people will choose to live in neighborhoods which not only have good public schools for their children, but where there are strong adult education programs for themselves and their parents.[16] The DRE creates learning experiences that meet the developmental needs (social, emotional, moral, religious, and so on) of parishioners so that all ages receive attention. The DRE should assist the local church to articulate both broad goals and specific goals for each age level, including all ages of adulthood.

Historically, the way churches have chosen to offer a new religious education program has been to announce a course that the pastor found personally interesting and then hoped that people would attend. Sometimes a popular program given in a neighboring parish was copied.

A sounder approach leading to a comprehensive religious education program is to mesh the needs of the parishioners with the overall goal of the parish's religious education program—a program which necessarily combines the community's story with its mission in the world as faithful God's people. Working from the broad goals, the specific programs and educational opportunities can be arranged to meet the developmental levels of all learners. The research on life-cycle needs and interests may guide the church in reaching the various age groups with topics of interest, leading to appropriate levels of commitment.[17] The broad goals also allow the church to arrange specific programs and educational opportunities over a period of several years to meet the developmental needs of learners. A long-range curricular design allows for the creation of a comprehensive religious education program that relates to spiritual formation, development, and renewal, personal growth and interpersonal relationships, institutional concerns (such as teacher or usher training), and education for discipleship or service.

Long-range plans include both ongoing activities and proposals for short-term programs. Each year the DRE must review and evaluate the plans so as to decide whether they should be dropped, modified, or continued. Because these plans represent projections of three to four years in the future there can be flexibility in their details. However, a timeline for leadership recruitment, sequence of programs, publicity, etc., together with a general budget for each project, should be prepared by the planners. The budget is necessary for most local church's budgeting procedures. These long-range plans provide time to recruit the desired leadership rather than waiting until the last minute.

Comprehensive Curriculum Creates Alternatives

Comprehensive curriculum planning enables the religious educator to prepare a variety of formats and methods for learning. In building curricula, the religious educator should consider both the cognitive ability of leaners, their emotional level, and their religious development level. There is research which suggests that 60 percent of American adults are unable to read well enough to meet everyday demands without difficulty (functional illiteracy.)[18] This fact is sometimes difficult for many DREs with advanced academic degrees in education to comprehend because reading skill is central to all formal education. The reading level of children, youth, and adults should influence the type, selection, and use of print materials, as well as methods of recruitment for attendance.

Emotional Factors in Education

One result of long-range planning is attention to the emotional factors related to education. The emotional factors include the feelings that persons have about the experience, the substantive-content, or the group. For instance, a value of ongoing classes, such as the adult Sunday school class, is the emotional commitment to each other developed by the class members. The building of relationships is important in a course on communications or for spiritual journeys in community. On the other hand, short-term programs are often focused primarily on the sharing of substantive-content. But even here, attitudes are often developed and personal emotional factors in the setting and about the topic are important. For instance, a simple thing like changing the room for meetings gives the group a different feeling. One parish taught its board members about the various groups in the church by holding board meetings in a children's classroom, the choir room, the youth center, etc., throughout the year.

The emotional factors of a class can be influenced by two other details that may receive attention in long-range planning. Long-range planning provides the opportunity to build intermediate and advanced courses into the design. Recognition that persons have completed the initial studies in a topic by offering an advanced course enhances the feelings of accomplishment and increased emotional commitment to the topic. It is suspected that absence from many teacher training events is based on the fact most courses assume that the participants have never had any experience or training. Courses reserved for those who have participated in a previous course will change the emotional level of the students. Bible study and arts and crafts also seem to have both beginning and advanced level possibilities. The emotional level is also changed by the charging of a nominal fee for a certain course as the members share a greater ownership of the project, even when the church subsidizes the overall cost. Advertising and promotion of a program should indicate the affective environment of the program in addition to featuring the substantive and structural content, and indicating the names of the leaders.

Plan for Different Learning Styles

Creative planning should provide for different learning styles. People learn differently. Some are visual learners while others are primarily auditory. Some people are analytical while others are more global and learn through relational experiences. Likewise, teachers teach differently, often the way they have been taught. It is important to recognize that each person learns differently and to plan opportunities for a variety of styles.

Long-range curriculum design enables the DRE to plan experiences that intentionally use a variety of teaching-learning styles. Some people enjoy discussion groups, while others are intimidated by discussion. Lecture series, sharing/personal growth groups, church nights, choir and/or dramatic groups all appeal to a wide spectrum of interests. Social action groups need to learn information about the people they serve as well as effective intervention methods. Some people will pursue a planned course of independent reading such as sponsored by several denominational women's groups, i.e., the United Methodist Women, while others will only participate in large forums. In research conducted by the present writer, it was found that in larger churches, there was a correlation of church growth with the offering of a wide variety of programs for the congregation. Lyle Schaller recommends that in a church of 1,000 members there should be approximately 60 to 70 groups that meet regularly to meet the religious, personal-enrichment, and fellowship needs of the membership.[19] To develop this wide variety of ministries takes planning and constant evaluation to determine what areas should be emphasized.

An Example of Curriculum Development

Curriculum design that combines long-range and short-term planning can be illustrated by how one local church organized a young adult Sunday school class as part of its seventy-fifth anniversary. There were already several classes for young adults including a college group, a young adult group, and an early middle-aged group. The Anniversary Committee recognized the need to organize a new class for young adults between the ages of twenty-five to thirty. The project was coordinated by the DRE. Working closely with the pastor, a young adult who had expressed interest in creating such a class was invited to help in the planning. Decisions were made that the new class would be different from the existing one. A pedagogical decision was made to use the discussion method in contrast to the lecture format currently used and to include a variety of topics rather than be restricted solely to a Bible study. A potential leader who would be able to combine a knowledge of theology, the Bible, religion, social issues, and discussion methods was selected as the resource person. A meeting was arranged with the potential leader (the present writer) to explore the next steps.

Following the leader's acceptance of the teaching role for the new class, additional plans were made. Two additional goals were added for the class, namely 1) to enable the class to become theologically aware in ways that would affect the church's decisions and 2) to encourage learners to become a support ministry for those who would be developed as leaders in the church. The class would empower the creation of a pool of resource leaders for the entire church who could think theologically as well as creatively, using their respective talents. This twin goal was not published officially, but would be an intentional part of the curricular design. A planning committee of those interested in such a class was invited to an informal coffee-dessert on the following Thursday night. Letters describing the intention of the meeting were sent with the signature of the young adult who had been part of the planning from its initial stages.

Five young adult couples, plus the prospective teacher and his spouse, the DRE, and the pastor attended the planning meeting. At that meeting, curriculum resources available through the church were displayed for selection. Ideas for substantive content and format of the class were chosen. A commitment to attend for four weeks was received from each prospective class member. When the class met for the first time ten days later, the teacher knew that at least ten persons would be present in addition to any others who might respond to the open invitations. More letters were sent, along with telephone calls, general invitations in the church newsletter, and pulpit announcements were made. Twenty-five prospective members attended that first Sunday.

Eight years later, the class had grown to fifty-three members. All of the group that met for the initial planning night and who still live in the city are still active members of the class. Furthermore, all the original attendees have become parish leaders. The class meets annually to select its curriculum for the following year. The group has studied materials in human sexuality, field-tested Bible study literature, developed units in process theology, shared an intergenerational learning event with fifth graders during a Christmas season, and a year later did another intergenerational study with a class composed of many of the young-adults' parents (fifty-five to sixty-five year olds), studied the history of Christian theology, and explored areas related to religious faith in personal life. These topics all relate to the initial twin goal of enabling the class to be theologically aware and to encourage the learners to become a support ministry. Except for the newest members, most of the class has served on the various committees of the church, including the chairing of a million dollar capital fund drive, and have served as Sunday school teachers and leaders of other church learning experiences. In addition, the class has commissioned some of its own members to create a second successful young adult class.

Short-term Curriculum Planning

The comprehensive curriculum design is implemented in the programs for a specific year. The DRE functions as the program developer to arrange the short-term design.

Short-term Settings

There are several categories of educational settings related to the use of the DRE as a resource in planning. Some settings may be ongoing such as the CCD program or the Sunday school, a mid-week share group, or a dramatic group. These educational settings often use a "standard" curriculum from a printed resource. Although the DRE typically has a major role in children and youth ongoing classes, many Protestant adult Sunday school classes view the DRE as an occasional consultant. For these adult classes the DRE may guide the selection of the specific curriculum but is not directly involved in an ongoing planning role as the class officers and teachers perform these tasks.

Another category of educational settings is the elective or occasional setting. This may include new member inquiry classes, mid-week older adult fellowships, vacation Bible school, summer youth programs, leadership and teacher training events, parenting and marriage enrichment seminars, or special religion courses which last several weeks. The ongoing youth program is a part of these elective settings. This later program typically utilizes the resources of the DRE directly in planning and generally employs a short-term program design. The DRE may become the actual instructor in the settings mentioned in this paragraph or may only assist in recruiting other leaders.

Each year at a planning conference, many churches find it helpful to schedule the year's program events. Special seasons call for new as well as traditional religious education programs to be scheduled. New programs to be started can be assigned specific planning dates throughout the year. The short-term program planning design then can be evaluated by comparing it to the comprehensive curriculum design to see if there are additional areas of concern that have been unintentionally omitted.

Session Plans for Specific Events

A plan for each specific event or class meeting also must be developed. Such planning may be in the form of a lesson plan for a single class meeting or in the form of a program agenda for a larger series of meetings. Planning of this sort is sometimes performed by the DRE as an individual teacher developing lesson plans and sometimes by the DRE acting as a coordinator of the planning committee. The task may be described as program planning, course design, or lesson planning.

Program planning, used here as a generic term, is concerned with the details related to the preparation of a specific class such as a teacher preparation workshop, a program such as the vacation Bible school, or a general educational program such as preparing volunteers to be an evangelism visitation team. Program planning is not limited to a specific age level or a specific event. Program planning parallels short-term curriculum design in most of its steps. It becomes the plan to implement the curriculum in a specific setting. The steps in program planning typically include setting general goals, selecting specific learning objectives, choosing resources, selecting appropriate educational techniques, preparing a detailed timeline, and finalizing a budget.

Set Objectives

Using the broad goal that guides the comprehensive educational program, the specific needs and interests of a learner group are identified. The DRE assists the responsible committees to articulate the desired learning objectives for each group or event to be planned in the context of the global educational goals and objectives. From these goals and objectives the scope and the sequence of the topical content is planned for each learning setting. Ideally, planning should be done together with potential learners, even with children.[20]

The setting of learning goals and objectives is important for educational events. It guides the selection of resources and methods of teaching-learning in addition to serving as a check on whether the learning was achieved as planned. Learning goals describing what the students will learn from an event are different from teaching goals that describe what the teacher/leader will seek to do during a session.[21]

It is in setting general goals and specific objectives that the DRE can influence new directions in teaching and learning. Conventional religious education has been based on the transmission model that primarily stresses pumping cognitive content into the heads of learners.[22] This is the model that most teachers have been taught, as well as most DREs. Although the transmission of knowledge about the faith's heritage is important, the setting of goals that call for models which move beyond teacher-centered transmission procedures to methods which stress the learner's participation in the identification of transforming possibilities will push-out the limits of learning that have been part of the transmission model.[23] In a religion that teaches the belief in new creations, the limits of goals that relate only to the transmission of ideas for knowledge of the familiar are often deadly. Effective religious education calls for goals that encourage people to think in new ways, for ideas that will cause learners to look at the implications of their actions, and for creative new ways to encounter life.[24]

Choose Resources and Teaching-Learning Settings

When it has been decided what a new program is to accomplish, the design moves to the choices of resources and strategies for presentation. In addition to popular speakers, print or multimedia resources, one of the most valued resources is the people who attend a program. The DRE assists planners by providing information on what resources are available and how to obtain desired resources. Resources should be chosen to meet the needs of the group and the learning goals designated.

The choice of teaching-learning strategies will also be based on the learning goals. There is not any single teaching strategy or technique for learning that is always better than all the others.[25] The clue to the selection of a teaching method lies in the degree to which it produces a desired learning outcome. A workshop, an evening lecture, individualized reading, an encounter group, laboratory school, or a field trip can all be used to meet different goals.

Teaching strategies refer to the very specific teaching-learning procedures used to communicate the content in a class such as lecture-discussion, role play, a symposium, storytelling, painting a class mural, or participating in a Los Posadis during the Sunday school hour as an intergenerational activity. Formal adult and youth religious education have typically been locked in a lecture-discussion technique, but fortunately this is beginning to change.

In children's religious education, it can be said that the most important parts of the lesson are the techniques that are creative responses to the teacher's verbal and nonverbal presentations. These include teaching strategies such as making and sharing pop corn, artistic projects, e. g., molding figures in clay, or making a diorama; dramatic or puppetry presentations; or musical expression (all ways in which children respond to the content through affective experiences). James Michael Lee challenges the traditional practice wherein religious education techniques for children, youth, and adults are primarily and in some cases exclusively verbal. Adducing a large mass of empirical research evidence, Lee shows how nonverbal teaching procedures and nonverbal substantive content have far more power than verbal content to create holistic religious education.[26]

The background of the potential learners influences the choice of organizing teaching techniques. Is the group familiar with the topic? Are the teaching procedures based on the way in which a specific age group approaches reality, e. g., do we use concrete techniques with children since persons of that age encounter the world concretely rather than abstractly? Is the group comfortable with doing individualized learning or is it dependent on an authority to explain ideas?

Another important factor influencing the choice of teaching-learning techniques is the physical arrangement of the proposed instructional site. The size of the room, acoustics, seating arrangements, and visual concerns such as distance to a chalkboard influence the choice of techniques within a setting. Many religious education programs can use either a large-group format that includes opportunities for interaction among the participants or a small-group format that is based only on discussion. On other occasions, to reach a certain objective the size of the group must be limited or extended to include the appropriate number of participants. The key to the final choice of techniques to choose from a large catalogue of options is that they represent the best way to reach objectives planned for the activity.

Planning Calendar

When the objectives are established and desired resources and learning formats are chosen, a detailed planning calendar and time-table of the event is constructed. The calendar is especially important for meetings when larger groups or programs cover several days. The planning calendar includes the details of each part of the program from its initial planning stages through its final evaluation. It includes listing the names of any support personnel needed to serve the program, such as members of the publicity committee, registrars, ushers, set-up committees and clean-up committees, or refreshment committees, in addition to any program leaders such as major speakers and discussion leaders. The planning calendar also includes dates for publicity preparation and distribution, dates for completion of recruitment, and other key preparation dates.

To help the program (class, workshop, seminar, etc.) move successfully from point to point, a time-table similar to a detailed lesson plan of the event should be made as part of the program planning process. This time-table guides the leaders during the actual presentation of a program. The time-table guides moderators and chairpersons during the program as well as any speaker. Designating how many minutes will be used for the introduction in a two-hour program that includes symposium and a forum guides the leaders in keeping the program from being too crowded and keep it moving smoothly. A similar time-table is recommended for the lesson plan of a workshop and even for a lecturer.[27]

Plan for Evaluation

The planning team also prepares for the evaluation of the program, both in terms of how the goals were fulfilled and how the next learning experience should be planned. The DRE has an important task in helping committees to complete the planning process as many times the temptation is to propose an idea, assign the project to some committee, and then wonder why some details that make for effective programs did not receive attention. Finally, the budget is reviewed to be sure that the plans fall within the estimated budget prepared by the comprehensive planning committee. At this time the total of any speaker's honorarium, cost of resources, and other anticipated expenses can be compared to any anticipated income.

An Example of Session Planning

The role of the DRE interacting with a youth group planning committee using this model can be demonstrated in the following example. The DRE met with the youth program committee on Monday evening. The youth council at its quarterly planning session had already chosen the topic for the regular Sunday night meeting to be held in two weeks. The DRE had obtained several books and program quarterlies on the topic in addition to having checked the denomination's media catalog and the city library for possible audio-visual resources related to the topic.

After refreshments, the DRE asked the students on the planning committee, "What do you want to learn about this topic?" In this way, the youth began to state their learning goals. Then the DRE asked the group, "What resources do you think we could use to help us learn these ideas, and how can we present the material?" Ideas from the youth were added to those gathered by the DRE and several ways of developing the session were shared in the group. When the major resources and techniques were selected, the DRE guided the students through the proposed hour's presentation by questions such as: How should the group begin? Who will lead this part of the program? What are some key questions we want to raise at this point in the discussion? How long should we spend in the small groups? Do we want designated group leaders or should the groups operate without any formal leader? How will we know if we are successful? Each part of the session is carefully listed on paper by the various students and the DRE.

A news article is now prepared for the church's newsletter/ bulletin to advertise the youth's program with the names of the presenters included. When the youth members of the planning team leave at the end of the planning period, they are prepared to actually lead the youth program next Sunday night. Some additional preparation work may be required by the youth as films are previewed, or time is spent in the library getting facts, but the students know what is expected of each member of the presenting team. The role of the DRE (or any other planning counselor) on Sunday night is to be an adult resource to facilitate the youths' success. The planning format and example questions to assist the youth in developing their own program can be the basis of similar procedures and questions used by the DRE to guide any age-level planning group from older children to adults, as well as the personal preparation of a lesson plan for an event to be taught by the DRE.

Media and Other Resource Materials Developer

The DRE often works behind the scenes to serve teachers and other leaders by providing a variety of print and audio-visual resources. Some of the resources are created by the DRE and some are obtained though other sources such as a media library, denominational publishing companies, or local book stores. Some of the resources are needed by teachers in the parish for their presentation and some are for the personal use of the DRE in a teaching-learning setting.

Print Media versus Alternative Media

Historically, the Protestant church has been dependent on print resources. The Guttenburg press enabled Martin Luther to communicate his ideas to the people. Luther's doctrine of the authority of the Bible also gave "the Book" a supreme place in Protestant religious education. The nineteenth-century Sunday school movement contributed to the emphasis on print models of cognitive education. The International Lesson series was coupled with the Bible each Sunday. At the start of the twentieth century, there was a battle for control of the Sunday school literature between the fundamentalists, who held the view of an inerrant printed King James Version Bible, and the modernists who sought to use progressive educational methods with emerging biblical scholarship in denominational curriculum. In most of the "mainstream/ liberal" Protestant denominations, the fundamentalists lost control of the curriculum by the end of World War I. The printed resources became a symbol of control and power in these denominations.

Ironically, as the persons committed to "progressive education" gained control of the denominational curriculum publishing committees an incongruous variation of the dependency on printed resources emerged. To expand their influence and express their ideas the early twentieth-century fundamentalists moved to the newly developing technologies of radio and film as ways to communicate.[28] For instance, the Moody Bible Institute became a major producer and distributor of 16mm religious films that could be used in a variety of settings while most denominational publishing houses only developed filmstrips to be used with specific lessons. When television replaced the radio as the mass media in the 1950s, many of the former fundamentalist radio evangelists were prepared to dominate the television religious broadcasts such as the 700 Club and organize whole religious-based networks such as the Christian Broadcast Network. In contrast, since 1980 only one mainstream Protestant church, First United Methodist Church of Shreveport, Louisiana, has developed a satellite up-link capability to develop the Alternate View Network.

The Catholic Church, of course, has been heavily involved in print and nonprint media throughout the centuries. The Catholic Church has sponsored catechisms since Bellarmine's time. Missionary tracts, pamphlets, scholarly and popular books, and diocesan newspapers have for many years been a staple of Catholic life. Because Catholicism is a sacramental religion par excellence, it has not placed as much emphasis on preaching as has Protestantism, especially those Protestant confessions which are nonsacramental in character. Still there have been notable Catholic television preachers ranging from Fulton J. Sheen in the 1950s to John Bertolucci in the 1980s. In the 1970s Mother Angelica, a nun in Birmingham, Alabama, established the first successful Catholic cable television network (Eternal Word Television Network).

Our era has been called the information age. Every progressive business uses a wide variety of computer software. Videotapes are consistently used for training, as are audio-tutorial tapes. No sales meeting would be complete without charts and often includes videotapes, slides, and/or overhead transparencies. Ironically, education, and especially religious education, is an area where modern communication and educational technology are not fully utilized.[29] Although most schools and many churches have well-stocked media equipment closets, the actual classroom use and/ or committee meeting use of the equipment is very limited. Other than the occasional use of the traditional chalkboard, relatively few religion teachers use any media beyond the printed curriculum resource.

Electronic Media Requires Teaching Strategy Changes

Mass electronic media are now recognized as the primary shaper of ideology and values in our culture rather than books or print media. Religious education based solely on print resources is really antiquated. "That means we serve an ideological structure that is being marginalized as the new media move in with their cultural power to form and shape human beings."[30]

The DRE must take leadership in enabling the church to enter the information society through the use of educational technology. The purpose of improvements in educational technology is to increase teaching effectiveness.[31] Most people teach the way they have been taught. In most parishes a large percentage of the educational staff, other than the DRE, are volunteers and are not trained in either public or religious education. When these volunteer teachers enter the classroom they typically are dependent on the models of teaching they experienced as children when they were in the CCD program or the Sunday school. Conscious effort must be made by these teachers to change personal behavior and to use alternative teaching-learning procedures and audio-visual resources.

A significant role of the DRE is to model in a wide variety of teaching-learning strategies how the various audio-visual media can be used in religious education. This means that the DRE must be professionally prepared in the construction and use of the emerging and currently available media. Professional religious education associations need to take responsible leadership in this area for the in-service education of DRE members. Such in-service preparation will have impact on the increased use of media as awareness and training usually precedes the purchase of the expensive items such as video cameras.

Providing Audio-visual Media to the Local Parish

The DRE serves as a media consultant to the church through several activities. One major service is the provision of catalogs from many sources for different types of media such as agencies to rent or borrow films and videotapes. Bibliographies and/or copies of supplemental resources for regular curriculum units may be collected for display in the church library or for additional purchase. Assistance in the use of church-owned projectors and production equipment would be available from most DREs. The DRE is usually the person who includes the purchase of major audio-visual instructional aids in the church's budget.

The DRE may be the channel that provides purchased or rented resources to leaders or may be responsible for the local production of certain media. Sometimes the best option for the DRE to provide resources for teachers and learners is the direct purchase of the media. Some criteria for selection of purchased materials include concerns for content usefulness and accuracy, how the resource could be used by the church in its religious education programs, and the degree of instructional value in relationship to its cost.[32] Some of the resources that normally would be purchased or rented/borrowed public, synod, conference or diocesan libraries include teaching pictures, maps, videotapes, filmstrips, and 16mm motion pictures.

Developing Local Media

There is also the need for the DRE and other parish leaders to develop resources in the local church.[33] The local production enables materials to be specifically related to the planned lesson content. Not every resource needs to be produced by an adult. Children or youth can plan and produce many materials that illustrate a lesson or unit. When students produce the materials, the emphasis is not on the finished product but on the learning process that is involved both in its preparation and in the content displayed. For instance, elementary children enjoy making write-on slides to illustrate a Bible story. Overhead transparencies with a larger drawing area enable younger children to participate in the same type of experience.[34]

Levels of Local Production

There are several levels of local production of resources by either the DRE or individual teachers ranging from the imitation of previously produced materials, through the adaptation or modification of existing resources for local use, to the invention of new resources.[35] Copying an outline map on to a transparency or a handout, or using a pattern for letters, or following printed instructions to construct a model are examples of *imitation*. Copying suggestions given in the curriculum resource or commercially prepared materials are easy ways for teachers to prepare media resources.

The second level of preparation, the *modification* of materials by the DRE or classroom teacher means that the materials have been altered in some fashion to be more useful to the specific session in which it will be used. A picture or an article in a book may guide the idea, but the leader must make the item without a published pattern and/or make adjustments in the content for the local situation. An example of adapted material could include creating a set of questions for a Bible quiz game patterned from a popular television show or asking a parent to make an easel for the children's class by showing one in the catalog but without having the dimensions.

The third level of preparations, a creative *invention* of learning resources, happens when the DRE or teacher develops an original teaching resource or project to present ideas or solve specific problems. Writing a special curriculum for a children's study on "Children and Death" following the suicide of a youth in the community, developing a videotape based on an event in the church, or creating a sound-slide show would all be examples of a creative production. Student-produced resources based in problem-solving situations may also be sources for original resources.

The Church Library Is a Media Resource

The church library is central to an effective media program. A sad commentary on the availability of media resources in many churches is the comment attributed to one Sunday school teacher that "the hardest thing about using audio-visuals in our church is getting the key to the media resource closet." A critical need is for the media resource library to be open and available near the church library whenever the major programs of religious education are happening in the church. A library that is equipped with resource books for teachers and students of all ages along with audo-visual resources such as tape recorders, projectors, and even a video cassette recorder and "mini-cam" is now needed for effective religious education.

Libraries have historically been centers of education and when guided by the DRE still continue to be a major educational resource. Effective use of the church library in general, and of the religious education library in particular, necessitates that both kinds of libraries exist and that they are well-stocked with the lastest audio-visual and print materials of high quality. All too often, unfortunately, church libraries and parish religious education libraries are nonexistent or are threadbare. One important role of the DRE is to see to it that at least the parish religious education library contains a good variety of up-to-date quality audio-visual and print materials.

Nonbroadcast Video in Education

In the future the DRE as a media and resource developer must become familiar with techniques for using video in educational settings.[36] Either through the purchase of a mini-camera in the church's budget or through the services of a parishioner, a VCR with a video camera will be available to local churches served by a DRE. The DRE must become familiar with how to script, produce, and direct a video production for the local educational endeavor. The DRE will also want to develop a pool of trained volunteers to actually run the technical equipment for use in the religious education program. This is in addition to any use that the church makes of television in broadcast of services or other programs either on cable or commercial television.

Some examples of the religious education use of nonbroadcast video include videotaping the pastor presenting a fifteen-minute background on the Bible passages in the next curriculum unit to be shown at the quarterly teacher's meeting. A workshop for beginning teachers can be video recorded so that the same information can be shared with those not present. A class invites a speaker in for a topic that is likely to be repeated in other classes and the DRE arranges for the session to be taped and edited for other classes. A teacher with confidence requests a tape be made of her teaching a class so that she can watch it next week at home to improve her own skills.[37]

Computers in Religious Education

Computers are another area in which the DRE must become competent. The DRE should be as concerned about the educational use of the computer as well as the administrative and word processing uses. Public schools have expended a great amount of funds for computing equipment. In 1988 over 2 million microcomputers were installed in public schools.[38] However, in elementary schools they are most often used for drill and practice of basic skills and at the high-school level they are used to teach computer literacy, with the rare anecdotal exception.[39]

Marylu Simon, Program Administrator at Educational Testing Service describes the central issue or problem related to the low level of use of computers in education. Most teachers are not aware of the possibilities of using the computer software to facilitate productivity in their own professional tasks.[40] In a society where children and youth are common computer users, a high percentage of teachers report anxiety about using computers. There is a high need for in-service education for teachers to learn to use word processors, data base skills, graphics, and basic types of educational software that will change the teachers' orientation to textbook/print media.

Religious education is also faced with similar limitations. Many volunteer teachers are not trained in the use of computers. In addition, there is a limited amount of software related to religious education whether it be games or drill.[41] Too often the literature assumes that the religious classroom teacher is a computer programer.[42] Although several companies sell disk copies of the King James Version of the Bible, neither the Revised Standard Version (RSV) nor the Good News Bible: The Bible in Today's English Version (TEV), translations typically used by the mainstream denominations as the biblical reference sources for their literature, have been widely distributed, if at all, in computer software. Both religious education and public education need editors of the standard curriculum to prepare software that is integrated with the traditional lesson materials with guidance for the classroom teacher in its use.

While both public and religious education are facing the lack of software that deals with problem solving beyond the drill level and computer anxiety by teachers, a cultural change is happening caused by the availability of computers. Although many schools have expended large funds for computer hardware, and have established computer labs, students still are able to use a computer for only thirty to forty-five minutes per day, provided they are enrolled in a computer literacy class.

The real revolution in computer learning is taking place in homes. Many middle- or upper-middle-class families are purchasing computers for their children which are regularly used for learning and other daily activities. In contrast, lower economic homes have not bought computers, except those primarily used for games.[43]

As computer software, videodisks, and videotapes increase for use in the home market, there will be a wider gap between the haves and have-nots. This gap will affect the learning styles of the children and youth in most of our churches by the end of this century. Books will become more expensive. In addition to the justice concern regarding social/economic class and the use of the computer, the DRE must be concerned that girls as well as boys are able to use the computer for religious education as well as public education. Since teachers tend to teach the ways they have been taught, it is important that in-service opportunities be given to religious educators in assisting them to up-grade learning opportunities using this resource.

The development of computer software for religious education needs to follow a careful curriculum design procedure that includes the interaction of content specialists, teaching-learning specialists, and software programers.[44] Religious education must relate both to affective and cognitive learning, as well as have concern for the religious/spiritual life of the learner. Concern should be raised for religious education programs to be developed using holistic education theories where the student and computer program are interactive in both problem stating and problem solving rather than stimulus-response theory as most drill (workbook style) programs are today.[45]

Effective teaching using computers will be based on the classroom teacher's ability to use quality instructional methods for the learning needs of each student. Helping students to develop, articulate, and test their own ideas rather than being told by either the teacher or computer is still the central means of effective teaching whether computers are used or not.[46] These concerns require that people knowledgeable in the techniques of computer software development and in religious education with an understanding of religious studies (including theology and biblical studies) take the lead in developing software that can be used to meet the vision of religious education.

Church members will increasingly be exposed to the use of audiovisual resources through general education and business experiences. To avoid becoming a marginal institution, the church must become skilled in the use of audio-visuals to enhance learning. The task of improving the communication skills of the church will increasingly become the DRE's responsibility.

Classroom Teacher

Teaching Is Central

One of the most significant roles of the DRE is that of classroom religion teacher. In this role the DRE is responsible for the communication of the religious content to persons of all ages. The role of a teacher first and always is to facilitate desired religious outcomes in learners. The DRE by virtue of high-quality professional preservice and in-service preparation skillfully integrates teaching procedure with holistic religious content, namely, religious content which combines the cognitive, affective, and lifestyle domains.

There are a variety of sources which bid the DRE to assume the role of classroom teacher. Many DREs began their entry into the profession as a result of a commitment to the Christian faith and meaningful volunteer experiences of teaching either in the Sunday school or the CCD program or by serving as a counselor in the youth ministry. For many, serving as age-level superintendents or coordinators meant larger blocks of volunteer time serving the church. Finally, a sensitive pastor recognized the person's graces and gifts. The pastor encouraged and invited the person to prepare for a professional ministry. Many women responded to the invitation by seeking graduate training in religious education with courses in theology, Bible, church history, and Christian social ethics, in addition to studies in teaching and learning with each age level. To claim the role of teacher is to reclaim the commitment that led to a person's assuming the position of DRE.

Robert Wood Lynn asserts that the emphasis on the manager role rather than on a ministry of teaching at mid-century was a major cause of the profession's loss of stature and thus of status.[47] Charles Foster relates the contrast of the vision of the roles of teacher and manager in biblical motifs.[48] During a time of crisis the DRE becomes more concerned with teaching or rehearsing for "the people those stories that reclaimed and affirmed their corporate identity, meaning and purpose." The educator as teacher was "one who urgently and deliberately transmits the heritage of a people with the expectation of its continuity and renewal."[49] The biblical experience of the Exodus from Egypt and other times of crisis shape this perspective.

In contrast, states Foster, the times of political stability and economic growth, such as during the period of the United Kingdom of David and Solomon, the emphasis was on remembering the blessing of God's graciousness, according to Foster, which leads to a model of the educator as a director or manager. In this model the director as manager is more concerned about "creating environments for learning than with the transmission of a threatened heritage."[50]

The role of teacher is central to the whole life and mission of the church. Teaching (or instruction, to use a synonym) happens when the DRE coaches a CCD teacher on how to handle a discipline problem in a classroom, it happens when the DRE consults with a parent on how to improve communication with a teenager regarding values, or it happens in the parent's-day-out program as the child is taught to share by taking turns. The role of teaching should not be confused with, or limited to, schooling models.

The DRE Models Teaching

Although teaching is not limited to the classroom, the DRE must intentionally serve as a classroom teacher on a regular basis in one of the traditional content areas of the Christian faith. Mary Boys describes the importance of the professional educator who brings sound educational philosophy and teaching skills to the world of biblical scholarship. How are the significant findings of biblical scholarship to be made accessible to the laity in the church? In order to move from the arena of biblical specialists, "it needs the perspective and expertise of the religious educator."[51]

The audience for the DRE as classroom teacher must regularly include adults in addition to teaching children or youth. Randolph Crump Miller points out that "unless there is a body of informed adults, nothing much of importance will happen."[52] The significance for adults to be studying in the church's religious education program can be appreciated at several levels. First, our society places the highest importance on what happens to adults as that is where decisions are made. Second, as the church seeks to fulfill the goal of developing discipleship through participation in the ministries of God in the world the DRE, along with the pastor, must use the best educational methods "to engage the community of faith in a process of interpretation and formation of its shared life and thought in ways that express the vitality of the Christian tradition and lead to transformation of the world."[53] And perhaps most importantly, in a world where Christianity is a minority religion, teaching adults "is central to the survival of the faith community . . . in preparing persons to participate in, perpetuate, and renew corporate worship and mission which give the church its identity and task in the world."[54]

The congregation needs to consistently see the DRE as one who is religiously, theologically, and biblically literate as well as an expert in the methods of teaching. The congregation's perception of the DRE as a teacher of the broad religious issues and topics is important for the enhancement of the DRE's status in the local church and for the profession. The DRE brings to the church the trained skills of teaching and educational philosophy along with knowledge from the broad fields of biblical, religious, and theological scholarship through high-quality graduate-level education. Good stewardship of the church's resources and return of the investment in the training of the DRE sponsored by the church requires a greater emphasis on the teaching role.

Substantive Content Areas of Teaching by the DRE
Some of the obvious content areas for the DRE to give teaching leadership include spiritual formation and development for

all ages. In these settings the story of the community can be heard and the vision of God's shalom can be shared.[55] In her book on teaching, Sara Little declares "that the existing situation calls for more direct, conscious attention to belief formation as an emphasis of the teaching ministry of the church."[56] Preparing learners for baptism and confirmation, in addition to concern for their growth in spiritual disciplines such as worship, study, prayer, and meditation are part of spiritual formation and development.

Traditionally, institutional concerns such as training Sunday school or CCD teachers, acolytes, or church officers to perform organizational duties have been standard areas of instructional activity for the DRE. Teaching groups of children in vacation church school or teaching youth as part of their Sunday evening fellowship would also be part of this regular ongoing teaching role. These institutional concerns will continue to be important.

The DRE also participates in education for personal growth and training for interpersonal relationships. Much of young adult ministry is concerned with these areas. Teaching must intentionally be planned to integrate cognitive and affective activities so that the whole person is developed. The concern for the vision of an inclusive church and society will be represented in religious education for personal growth and for more focused spiritual formation. Sharing stories with children and youth that are rich in alternatives for role models, vocational options, and creativity will enable persons of all races and sexes to come to a vision of that kind of future which more adequately reflects God's shalom for humankind.

The area of religious education that needs special attention in most churches is education for discipleship or ministry in areas outside the institutional church. Teaching must be planned to develop personal resources for congregational members to be involved in the peace and justice issues of life. Most people tend to avoid engaging in critical thinking on controversial ideas, and the DRE cannot assume that people will automatically deal with controversial issues in a fashion enlightened by Christian principles.

The importance of educational models that include the "wrestling with the issues in discussions among the lay members" cannot be underestimated.[57] Studies have indicated that white

Protestants who can be labeled politically and economically conservative have a high degree of involvement in their local churches.[58] It is recognized that many other factors cause conservative responses. Yet most of the major mainstream Protestant denominations and also the Roman Catholics have adopted official social statements that vastly differ from conservative viewpoints. It would be a fair assumption that at least some of the ministers and priests have communicated their own generally progressive attitudes, as well as the official statements of their denominations, to parishioners during the course of their sermons. Indeed, many denominational newspapers include letters to the editors about social topics. The research asserts "that preaching and other monological means of communication, forming as they do the major means of communication in most churches today, are relatively ineffective in changing people's attitudes and opinions on social questions."[59] If religious education does not address the social-ethical issues, then where can a morality based in the Christian vision be heard?

Religious education encourages learners to think, to challenge ideas, and to create new ways to see life.[60] Although teaching includes the passing on of the tradition of the faith community, with the goal of incorporating people into the community, there is also the sense that the tradition can be challenged and transformed. The models of teaching that the DRE must use include ones of inquiry, of heuristic commitments in the pursuit of truth. This creates the possibility of doubt, of challenge to the tradition as the learner is led to search for meaningful answers. Churches and parishes which expect educational models to indoctrinate will not accept this open and growth-oriented premise of religious education. The interplay of the heritage of scripture and tradition, with personal experience and reasoned thinking makes religious education a dynamic activity.

Components of the Teaching Act

In every teaching event in addition to the persons of the teacher and learner there are three major interactive components. These three are the subject-matter content, the teaching strategies, and the classroom dynamics, or the process of interaction in the teaching environment. The way in which these three major components interact depends on the goals and texture of the particular teaching-learning activity.

Substantive-content Component

Substantive content generally describes *what* is being taught, the subject matter.[61] The content may be cognitive learning of certain periods of church history, or the content may be a motor/ skill such as making a stained glass window in a youth week. There are several levels of content to which the DRE must give regular attention in each teaching event. Obviously there is the verbal content. This is what the lecture, the discussion, or the storytelling is about at the verbal level. The DRE must do the necessary background research to assure that the facts are presented accurately.

Another content consideration is at what level is the material taught. Benjamin Bloom, David Krathwohl, Anita Harrow, and their associates have developed taxonomies for the cognitive, the affective, and the psychomotor domains of learning.[62] Most schooling unfortunately operates at the lower levels of the cognitive taxonomy which is basically learning facts or being aware of affective stimuli. Because religion is more than knowing facts, religious education classes should offer classes which operate at all levels of the taxonomies, especially the higher levels of the taxonomies.[63]

As a teacher, the DRE must model in teaching the practice moving toward the higher levels of the taxonomy.[64] Thus, in relationship to cognitive learning, goals should be pursued that lead to ways to apply the knowledge and to be able to analyze the ideas so that the individual elements can be put together to create a whole pattern that relates to the person's life. Finally, the higher taxonomy levels of cognitive learning enable the students to make judgments about the value of a set of ideas through comparisons with other objective data that are recognized as authoritative. In terms of affective learning, the higher taxonomy levels relate to making value commitments, developing a personal value system, and finally being characterized by a ethical or value system that is internalized independently from the group's pressures.[65] Incidentally, these upper levels of instructional objectives have many corresponding elements with the upper stages of moral and faith development.[66]

Unintentional Curriculum

One additional content concern involves the hidden content. While the intentional curriculum is the set of learnings which the church consciously intends for the learners, the hidden content generally is not consciously intended. Sometimes, the church teaches things it is not intending nor is it even aware it is happening. For instance, the location of classrooms may invite older adults to stay away due to a large number of stairs.

One of the key parts of the hidden curriculum is the ideological assumptions of the church and society that are not articulated. Concerns for sexism, racism, ageism, anti-Semitism, and the many other intentional and unintentional biases that lie hidden under the overt content are now curriculum issues in both religious education and public education. The DRE models a caring sensitivity for others by attention to language and styles of organization that are inclusive rather than cause separation both in the classroom and in the general administration of the educational activity.

Teaching Strategy Component

The teaching strategies or instructional procedures are the second component of every teaching-learning event. Teaching strategies are the microset of learning experiences designed by the teacher to achieve specific objectives.[67] Some of the older pedagogical literature used such terms as methods, techniques, devices, and so on, with subtle distinctions, but most of the contemporary literature uses teaching strategy to describe the instructional methods teachers select and organize to present the content.[68] Some of the many strategies that the religious educator might use might be found in this list of procedures:[69]

lecturing	discussion
simulation games	problem solving
use of audio media	use of video media
laboratory	field trips

questioning	creative movement
dramatization	storytelling
learning centers	creative writing
case study	research and reporting

It is obvious that the above list is only suggestive of the wide varieties of teaching strategies available to the DRE both as teacher and counselor to other teachers in the church's educational program.

When serving as the instructor of a group, it is important for the DRE to help students to reconcile their learning expectations with what is intended for any instructional event. Sometimes the objectives need to be modified based on the particular participant's needs and this is part of the procedures. The DRE activates in the church's life the norms for using a wide variety of teaching strategies in learning settings. Teaching strategies that include the opportunity for children, youth, and adults to practice implications of learnings are essential for the internationalization of learning. Creative choices of teaching strategies enable the DRE to communicate the substantive content in the learning session.

In the open system of teaching-learning advocated in the religious education model, the DRE must provide feedback to learners in order to facilitate the student's growth.[70] The collaborative style of sharing information about the learner's progress toward achieving the objectives of the session is the most appropriate form of feedback with the learner. Since most religious education does not include classroom testing, learners need some guidance on their learning progress. In the church, the DRE functions primarily out of persuasive moral influence so that positive reinforcement techniques are the most productive.[71]

One part of religious education is helping students to relate their subject-matter content learning to their personal life situation. To be able to articulate one's beliefs and feelings about ideas and interpretations requires learning to think independently. This skill is begun in childhood and its development is lifelong. Although students can only think for themselves, they use the relevant fund of knowledge and the diversity of models of thinking and relationships developed as the teacher challenges them to open attitudes and intellectual responsibility.[72] In religious education, the teacher seeks to relate subject content to the personal lives of the learners, moving from stories about biblical characters to inviting students to reflect on the actions of the characters from the frame of reference of the learner's life. When providing feedback in the area of personal beliefs and feelings about a subject, the teacher must remember that personal feelings are not appropriate topics for debate in the same way that ideas, theories, or other objective content may be challenged.[73]

Classroom Dynamics Component

The process of a class's interaction is sometimes described as the classroom dynamics or learning environment.[74] What is the psycho-social level of the class? Is the atmosphere friendly or is it difficult to make friends in the class? Is the group task oriented, where they are limited in asking questions, either because of the limited knowledge/experience of the leader, or can the group relax and follow ideas that are suggested by the topic but not necessarily planned by the leader?

One of the helpful procedures that must be modeled by the DRE is leading a class or group in appropriate evaluation of its own learning dynamics. Helping participants to understand and name the dynamics of its interaction often renews its commitments to the basic learning task, or provides group-generated data to change the group's learning objectives. This important teaching-learning procedure is often ignored but often provides crucial information to both the teacher and learners about the next desired steps for learning.

The nature of the over-arching learning environment can be demonstrated in the toddler rooms by how nursery workers report the behavior of a child to parents following church. The practice of only giving positive remarks about a child when the parent meets a child in the nursery tells the child he is still loved in this place even if conflicts had happened during the hour. Parents are also reinforced in this policy that says it is all right to leave your child here. We like him and will help him grow in positive ways.[75] Injuries to a child, of course, would be reported. The process of caring then becomes part of the lived curriculum in the context of the specific class.

Empathy: A Key to a Caring Christian Environment

It appears that the mechanics, i.e., the strategies, of teaching are fairly easy to learn through a variety of options ranging from in-service education to formal academic courses. However, the human dynamics of teaching in which the teacher demonstrates empathy for the feelings and ideas of the learner, the empathy that reassures and helps students feel comfortable in the learning setting, the sensitivity to cultural differences in the classroom, and being sensitive to the needs of the learners as persons is more difficult to develop.

This form of empathy is not the result of simple cognitive training but can sometimes be developed through experiential learning events designed to stimulate awareness for the need for empathy and with opportunities to practice a model of sensitive responses to human resources.[76] A DRE who models the human resource approach of supervision with teachers and other staff members reflects a high value on individual differences and will generally find increased satisfaction among both staff and learners about the goals of the educational program.[77]

Frequently, the ability to relate to children, youth, and adults is the result of maturity rather than academic knowledge. Parents often laugh about their life as new parents in that they were anxious about doing everything right for the first child, but the second had to shift for her/himself. Self-confidence about the DRE's own personal being, in addition to confidence in one's preparation and knowledge of the content, all seem to be intertwined in the creation of a sensitive environment where there is a high level of concern about persons.

As a classroom teacher, the DRE models ways in which basic communication norms in a learning event may be established. These norms for a learning event typically include how the learning expectations of the teacher and the student are to be reconciled, how communication will happen between the teacher and students and between students, what topics will be allowed in today's session, what are the acceptable questions, and what questions should not be asked. For instance, a process norm of voluntary participation in healthy adult groups is that no one is ever called on by the leader to get a discussion going unless that person volunteers to speak.

It is in the process component that an unintended teaching content is often important. Unintended teaching content is something that is taught in the dynamics of the learning environment without the awareness of the teacher or educational system. Sometimes the unintended teaching content is desirable but often it blocks the intended curriculum. This fact underscores the importance of the teacher being constantly aware of what is happening in the ongoing pedagogical dynamic. Such unremitting professional awareness will alert the perceptive religious educator as to the unwanted intrusion of unintended substantive or structural content.

Teaching Serves the Community

Teaching does not happen in isolation. In public education, the teacher is part of the larger school district. The public school classroom teacher is expected to use an approved curriculum reflecting the values of the larger community, choosing the teaching strategies that are compatible for the teacher's skills and personality and appropriate to the development of the learners, reflecting the subject matter.[78] In essence there are two levels of authority in the teaching event: the authority of the larger community as it determines the metacurriculum and the authority of the classroom teacher as she or he implements the teaching event.

The DRE, or any religious education teacher, represents the faith community in the teaching act. The DRE is the incarnation of the community's story in the teaching setting as well as in the whole life of the community, seeking to enable persons to experience and transform the story and tradition into their daily lives.

A negative unintended environmental impact may be experienced when a parish fails to consider the representative nature of the teacher in the classroom. Charles Foster calls attention to the dilemma of the recruiters for Sunday school classes in many mainstream denominations that need large teaching staffs.[79] Sometimes new members of the church who are not familiar with the religious life and traditions of the congregation and in many situations have not attended any religious education programs since they were young teenagers are recruited as teachers. In some cases, a person who is not even a member of the local church has been recruited as a teacher. Teaching is more than

using good teaching methods or repeating the words of a curriculum resource. Although these people probably contribute in
some fashion to the life of the church, the skill and hence the
transformational quality of their teaching will be limited.[80] In
the church, teaching involves the tradition of the community as
well as empowering the people to transform that story for new
situations.[81]

The authority of the religion teacher, which is part of the educational environment, comes from beyond the classroom event
which is then personalized in the choices of teaching strategies.
Teaching for a Christian lifestyle seeks to enable others to identify
with and become characterized by the religious ideals that are
part of the community's experience.[82] Churches with a tradition
of emphasizing specific doctrines, such as Roman Catholics or
Southern Baptists, have many examples of how the church sets a
level of authority which determines the instructional content.
Other mainstream Protestant churches often lack that clarity and
frequently have teachers creating their own individual curriculum outside the authorization of the church. This practice under-
mines the traditions of the denomination's focus and of the specific congregation. Although teachers must personalize every
curriculum, it appears reasonable that teachers who are not comfortable theologically with the parish's approved curriculum
choices and who wish to impose their own brand of curriculum
should not be invited to teach in that setting.

The Search for the Effective Teacher

What makes an effective teacher? One survey of United Methodist religious education programs discovered that people tend to
judge the effectiveness of teaching on the basis of the expectations
that the members had for the church school.[83] A quality highly
valued by most of the persons (89 percent) was the teacher's
ability to love and be concerned about persons. Another study of
nine of the largest church schools including Assembly of God,
Independent Baptist, Southern Baptist, and Nazarene Churches
found that persons attend educational events because they want
to learn more about the Bible.[84] Members in these churches
ranked the teacher's knowledge of the Bible, along with skills in
lecturing, to be the key to effectiveness.

The data reported in the preceding paragraph represents subjective opinions of parishioners. There have been many scientific research studies examining the determinants of teaching effectiveness. Most studies have concluded that a particular teaching procedure in and of itself is not the primary determination in student achievement or instructional effectiveness. Rather, instructional effectiveness is determined on the basis of how the teacher uses the instructional procedures, how the teacher integrates the procedures into the overall instructional ecology, how the teacher moves between and among various procedures, how the teacher integrates the procedures into his/her teaching style and the student's learning styles, and so forth.[85]

When the research focuses on the interpersonal skills of teachers other characteristics tend to emerge. Teachers who have desirable chracteristics tend "to behave approvingly, acceptantly, and supportively; they tend to speak well of their own students, students in general, and people in general. They tend to like and trust rather than fear other people of all kinds.[86] Other studies indicated that effective teachers have an enthusiasm for the act of teaching, for the people they teach, and for the ideas they are sharing.[87]

The ability to organize a learning setting, to understand the substantive content to be taught, and to generate enthusiasm for learning are important for effective teaching.[88] Effective teachers tend to perceive their purpose as being one of helping students to discover ideas and learnings. Encouraging and assisting students to think independently and to work toward personal learning goals are ranked high in desired teaching characteristics.

The vision of the DRE as a learning specialist flows from the nature of religious education in its concern for lifelong learning of the whole person. The conceptual tasks of curriculum building require the DRE to vision long-range needs and to plan for the total congregation in ways that build bridges between the various parts of the church's life and ministry. The skills in human relations are used both in the negotiations between the various concerned planning groups and in the actual classroom. And in the classroom the technical skills of the DRE as teacher create both opportunities for direct learning of content and indirect learning of models of teaching. By developing skills in the work of teaching, the DRE will reclaim the vision that was the call to the vocation of being a religious educator.

NOTES

1. John P. Miller and Wayne Seller, *Curriculum: Perspectives and Practice* (New York: Longmans, 1985).

2. Johannes Hofinger, *The Art of Teaching Christian Doctrine*, rev. ed. (Notre Dame, Ind.: University of Notre Dame Press, 1962). Josef Goldbrunner also argues strongly for a transmission-based form of religious education curriculum and teaching practice. See Josef Goldbrunner, "Catechetical Method as Handmaid of Kerygma," in *Teaching All Nations: A Symposium on Modern Catechetics*, ed. Johannes Hofinger, revised and partly translated by Clifford Howell (New York: Herder and Herder, 1961), pp. 108-121.

3. Sara Little, *To Set One's Heart: Belief and Teaching in the Church* (Atlanta: John Knox, 1983), p. 32.

4. Ibid., p. 33.

5. Leon McKenzie, *The Religious Education of Adults* (Birmingham, Ala.: Religious Education Press, 1982), p. 128. McKenzie rejects the domination of theology over religious education. Well-versed in both theology and religious education, McKenzie places religious education activity squarely within the sphere of education rather than within the realm of theology.

6. Daniel S. Schipani, *Religious Education Encounters Liberation Theology* (Birmingham, Ala.: Religious Education Press, 1988).

7. James Botkin, Mahdi Elmandjra, and Mircea Malitza, *No Limits to Learning: Bridging the Human Gap* (Oxford: Pergamon, 1976), p. 30. This book utilizes the notion of participation learning which is related to social problems. Thus the thesis of this book has relevance to that kind of religious education theory and ideology which seeks social and political transformation of the world.

8. Mary Elizabeth Moore, *Education for Continuity and Change: A New Model for Christian Education* (Nashville: Abingdon, 1983), pp. 122-123.

9. See, for example, James Michael Lee, *The Content of Religious Instruction* (Birmingham, Ala.: Religious Education Press, 1985), pp. 746-766. These twenty pages form a chapter called "Epilogue to the Trilogy" and constitute a small, meaty overview of the more than 1500 pages (having about 4,000 scholarly footnotes) of Lee's trilogy.

10. James Michael Lee, *The Flow of Religious Instruction* (Birmingham, Ala.: Religious Education Press, 1973), pp. 196-205. See also James Michael Lee, "The Blessings of Religious Pluralism," in *Religious Pluralism and Religious Education*, ed. Norma H. Thompson (Bir-

mingham, Ala.: Religious Education Press, 1988), pp. 57-124.

11. Moore, *Education for Continuity and Change: A New Model for Christian Education*, p. 156. Moore suggests that the title program director is more narrow than director of religious education because education is found in the larger life of the church. "Program" is a functional term because it defines certain settings in the church. "Program" is also a descriptive term because it tells what happens in a certain event.

12. Iris V. Cully, *Planning and Selecting Curriculum for Christian Education* (Valley Forge, Pa.: Judson, 1983), pp. 63-74. The confusion can be demonstrated in the practice of the National Council of Church's own description of its vision statement as "Statement of Objective." Cooperative Curriculum Project, *The Church's Educational Ministry: A Curriculum Plan* (St. Louis: Bethany, 1965), pp. 7-11. It also appears that literature for Protestant K-12 typically uses goals as the broad term while literature for adult religious education tends to use objectives and goals almost interchangeably and with less precision or delineation, depending on the definition and viewpoint of each individual writer. Compare Donald Griggs, *Teaching Teachers to Teach* (Nashville: Abingdon, 1974), p. 13, with Malcolm Knowles, *The Modern Practice of Adult Education* (New York: Association Press, 1980).

13. Warren J. Hartman, *A Study of the Church School in the United Methodist Church* (Nashville: United Methodist Church, Board of Discipleship, 1972), p. 39.

14. Dorothy Jean Furnish, "Study of Local Church Educators in the United Methodist Church" (Evanston, Ill.: Garrett-Evangelical Theological Seminary, 1976), p. 54. (Mimeographed.)

15. Margaret Mead, "Thinking Ahead," in *Selected Educational Heresies*, ed. William F. O'Neill (Glenview, Ill.: Scott, Foresman, 1969) p. 366.

16. Marvin Cetron, *Schools of the Future: How American Business and Education Can Cooperate to Save Our Schools* (New York: McGraw-Hill, 1985), p. 15.

17. Lawrence Losoncy, *Religious Education and the Life Cycle* (Bethlehem, Pa.: Catechetical Communications, 1977), provides an example of the application. See also James W. Fowler, *Becoming Adult, Becoming Christian* (San Francisco: Harper & Row, 1984).

18. Cetron, *Schools of the Future*, p. 70.

19. Lyle E. Schaller, "Reviewing the Group Life," *The Parish Paper* (Naperville, Ill.: Yokefellow Institute, 1983), p. 2.

20. Donald L. Griggs, *Basic Skills for Church Teachers* (Nashville: Abingdon, 1985), p. 18, applies the concept of participative planning to the classroom teacher.

21. Donald E. Miller, *Story and Context: An Introduction to Christian Education* (Nashville: Abingdon, 1987), p. 278, states that learning happens whether or not teaching is attempted while the opposite is not true.

James Michael Lee, *The Flow of Religious Instruction*, pp. 39-57, contrasts a theory of teaching with a theory of learning indicating the actions are different.

22. Paulo Freire, *Pedagogy of the Oppressed* (New York: Seabury, 1968), pp. 57-74, describes this as the "banking model" and James Michael Lee, *The Flow of Religious Instruction*, p. 25, describes it as the transmission strategy of teaching.

23. Miller, *Story and Context*, pp. 269-291.

24. Charles R. Foster, *Teaching in the Community of Faith* (Nashville: Abingdon, 1982), p. 125.

25. Sara Little, *To Set One's Heart: Belief and Teaching in the Church*, presents a variety of teaching approaches that incorporate many different procedures.

26. Lee, *The Content of Religious Instruction*, p. 455.

27. Griggs, *Teaching Teachers to Teach*, presents a model of this approach in the preparation of a lesson plan for a single class session with children or youth including the use of the time-table.

28. Ronald A. Sarno, *Using Media in Religious Education* (Birmingham, Ala.: Religious Education Press, 1987), pp. 215-232, describes the issues related to positive and negative effects of religious television broadcasting.

29. Calvin Dellefield, "New Aids to Learning," *Materials and Methods in Adult Education*, ed. Chester Klevins (New York: Klevins, 1972), p. 167.

30. William Kennedy, "Ideology and Education," *Religious Education* 80:3 (Summer, 1985), p. 343.

31. Rex Reynolds, "Educational Technology," *Materials and Methods in Adult Education*, ed. Chester Klevins (New York: Klevins, 1972), p. 176.

32. James W. Brown, Richard B. Lewis, and Fred F. Harcleroad, *AV Instruction: Technology Media and Methods* (New York: McGraw-Hill, 1976), pp. 43-44.

33. Mary Jensen and Andrew Jensen, *Audiovisual Idea Book for Churches* (Minneapolis: Augsburg, 1974), presents ideas for the creative use of AV equipment and materials in a wide variety of settings ranging from the worship service and church school or teacher training to confirmation, outdoor education, and nursing home visitation.

34. John R. Bullard, *Audiovisual Fundamentals*, 3rd. ed. (Dubuque: William C. Brown, 1984), gives step by step procedures for creating educational audiovisuals. Sarno, "Selected Printed Materials on Audiovisual Media," *Using Media in Religious Education*, chapter 5, is a set of selected books and periodicals helpful for making audiovisuals. Griggs, *Teaching Teachers to Teach* also presents detailed outlines on preparation of audiovisual resources as well as a model for a teacher in-service education workshop on audiovisuals.

35. Brown, Lewis, and Harcleroad, *AV Instruction: Technology Media and Methods*, p. 35.

36. Sarno, *Using Media in Religious Education*, pp. 226-231, describes how the broadcast television can be used by the church. Tom Neufer Emswiler, *A Complete Guide to Making the Most of Video in Religious Settings* (Normal, Ill.: Behavioral Images, 1988), describes the basic skills and equipment for local churches at the classroom level.

37. Daniel W. Holland, J. Ashton Nickerson, and Terry Vaugh, *Using Nonbroadcast Video in the Church* (Valley Forge, Pa.: Judson, 1980), presents both skills for amateurs in the local production of video materials and many ideas for use in the local church by lay groups.

38. Jonathan Goodspeed, "Two Million Microcomputers Now Used in U.S. Schools," *Electronic Learning* 7:8 (May/June 1988), p. 16.

39. Stanley Pogrow, "The Computer Movement Cover-up," *Electronic Learning* 7:7 (April 1988), p. 6.

40. Marylu Simon, "Let's Help Teachers Harness Computer Power," *Electronic Learning* 7:6 (March 1988), p. 6.

41. E. V. (Eldon Von) Clemans, *Using Computers in Religious Education* (Nashville: Abingdon, 1986), pp. 71-74, lists twenty-five companies which sell mostly Bible-based games or drill software programs. None of the publishers listed was either Protestant denominational publishers or major Roman Catholic literature publishers.

42. Ibid., pp. 55-59. See also Kenneth B. Bedell, *The Role of Computers in Religious Education* (Nashville: Abingdon, 1986). Bedell, founding president of the national Church Computer Users Network, describes the software issues of curriculum design for both public and religious education. He indicates that religious education software (the computer programs) is only in its pioneer stage, and lags behind public education. To move beyond the "creative individual" stage to mass-level importance, religious education will have to be assisted by a strong development in public education so that general education programs can be adapted for religious education. Educators who have learned to use the computer in these early stages will be prepared to use the developing resources in the future.

43. Cetron, *Schools of the Future*, pp. 30-31.

44. Barrie Jo Price, George E. Marsh II, and Anna C. McFadden, "Software Development: The Role of Curriculum," *Technological Horizons in Education Journal* 15:3 (October 15, 1987), pp. 84-89.

45. See Miller and Seller, *Curriculum: Perspectives and Practice*, pp. 117-172, for a description of transformational educational models in which students and ideas are interactive.

46. Stanley Pogrow, "How to Use Computers to Truly Enhance Learning," *Electronic Learning* 7:8 (May/June 1988), p. 6.

47. Robert Wood Lynn, "Tradition and Modernity: Managerial Images of Ministry in Protestant Church Education, 1900-1920," in *Minis-*

try and Education in Conversation, ed. Mary Boys (Winona, Minn.: St. Mary's Press, 1981), pp. 97-112.

48. Charles R. Foster, "Abundance of Managers—Scarcity of Teachers," *Religious Education* 80:3 (Summer 1985), pp. 437-446.

49. Ibid., p. 438.

50. Ibid., p. 439.

51. Mary C. Boys, "Religious Education and Contemporary Biblical Scholarship," *Religious Education* 74:2 (March-April 1979), p. 183.

52. Randolph Crump Miller, "Continuity and Contrast in the Future of Religious Education," in *The Religious Education We Need*, ed. James Michael Lee (Birmingham, Ala.: Religious Education Press, 1977), p. 31.

53. James N. Poling and Donald E. Miller, *Foundations for a Practical Theology of Ministry* (Nashville: Abingdon, 1985), p. 13.

54. Foster, "Scarcity of Teachers," p. 447.

55. See Thomas H. Groome, *Christian Religious Education* (New York: Harper & Row, 1980), for an elaboration of these terms. I am using them to mean the broad scope of the Christian faith that incorporates the biblical story, the story of the church's history, and the story and vision of the modern Christian's personal pilgrimage in light of the reign or shalom of God.

56. Little, *To Set One's Heart*, p. 31.

57. David J. Ernsberger, *Education for Renewal* (Philadelphia: Westminster, 1965), p. 42.

58. Gerhard Lenski, *The Religious Factor* (New York: Doubleday, 1961), pp. 109-111.

59. Ernsberger, *Education for Renewal*, p. 43.

60. Foster, *Teaching in the Community of Faith* p. 125.

61. For an elaborate and scholarly analysis of the content component the reader is referred to James Michael Lee, *The Content of Religious Instruction*. Lee describes the interactive components in detail. He lists nine global categories of content and develops in precise detail the categories of substantive content: product, process, cognitive, affective, verbal, nonverbal, conscious, unconscious, and lifestyle.

62. See Benjamin S. Bloom, ed., *Taxonomy of Educational Objectives: Handbook I: Cognitive Domain* (New York: McKay, 1956); David R. Krathwohl, Benjamin S. Bloom, and Bertram B. Masia, *Taxonomy of Educational Objectives: Handbook II: Affective Domain* (New York: McKay, 1964); and Anita J. Harrow, *Taxonomy of the Psychomotor Domain* (New York: McKay, 1972), for descriptions of the taxonomies.

63. Lee, *The Content of Religious Instruction*, pp. 608-735, presents an extensive description of "Lifestyle Content" which demonstrates the need for upper levels of both the cognitive and affective domains.

64. Norman E. Gronlund, *Stating Behavioral Objectives for Classroom Instruction* (New York: Macmillan, 1970) provides guidance in

writing objectives for the affective domain in addition to the cognitive domain in the taxonomies.

65. Allan A. Glatthorn, *Curriculum Leadership* (Glenview, Ill.: Scott, Foresman, 1987), p. 5.

66. Henry Giroix and David Purple, eds., *The Hidden Curriculum and Moral Education* (Berkeley, Calif.: McCutchan, 1983), p. 107.

67. Miller and Seller, *Curriculum: Perspectives and Practice*, p. 189.

68. Peter F. Oliva, *Supervision for Today's Schools*, 2d ed. (New York: Longman, 1984), p. 126. For an example of a taxonomy of the subtle distinctions in the concepts see Lee, *The Flow of Religious Instruction*, pp. 32-35.

69. For specific teaching strategies applied to religious education see Griggs, *Teaching Teachers To Teach*. Patricia Griggs, *Opening the Bible with Children*, (Nashville: Abingdon, 1987), presents strategies for biblical teaching. Little, *To Set One's Heart: Belief and Teaching in the Church*, presents five models of teaching based on the general education models of Bruce Joyce and Marsha Weil, *Models of Teaching*, 2nd ed. (Englewood Cliffs, N.J.: Prentice-Hall, 1980), which represents models appropriate across a variety of age ranges.

70. See Miller and Seller, *Curriculum: Perspectives and Practice*, in which the transmission model represented by a closed loop system is contrasted to the alternative curriculum models such as the transaction model which uses problem solving and analysis strategies and the transformation models which encourages divergent thinking, and emphasizes two-way interactive communication betwen the teacher and student that goes beyond the cognitive elements.

71. Ibid., p. 214

72. Stanford C. Ericksen, *The Essence of Good Teaching* (San Francisco: Jossey-Bass, 1984), p. 96.

73. Donald L. Griggs, *Basic Skills for Church Teachers* (Nashville: Abingdon, 1985), pp. 103-104.

74. Joseph Lowman, *Mastering the Techniques of Teaching* (San Francisco: Jossey-Bass, 1984), pp. 23-71.

75. See Lucie W. Barber, *The Religious Education of Preschool Children* (Birmingham, Ala.: Religious Education Press, 1981), for the complex interaction of cognitive ideas and psychomotor skills with affective behavior.

76. Robert A. Luke, "The 'Human Relations' Content of Teacher Training," in *Materials and Methods in Adult Education*, ed. Chester Klevins (New York: Klevins, 1972), pp. 121-122.

77. Peter F. Oliva, *Supervision for Today's Schools*, 2nd ed. (New York: Longman, 1984), pp. 394-395, describes how supervisors functioning as a human relations/human resources supervisor must function from a cooperative mode in which they are colleagues whose purpose is to improve the educational program so that together they may

enhance student learning; the final result will be an increase in teacher satisfaction.

78. Ibid., p. 129.

79. Foster, *Teaching in the Community of Faith*, p. 123.

80. Ibid., p. 124.

81. Ibid., p. 108.

82. Lee, *The Content of Religious Instruction*, p. 616.

83. Hartman, *Five Audiences*.

84. Marion E. Brown and Marjorie B. Prentice, *Christian Education in the Year 2000* (Valley Forge, Pa.: Judson Press, 1984), p. 122.

85. Miller and Seller, *Curriculum: Perspectives and Practice*, p. 230, indicate that congruence between the chosen theory of education and implementing the teaching strategies becomes the standard for effectiveness. In fact, they point out the evaluation procedures must be congruent for the theory orientation, or wrong implications will be produced.

86. N. L. Gage, *Teacher Effectiveness and Teacher Education* (Palo Alto, Calif.: Pacific, 1972), p. 35.

87. Lowman, *Mastering the Techniques of Teaching*, p. 71.

88. Ericksen, *The Essence of Good Teaching*, pp. 41-52.

Chapter 9

The DRE as Researcher, Diagnostician, and Evaluator

In our society information is a major source of power. The ability to generate, gather, analyze, and distribute information is vital to the decision-making concerns of the DRE in the local church. The church that will be effective in the future in meeting the needs of its members and in communicating the faith of that community will be a church that is skilled in information resource management.

The access to different kinds of information determines the broad perspective of the decision maker, whether that is the DRE, the pastor, or a lay person. The broad perspective creating a person's "model of reality" affects the decisions that a person is capable of making. The more accurate information available to the person, the greater the possibility of making a decision reflecting the true dynamics of any given situation.[1]

The DRE as Information Specialist

To avoid being dependent on intuition only, the DRE must be able to obtain and analyze data from a variety of sources. One image for the DRE is that of information specialist. An information specialist gathers and communicates the special knowledge related to a particular field, such as religious education. The information specialist typically uses computer skills to gather information. The information specialist serves as a link with senior-level executives to share information to be used in strategic-level decision making as well as an information link with persons in actual operational levels of the organization.[2]

The image of the DRE as a linker with knowledge and as an information resource manager is new for most DREs. The technical skills for an information manager have only recently emerged in the world of business. Information management involves both the technology for acquiring information and the policies and structures related to use of information.[3] It will be increasingly important within the next decade for the DRE to be skilled in computer data base management, to be able to create networks that generate information, and to communicate the developing knowledge to the congregation's membership.[4]

As a professional, the DRE must possess a body of knowledge related to the whole area of religious education ministry at an advanced level that surpasses personal experience. This will require a professional competence to "describe, explore, explain, and reflect upon the data which identify a field."[5]

With quantum leaps of knowledge and information, the DRE must create ways to access and organize the vast data. The DRE serves as a link with the resources and alternative ideas on structure and procedures. Today, most large churches employing a DRE have access to a computer or are making plans to acquire one. The use of computers and telecommunications provide the DRE with large amounts of data that can be communicated to the institution.

Information Management Serves Conceptual Planning

As an information manager or linker with resources, the DRE relates to the conceptual planning of the church. What are the long-range plans for the congregation that need information? Where will the church need information to move effectively into its next area of planned ministry? Using technical skills of research and data gathering, the DRE will be able to guide the acquisition of emerging information.

As the culture changes its understanding of the value of information as a specific resource and how information will be shared by knowledge workers, the church must also develop a policy on the use of equipment and on the staff's responsibility for the sharing of information. The decision of whether to have a centralized system for the church in contrast to each staff person having a personal computer with individual programs will affect control of data and the distribution of information. Perceptions of community ownership of programs and information data produced are different if the church has a centralized LAN (Local Area Network) compared to perceptions if each staff member uses individual programs on personal computers. For instance, who has access to certain restricted files. These policy decisions will affect the data stored in membership and stewardship lists as well as linkages with the vast resources in education.

One implication of information management is that significant assistance from most information systems requires the disclosure of essential facts and information that have often been considered the private knowledge of the pastor.[6] (This does not include privileged conversation information from counseling.) In the past, with the sharp division of the ordained clergy on the one hand and religious educators on the other, many DREs were not perceived as valued sources of information. Too often the image was one of distributor of curriculum resources, or player of games with children. The blame for this perception must be borne by both sides of the fence since often the DRE was not an effective communicator with the clergy. This was especially true of those DREs who did not receive graduate-level preservice and in-service preparation.

The issue here is that as information is increasingly available through many sources the church must make some intentional decisions on how it will manage information resources in the future. One critical religious education policy decision that must be made is whether or not the DRE is given authority by the church to develop and maintain innovations in information processing and communication. The authority to use the knowledge of innovations and evolving technology and information in appropriate educational events and settings must be provided to the DRE to make maximum use of the DRE's planning skills and leadership.

Information Gathering Functions

The DRE has three broad information gathering functions: research, diagnostics, and evaluation. These represent sources or three types of information the DRE needs to make decisions regarding educational policy and practice. The DRE must improve the current level of skills in these areas that are often neglected in congregational settings.

Unfortunately, most DREs possess only limited skills and interest in these areas. Several reasons for the limitation of technical skills are based in the nature of the academic preparation of the DRE.[7] One limitation is the result of academic institutions which have claimed that religious education is nothing more than theology. These institutions, therefore, aver that religious education is only a matter of making one or another educational deduction from theology. In this view, theology contains the sole source of appropriate knowledge, the sole source of truth, the sole source of norms, and the sole source of scholarly based practice for religious education. In reality, theology is incapable of generating or assessing teaching practices. Indeed, there is not a single instance in the millenia of religious education history in which theology has ever produced directly an educational technique.

Another reason is at the general graduate academic level research has the primary connotation of involved use of complex statistics and abstract theory. However, many are challenging traditional scientific models of research as inappropriate for organizational and human resources studies.[8]

There is a critical role in the local church for each of the information sources. In the local setting, the emphasis is not on statistics and theory but on information generated by the basic questions guiding each function. The key questions guiding research, diagnostics, and evaluation relevant to the DRE's planning are: "What can be done? What should be done? How well is something being done?"[9] The methods or tools for gathering information may be similar for each of the questions and typically in the local church will be narrative in form. The methods and tools are grounded in the social-scientific theories of organizational and systems theory as well as educational theory rather than theology.

The DRE as Researcher

Beginning with the question of "What can be done?" research studies possibilities or alternatives. Research is concerned with knowledge, insight, and ideas leading to generalizations and predictions on why something happens, how something will work, or will something be more effective than what is currently being done?[10] Functioning as an educational researcher, the DRE seeks answers to educational questions related to educational theory, program design, teaching-learning activities and strategies, and the environmental structures of educational activities.

Types of Research

Four types of general educational research have been identified. These four research types are as follows:[11]

Basic research. This is often described as pure research. It is the traditional style of research, carried out in laboratory settings, often using animals, with the purpose of producing theoretical knowledge. In education today, there is resistance to being dependent on research based in abstract empiricism such as found in pure scientific studies. To avoid the time- and circumstance-bound nature of most studies researching a single program, current strategies seek comparative studies or longitudinal studies.[12] Few classroom teachers conduct basic research studies.

Applied research. This represents the major reported research in education. Using generally accepted principles and methods of scientific research, applied research studies the applicability of learning theory and instructional principles in the classroom. Its purpose is to improve the curriculum or the instructional process. Typically, this research is conducted for a school board or textbook publisher but is often published in educational journals.

Action research. Using less controlled methods of research, the classroom teacher generally engages in this level of research. Trying out a new teaching strategy or comparing one textbook with another within a specific classroom or school are examples of action research. Because it controls the variables in a limited manner and its results are not usually able to be generalized beyond the immediate setting, action research is often rejected by the "academic specialists" in measurement and research. (It might be noted in passing that most Doctor of Ministry projects use an action research model.) The value of this type of research for the DRE is that it is generated locally and the dissemination of its results is quickly available to the participants. The value of action research is that scientific methods are applied to real life problems which goes beyond subjective, intuitive thinking to make decisions.

Descriptive research. A study describing the extent of a selected item in a defined situation that results in an accurate accounting of the item is descriptive research. A study of sexism in a series of curriculum resources or a survey of how many churches have programs for children with a specific handicapping condition would be examples of descriptive research. Sometimes a descriptive report of the actions in a particular classroom has been called process research, a form of descriptive research. Descriptive research is often used by DREs to prepare reports to education committees and other parts of the church's administrative structure. It would be a central part of information management.

Research Types in Local Church Religious Education

Sometimes the DRE will personally decide on the type of research needed for the local congregation's educational program. Pilot studies, field testing a new curriculum that is being prepared to be published, comparing curriculum resources for theological perspectives or surveying parents on attitudes about a proposed drug education program are examples of research originated by the DRE in the local congregation.

On other occasions the research may be generated at the judicatory/denominational level or interdenominational agencies. The Joint Educational Development (JED) project provides an example of a research project that originated at the judicatory level but gave research information to local congregations. The joint venture of twelve judicatories including the Episcopal Church, the United Church of Christ, the United Presbyterian Church in the U.S.A., and others, introduced new curriculum components in the series, Christian Education: Shared Approaches (CE:SA).[13] In CE:SA there were four major approaches: 1) knowing the Word, 2) interpreting the Word, 3) living the Word, and 4) doing the Word. Prior to the purchase of any printed resources each local congregation was provided vast resources to research the theological and educational affirmations in that congregation and its understandings of its educational philosophy and mission. After the local church analyzed its data, it was prepared to make informed choices on the literature options available.

Methods to Gather Information

The DRE can gather research information in a variety of ways. Some of the more common basic methods that are used to gather data include questionnaires, interviews (with structured, closed questions or with open-ended questions), observations, and the analysis of records and documents in the church.[14] Collecting data on the interests and needs of the membership is a vital ongoing task of the DRE. In the normal course of meetings and visiting members the DRE has the opportunity to informally interview and question a wide range of the church's membership. One DRE kept blank 3 x 5 file cards available for brief notes on which to record the interests of persons or comments about emerging issues. Following the conversation the cards were placed in a file box under general titles. Later they became resources for prospective teachers or for prospective members of a new program as the notes recalled brief references made about the topic in earlier conversations. The DRE is cautioned to remember that when using interest questionnaires that responses on surveys do not equal the commitment to actually participate in a program.[15]

Observation is another common form of research. A new teacher observes a master religious educator in order to gain new teaching methods. A DRE can visit another church to see how that staff performs its religious education work. The creation of pilot projects to test out ideas is common in many churches. Formal research projects such as those in basic or applied research often use a control group that parallels the research group. It should be noted that the awareness of being observed has an influence on a group and often causes the "control group" to change as much as the official research group.[16]

Sources of Research Information

Membership in professional associations that are related to the primary task of the DRE as well as membership in a professional group in a related field are essential for the effective information manager. These contacts will enable the DRE to learn emerging trends in religious education as well as receive ideas of current programs that are working in other settings through contact with other professionals outside the local church. It is anticipated that religious educators will soon follow the lead of public school educators in forming telecommunication networks that will make data bases available on research available to local DREs.

Another source for research information is the DRE's professional reading. The DRE must systematically seek out research that reports emerging trends. This requires a change in the reading habits of most DREs.[17] Professional reading should reflect the balance of program ideas and ideas to improve the communication of ideas. Professional journals such as *Religious Education* or *Living Light* that often provide information beyond the how-to-do-it reports should be part of the regular reading of the DRE.

Book publishers also issue volumes on religious education. Many articles in professional journals and many religious education books are of low quality. The DRE should not waste time reading these. Rather, the DRE should concentrate attention on reading top-flight articles and especially top-flight books. Indeed, first-class books in religious education have influenced the field over the long haul more than any other single source. It is well-known that most effective DREs devote one hour a day reading serious religious education books or articles. Research reading should assist the DRE to develop criteria to evaluate and compare emerging trends so that an evaluation of the feasibility of suggested approaches can be predicted.

Using Research in the Local Church

Being able to anticipate the results of performing a task in a certain way should be part of the professional skills of the DRE. This ability is gained by reading the results of research in one's field. An example of integrating research knowledge to make decisions would be the consideration of the anticipated impact of moving sixth graders from an elementary program into a youth program. Many cities are moving into a middle school public education arrangement. Should the local congregations follow the public school pattern or continue to follow the pattern of many denominations which define youth programs as being for students in seventh grade through twelfth grade. What are the anticipated results of merging sixth graders into a youth group of either seventh and eighth graders or a group of seventh to twelfth graders? Using information on the sociology of group memberships, adolescent maturity, intellectual development, and religious development the DRE should be able to predict the possible problems and generate alternatives for such a move, rather than just conveniently following the public school.

One type of descriptive research that needs to be conducted by the DRE is forecasting. Simple studies of church membership trends can guide many decisions of programs for the DRE. Based on current growth rate of the congregation, how many adults, youth, and children can the church expect in the next two years, five years, and ten years? What kind of issues for room space do these data answers raise? Has a church which wishes to build a new children's building conducted a study of married couples already in the church in addition to the neighborhood study? How many children are currently in the nursery? What will be the number of children in the elementary level in five years and youth in the church in ten years? What does the number of children currently in the first grade mean for the church's junior-high ministry six years from now regarding staffing and space? Decisions made now will commit resources for several years, and information needs to be gathered on anticipated needs as well as apparent current needs.

The research function of the DRE provides the church with valuable information for making informed decisions. It is possible to conduct research without the use of elaborate statistical tables, although these are sometimes necessary. Assistance from local members who regularly work with statistics can usually be obtained for those few occasions when statistics are needed. The management of research ideas includes regular communication of the information to appropriate committees so that the whole church benefits.

The DRE as Diagnostician

Diagnosis is primarily concerned with the development of the organization's ability to meet its broad goals and specific objectives. It may consider the whole organization, or a specific administrative situation, or a learning group. While research tends to relate to learning theory and learning strategies, diagnosis focuses on the structural level of the educational system. Diagnosis, in this context, seeks to improve the organizational effectiveness of the church in meeting its educational goals and objectives.

The DRE is far more than a classroom religion teacher. The DRE's primary concern for diagnostic activities is of course related to the broad religious education work of the church, although the diagnostic techniques may be applied to a wide area of the church's organizational life. The key areas of diagnosis are the processes of 1) communication; 2) member roles and functions in groups; 3) group problem solving and decision making; 4) group norms and group growth; 5) leadership and authority; and 6) intergroup cooperation and competition.[18] In addition to the organizational level, the DRE is responsible for diagnosing the religious education needs of many groups in the church.

Throughout the activities of planning, organizing, and administrating the religious education program the DRE must constantly make diagnostic decisions. The focus of the diagnosis may be to improve a study group's effectiveness, to provide data for organizational or structural alteration such as changing the chain-of-command for a youth director's supervision, to identify leadership training needs, to discover new areas of needed or desired programs, to improve the operation of a department such as the day care center, to develop content goals and objectives for learners across the age span, or to discover the needs for a community outreach ministry which includes the educational requirements of the volunteers and the people to be served.

Generally, a model that involves collaboration between the DRE and the unit being diagnosed is desired.[19] In the joint diagnosis model, the DRE typically provides a system of questions and procedures for a group to follow to assess its own situation and to discover ways to be more effective. The role of the professional is to teach the group how to solve its own problems using creative problem-solving techniques. The assumption is that when a group generates remedies to solve its own problems, the solutions will be based in a greater reality of the situation and will be more permanent.[20]

Because many laity are hesitant to make judgments about "religious" behaviors or religious leaders, the DRE's role as guide and advisor is essential both to structure the format and to guarantee permission for the collection of information and its analysis. However, it is essential for the members to own the ideas generated from the diagnosis to enhance their willingness to change or accept the goals planned.

Those who plan and conduct the diagnosis must be clear at what organizational level the diagnosis is taking place. The diagnostic procedures can focus on the church and its organizational life, the educational ministry as part of the larger organization, the specific program or educational event at the classroom level, or the personal situation of the learner.[21] The decision concerning which sub-system to diagnose will guide the questions and standards that will be used.

It is important to distinguish between educational needs, such as problems which may be addressed through religious education programing, and other variables, such as organizational structural needs related to control of decision making, technological impact of introducing new methods or equipment for job performance, or task performance problems where the person has the knowledge but chooses to act in another fashion.[22] For instance, a youth worker who is constantly late for meetings and assignments may not be reflecting carelessness in time schedules. Instead the worker may be acting out a form of rebellion based on an issue of authority over program plans. When mutual diagnosis is conducted, the focus for change would not be classified as a learning problem but an organizational concern. Multilevel diagnosis helps to move from observations of symptoms to identification of the cause of problems

Even when a problem has been defined as related to educational concerns, the diagnostic process needs to consider multilevels of the situation. The DRE must decide if the observed behaviors constitute the real problem or reflect symptoms of a problem at a deeper level of the organization's life which must be addressed at the structural level.

An example of how observed behavior may not itself constitute a real problem is the difficulty in recruiting Sunday school or CCD teachers is most churches. First, the diagnostician should consider if there are enough families with children in the program to recruit an adequate number of teachers. If there are, then the problem may range from the lack of training to poor recruitment methods. In one setting with enlistment problems, the leaders diagnosed a deeper level of concern. The low public recognition that volunteer teachers of children receive gave the position limited desirability. Recognition is considered a means of saying that those who serve in this capacity are appreciated. The recommended change solution was to increase the number of times and ways that teachers were publicly recognized for their teaching.[23] Most problems are complex and the observed behavior is usually less than adequate to explain the situation.

An accurate diagnosis of the real problem is the critical first step of decision making. Correctly identifying the real, basic problem is essential to the success of the subsequent proposed solutions.[24]

Reasons for a Diagnostic Procedure

The motive for initiating a diagnostic procedure may come from various sources. One source may be a crisis in a group which may cause a diagnostic action to be taken. Diagnosis may result if the church failed to meet a certain goal or objective set at its annual planning meeting related to religious education. If after evaluation the goals are still valid and appropriate, the diagnosis of causes and alternatives may be pursued. Another motive may be the intuitive feeling of the DRE to improve the operation of some part of the educational system. A fourth motive may be to expand the educational program after comparsion with other churches.[25]

A diagnostic activity may be limited to symptoms, problems, or issues that initially led to the diagnosis or it may be a comprehensive investigation of the full range of the organization's activities from strategic level planning to specific needs of individuals. In both cases, the purpose of diagnosis is to bring about change.[26]

Format of Diagnosis

Using social-science skills, the following format provides a simple outline for conducting a diagnosis:[27]

1. Identify symptoms of the problem or issue.
2. Determine the subsystem focus and the range of diagnostic activity.
3. Collect the appropriate information.
   a. What criteria of adequacy will be used?
   b. What symptoms and patterns of symptoms can be identified related to the problem?
4. Analyze the data to determine causes and needs. Especially religious education needs.
5. Use the information to bring about change.

Using this format, several diagnostic models emphasize different specific concerns.

The Gap Model.[28] The gap model begins by establishing an ideal model of excellence (or adequacy). It is important to clearly state the desired level of adequacy so that it may be compared with existing actual performance or the predicted new situation. Next the diagnosis asks what are the basic, root cause, and the intermediate related causes of the gap between the desired level and the actual level of performance. Then, by analyzing the data, the diagnosis generates suggestions for the alternative solutions that may be applied.

In the diagnosis it is helpful to check both where the ideal is met and where it is frustrated. When a hypothesis has been developed on the basic cause of a problem, rather than seeking to prove the hypothesis, the model asks the diagnostician to endeavor to disprove it as the root cause.[29] If there is any reason to suspect that the hypothetical cause might not be the real one, it can be eliminated and a more accurate one can be tested. This usually means that several layers of reasons must be worked through before alternatives for a solution are generated.

The next step is to develop alternatives for a solution. Again, early closure can make the process ineffective. Often the alternatives come from the DRE's past experience. If the DRE is mature and has had successful experiences in other settings this can be very effective. A similar source for solutions is the imitation of other churches which have initiated similar programs or solved similar problems, along with the necessary adaptations to make it work in the DRE's current church.

The gap model would guide a church that wished to increase the number of adult classes in its Sunday school. For instance, the education committee might determine that for a church of its size there should be seven adult study classes in its Sunday school. However, only four classes exist and one of them is weak. The church could conduct interviews of members not attending classes to determine why people don't attend or join classes, check the space assignments for classes, or a variety of other activities to generate data on the basic problem. Now it is ready to seek and propose alternative solutions. These may be generated by ideas proposed by the experiences of members of the education committee, through visits to churches with successful class development, or by reading research that describes the value of organizing new classes or opportunities based on parish needs and goals whenever twenty new members regardless of their specific age, sex, or family grouping of any type are added to the parish's membership. Finally, the committee must decide to implement the decision they have reached based on the diagnosis.

Action Research Model.[30] A data-based, problem-solving process model action research uses the social-science methods of data gathering. The initiation of the action research may come from someone within the organization desiring to improve how things are done or in response to an organization crisis. Its focus is on the members of the organization and their involvement in the total process is fundamental.[31] The diagnosis begins by gathering information about problems or desired changes from the members of the organization. The key part of action research is its involvement of the group members in each step. The data is gathered and then shared with the members involved so that they are aware of the relevant information. Finally, the group plans and carries out specific actions to correct identified problems. This model helps groups develop and sharpen communication patterns and problem-solving skills.

Curriculum Assessment Model.[32] This diagnostic model serves as a curriculum development model, based on the learning needs of the diagnosed system. The model is based on an idealized criteria of adequacy. Through professional literature and other sources of information, the idealized goals, objectives, and standards for a church's religious organizational structure and procedures and teaching-learning processes are defined. The content concerns are on improved skills in problem solving and task performance, rather than core religious knowledge. In the second step data is gathered on the current levels of learning and organizational life to be analyzed by comparing them with the ideal. Information is gathered about the general characteristics of the population, the instructional patterns and strategies used in the church, and how the educational program is administratively organized. Data is typically gathered through the techniques of observation and questionnaires. The results of the analyzed information are shared with the specific groups being diagnosed and their related components, e.g., a diagnosis of a children's program would be shared with parents. Both the ideal criteria of adequacy and the results of the diagnosis can then be used by program planners to develop new workshops or to improve existing programs in the church.

The model serves the church at two levels: in establishing religious education needs at the local level and in developing teaching-learning strategies for religious education opportunities beyond the local parish.

When used in the local parish, the criteria of adequacy are applied to a specific group and generally involve the groups' collaboration in determining the educational needs. Some examples the issues confronted by this diagnostic model might include: What do our sixth-grade children need to know to more meaningfully participate in communion? What do the volunteers working in the church's pantry need to know about their own feelings toward those on welfare and the anxieties of the unemployed? What basic knowledge does a new member of the parish's administrative board or council need regarding the local church's structure and polity or of the church's position on specific social issues to serve effectively on the council? What people need to know in this church regarding how certain tasks such as taking up the collection by ushers, or the lighting the candles by acolytes, or scheduling rooms for meetings by group presidents would be diagnosed by this model. The educational needs to improve specific communication skills that would enable members to articulate their religious faith as well as the whole area of leadership skills, such as leading committees or teaching a group, could be subjects of investigation using this diagnostic model.

An example of the model serving the parish in the larger context is demonstrated in how a workshop is typically planned at the denominational level to train teachers. The leaders prepare their workshop classes based on their professional knowledge of what a "good teacher should know," which functions as an ideal criterion or competence. The planners of an educational event use these standards to create a minimum achievement level for all who attend the event. The typical solution to the diagnosed needs in the model assumes that people need assistance on how to organize information and to structure certain types of knowledge. This leads to a teaching-learning strategy such as found in information-processing teaching models.[33] In this case the advanced organizer may be aware that some persons attending the event may be beginning teachers and others experienced teachers. Still, the substantive content and the teaching procedures are all controlled by the leader's understanding of the idealized criteria of adequacy.

The model may be modified when used to invite in an outside resource person to do a workshop for the local parish. In this example, the youth counselors wish to be trained to prepare a set of curriculum resources for their youth program. The resource leader will receive a set of questions from the counselors to build the session's content. The counselors' stated objectives will shape the planned event, along with several built-in opportunities for the harmonious reconciliation of objectives during the actual event.

Diagnosing Real and Felt Needs

Sometimes the diagnosed needs will be recognized or felt by the persons involved and other times it will be the responsibility of the planners to convince potential participants of their real needs.[34] Although it is inappropriate for the DRE to manipulate learners to attend training events, the effective advertising and promotion of these events that identify the real needs and create a positive commitment response to legitimate needs is appropriate. A value of collaborative diagnosis is the mutual identification of real needs which reduces manipulation.

The diagnostic models that most effectively diagnose real needs leading to acceptable solutions are those which involve the people most affected by the problem and its resolution. These models encourage open two-way communication throughout the various levels of any organization. The leadership recognizes that feelings and attitudes may well be more significant in defining a problem than simply observable factual behavior. In other words, the feelings and attitudes of the participants are part of the solution, just as observable facts are part of the solution. Successful diagnosis often depends on generating sufficient alternative perceptions to provide a greater flexibility for creatively diagnosing the problem. Because of their involvement from the early stages, those most affected are also trusted to evaluate the data and then plan and implement the decisions flowing from the diagnosis.[35]

The DRE and Diagnosis

The DRE contributes several skills to the successful facilitation of joint and individual diagnostic activities.[36]

Technical Skills. At the technical level, the DRE brings skills in the procedures of organizing a diagnostic project and in gathering and analyzing information. These skills can be used to guide groups or to conduct individual diagnostic projects. Being able to observe and describe symptoms as separate from causes is basic to diagnosing real problems. The DRE should possess skills to gather reliable data about organizational objectives, to insightfully observe the behaviors of groups, to analyze gathered information, to communicate findings and recommendations to appropriate units, and to generally administrate the completion of a diagnostic project.

Human Relations Skills. At the human relationship level, the DRE brings skills in group process. The DRE helps the various concerned persons and groups to work together in a collaborative effort. Skills in small-group dynamics and negotiation are central to the process level when the problem involves personalities rather than cognitive content limitation. Process skills are especially concerned with attitudes and feelings that may surface during a diagnostic project. Skills in conflict management facilitate groups in keeping communication open. The DRE may provide access to certain types of legitimate information available at the staff level in the process skills area such as enabling people to evaluate religious practices. Central to this function is communication between the DRE and the various units involved in the diagnostic activity.

Conceptual Skills. At the conceptual level, the DRE brings two skills that serve the diagnostic process. First is the conceptualization of how this diagnostic project fits into the whole life of the church. To guide the strategic planning, diagnosis involves the skill of selecting data and characteristics that describe symptoms of problems relevant to the church at the organizational level. To envision the connection between individual needs and group needs and church needs requires the ability to conceptualize the whole and its sub-parts. The conceptual level includes the ability to make philosophical and ethical reflections about the diagnostic procedures based on the values of the church.

Creativity. The second conceptual skill is creativity. Creativity is related both to the design of the diagnostic procedures and to the vision of all religious education activity. In addition to being able to envision the whole and its parts, creative people tend to be able to synthesize the parts into new combinations. Creativity is both an attitude and a style of functioning.[37]

Many of the things people have considered to be the natural result of being a "creative person" are actually the result of deliberate activity on the part of the leader.[38] Creativity is fostered as the DRE intentionally seeks ways to enable the congregation to be more effective in its mission. Some organizations have a climate that rewards creativity and initiatives by individuals while other organizations stifle attempts through the executive decision process.[39] A creative DRE is flexible and is typically willing to risk that many programs will fail or not attract large attendance. They are persons who share leadership easily, enabling many small projects to serve the needs of various members.[40]

Creative DREs tend to always be on the lookout for new programs. Through involvement in professional associations, the creative DRE learns new developments in various areas. When preparing to attend a conference, a creative DRE typically makes a list of several persons to visit with the intention of gathering information on creative opportunities. These may be seminary professors, curriculum editors, or outstanding DREs in churches in other parts of the country. The information from these visits may be more sgnificant than the actual conference.

Creativity at the conceptual level also gives the DRE an awareness of how the organization will predictably react to changing environmental situations so that alternative approaches may be developed. Understanding how the responses of congregations composed primarily of blue-collar background persons differs from congregations composed of professional managers in their responses and expectations provides information on how to creatively challenge each congregation. The professional awareness that a church facing a large loss of membership experiences a grieving process that handicaps its rational problem-solving processes enables the DRE to diagnose needs and to create religious education activities that are significantly different in feeling from the growing suburban church.[41]

Creativity is reflected in the planning of the actual events and in the related training experiences preparing for the events. Creativity also affects the procedures of diagnosis. As the facilitating guide, the creative DRE requires groups involved in the diagnosis to consider many alternatives as part of the procedures. Marlene Wilson defines creative problem solving as "the degree to which one can think up different, more effective approaches."[42] Building into the model the requirement for generating alternative perspectives as well as solutions assists the diagnostic team in generating creative answers.

The DRE as Evaluator

The third information-gathering function of the DRE is evaluation. Evaluation gathers information in order to discover how well something is being done or was accomplished. Evaluation is always concerned with how a specific program, curriculum resource, teaching behavior, and the like, compares in actuality to a stated criterion of value.[43] Both the intentions and the outcomes are considered in evaluation.

In contrast to research that seeks to discover how something may be done, evaluation always has a set of criteria that serves as a value standard. D. Campbell Wyckoff defined evaluation as the "process of comparing what is with what ought to be, in order to determine areas and directions for improvement."[44] Evaluation considers both the value of the intended goals and the actual effects of the program. By determining the actual effects of a program in meeting educational needs, the evaluation considers both the main goals and the unanticipated effects of its implementation.[45]

The importance of evaluation has been increasingly recognized during the past few years. Yet many activities that educators have called evaluation are more accurately labeled the measurement or the assessment of what students learned. Measurement places no specific value on what is being measured. Evaluation, in contrast, studies the major issues or conditions precisely because they represent educational values.[46] Checking the ability of the children to recite certain Bible verses that have been taught or to determine if the members of the Adult Inquiry Class can describe our church's doctrine of Eucharist are examples of measurement rather than evaluation.[47]

Objects of Evaluation

There is a wide range of objects that may be considered in the evaluation. It is important for the evaluator to understand which object reference is the focus. Evaluations are often conducted on the following range of educational objects:[48]
1. Instructional procedures
2. Curriculum materials
3. Programs and organizations (e.g., Parent's Day Out, teacher training, or the youth fellowship)
4. Educators (lay volunteer teachers and professional staff)
5. Students (all ages)

Purposes of Evaluation

Evaluations can be designed to gather information for a wide variety of decisions. Each set of decisions requires a different set of questions to be investigated in the evaluation. For instance, an evaluation may be used to justify a certain program and the amount of money the program receives in the budget. Or an evaluation may seek to discover ways to improve a program, or the evaluation may serve as a diagnostic means to discover what new programs need to be planned.[49] An evaluation may also serve as an internal organizational audit to improve the operation of the religious education program.[50] If appropriately conducted, an evaluation report can be used to provide justification to expand the religious education activities either in terms of budget or personnel. (It can also be used to explain why a particular religious education activity should be discontinued.) Most often the overarching purpose of evaluation for the DRE is to improve how a program meets its overall goals and specific objectives.

Every teacher or group leader is responsible for both the assessment of learning and the evaluation of each teaching-learning experience. By checking what students have learned, leaders can adjust pedagogical procedures that may improve the level of learning. Children's teachers must evaluate which teaching-learning strategies are appropriate for their class based on the reading and experience level of the children. Adult Sunday school or CCD teachers must constantly assess whether their students have already mastered the information given in a particular lesson so that they may choose appropriate content and methods for each session. These teachers also evaluate whether the goals suggested are appropriate for their class, as well as whether a certain suggested teaching-learning strategy assisted in reaching the desired goals most efficiently. For instance, to improve understanding of the Last Supper of Jesus in the Upper Room the class held a model Seder (the Jewish Passover meal). The evaluation considered whether the time of preparation was worth the level of learning that took place or if an alternative demonstration of the meal during a regular class session would have resulted in similar learning.

Through evaluation, the program leaders receive feedback. There are two major types of evaluation: Formative evaluation, which is used to improve the program while it is being developed and in progress, and summative evaluation, which appraises the worth or value of the resource or educational activity at its conclusion.[51] Both types of evaluation contribute to the decision-making responsibilities of curriculum and program developers.

By using the two types of evaluation, programs can build in feedback at key times.

Formative Evaluation

Formative evaluation makes possible improved program effectiveness through constant feedback opportunities. Programs should be evaluated at each step of their development. The quality of the goals, the progress of planning and recruitment, the actual enrollment, the progress toward goals by the participants, the methods of presentation and/or operation by the group leaders, are all points of formative evaluation. Changes can be made in the rate of presentation based on the speed of comprehension and experience level of the people who actually attend. If the attendance of the latch-key children's program drops, a formative evaluation of the program and its staff can enable adjustments that may cause renewal.

Summative Evaluation

Summative evaluation examines the merit of a program at its conclusion. It might review the list of programs and activities offered during the past year to make decisions about the balance for all age groups or religious education work with certain populations such as singles. A summative evaluation might be used to determine how worthwhile a program is, especially in comparison to another similar program.[52] For example, a summative evaluation might appraise how cost-effective the weekly church-night dinner format is compared to a once-a-month format for the building of community and the quality of the courses offered.

Observations on Public Education Evaluation Approaches

Two polar positions have been identified in approaches to evaluation models based in public education. Lee Cronbach identifies two basic approaches to evaluation: 1) the scientistic ideals approach and 2) the humanistic ideals approach.[53] The scientistic ideal approach tends to concentrate on the learner using quantitative, statistically analyzed data. The humanistic ideal approach, on the other hand, studies programs already in place, using few experimentally structured models but seeking to describe the phenomenon located in the local setting. Scientific evaluation methods are typically used to provide information on student outcomes, whereas humanistic evaluation approaches tend to recognize a program is holisitic in its environment and focuses on the success of the methodologies being employed.

Several models are popular in public education.[54] Each is grounded in an educational philosophical theory and serves that particular perspective best. In actual practice, some evaluators follow these models closely, while others mix the models creating an eclectic model.[55]

The Discrepancy Model. Malcolm Provus presents the discrepancy evaluation model which is useful to evaluate transmission types of educational programs.[56] Provus's model evaluates the extent of the discrepancy between program standards and program performance.

The CIPP Model. Another popular evaluation model used in many school systems is the CIPP Model.[57] The acronym CIPP describes four types of educational evaluation used for the improvement of curriculum within a school system. The four types of educational evaluation included in the model are: 1) *context evaluation* which studies the environment in which the program takes place; 2) *input evaluation* which concerns judgments about the teaching-learning strategies and resources used to accomplish the stated goals and objectives; 3) *process evaluation* which is held during the implementation phase of a program examines the congruency between the planned and actual teaching-learning strategies used; and 4) *product evaluation* determines the extent that the outcomes of the program compare with the intended or desired goals and objectives. The prepared analysis of the data is submitted to system level supervisors and boards for their decisions.

Evaluation in the Church

Collaborative Evaluation Is Basic

Collaborative evaluation is essential in volunteer groups such as the church. Individuals and groups who are responsible for various aspects of the religious education program along with participants and group leaders should be part of most program evaluation efforts.[58] It is an absolute requirement that when staff evaluations are conducted that everyone concerned be involved both in the setting of standards and in the annual performance review.[59]

Formal Evaluation

In the local parish an evaluation may be formal or informal.[60] A formal evaluation typically involves a committee and uses traditional research data gathering techniques. In the church it may be done as the annual review of the total religious education program or the church's program, or it may be done on a weekly basis as a report made either to a supervisor or executive board. A formal annual evaluation might be conducted by the education committee or a parish council over a period of several weeks using interviews and questionnaires to evaluate the previous year's program.[61]

Informal Evaluation

Although evaluation textbooks tend to leave the impression that all evaluation must be of the traditional, formal, research variety, realistically it is the informal models of evaluation that are the most common. Informal evaluation happens daily and with multiple levels of detail.[62]

An informal evaluation might be a report of an ice cream social filed by the DRE in her office which includes a list of supplies used, the attendance, and a few suggestions to make next year's event go more smoothly. Another informal evaluation example is the discussion with the youth planners during the clean-up time on what they would like to try the next time based on their experience in this program. Sometimes informal evaluations are conducted through surveys such as the end of a workshop questionnaire completed by participants, or a self-checklist completed by the teacher on personal attitudes or skills. The informal survey primarily is concerned with generating information on its value to the total program and ways to facilitate and improve its implementation in the future.

Evaluation of Organizational Life

Although evaluation by the DRE is important in the classroom, as the administrator, program-developer, and general educational consultant for the church's educational program, his or her primary concern is evaluation at the general program level. The DRE typically is administratively responsible for most evaluations beyond the classroom level. Assisting the church to evaluate its organizational life and group work activity are special areas of service for the DRE.[63]

Effective models for evaluating organizations go beyond the traditional research designs that stress quantitative measurement and experimental paradigms. Evaluation at the organizational level seeks to provide feedback to the organization that is helpful for it to make modifications in its own program.[64] Organizational evaluation or organizational behavior management uses feedback models based on organizational performance problems. The models include verbal feedback, written feedback, mechanical (e.g., videotape) feedback, and self-recorded feedback.[65] It looks at changes in the context of the task and how people change over a period of time or how people are affected by a particular program or procedure. It is aware that there will be alternative answers for different parts of the system.

The approaches for evaluating human organizational systems function on the awareness that real organizations are interactive.[66] A change in one part will impact other areas of the system. The church is not a static organization. A decision to start a young couple's class, for example, will not only affect adult education. It will also affect the young children's program, requiring staff and space in both areas for expansion. Effective evaluation of organizations is based in feedback and a learning system that enables the system to make adaptations in its own program implementation.

Steps in Evaluation

The steps in an evaluation procedure are similar regardless of whether it is done by a formal administrative committee, a program planning committee, or individually by the DRE. As part of the preplanning for the evaluation, the object and the purpose of evaluation must be carefully chosen, just as is true for a diagnostic project. The decision may be made to evaluate a Sunday school or CCD class session (e.g., focusing on the teacher's discussion leadership or giving directions, or on the new curriculum's effectiveness, or on student achievement), a church-wide program such as a parent's seminar, the religious education program for older adults, the comprehensive educational ministry, or the professional and volunteer staff. The careful delineation of the unit and the area to be evaluated enables the design to be focused on the appropriate issues and concerns. It is also important to designate the purpose of the evaluation and to identify its intended audience.

State Goals and Standards

The first step in evaluation is to articulate the goals and specific objectives of each program to be evaluated and the basic standards of quality performance. Implied in the evaluation process is the evaluation of the quality of the goals. It is not enough that a curriculum meet its goals but that the goals are worth obtaining.[67] A Bible curriculum which leads only to the memorization of selected verses without developing the ability of the youth to apply them in reflective thinking would be of limited value.

The importance of stating the church's broad outreach-ministry goals, as well as specific program objectives, to guide the evaluation is demonstrated in the assessment of the parents-day-out program found in many churches. For instance, a church may state a value-goal to serve the near-by neighborhood with its ministries. Many of its members live more than a mile from the church building. The enrollment statistics in its parents-day-out program report only twenty church members, but sixty neighborhood children are enrolled. If the goal is to serve its own membership, this program is not successful, but with the value of community service it would receive high marks. The specific operational objectives describing what children are to learn in the program would be evaluated as well as the general goal. The same program has different criteria of excellence in different settings.

Formulate Evaluation Questions

The second step is to formulate the questions to be answered during the evaluation along with specific plans on how they will be organized for analysis.[68] Formulating questions that will achieve the desired information is often difficult for lay persons not trained in research or general education. It is also important to understand how the specific evaluation relates to the strategic conceptual vision of the whole religious education program.

The DRE as a consultant typically contributes the technical skills necessary to ask the appropriate questions for the information desired, as well as having a conceptual vision of the total educational program. The questions define the scope of the evaluation. In formal evaluations this step includes developing the various forms and documentation that will be used to gather information.[69] Questions for informal evaluations might relate to the adequacy of the content that was presented and whether the program achieved its desired objectives; the adequacy of resources, techniques, and preparation; what changes could be made in the design of the activity; and the overall value of the program and suggestions for revisions if repeated.

Gather Data

The gathering of the data to make the evaluation is the third task. Information can be obtained through the observation of members of the planning team, comments made during breaks, concluding panel discussions, end of meeting student evaluations, group leader evaluations, formal questionnaires, surveys, written records, and occasionally, tests.

Analyze Data

When the appropriate data has been gathered, the fourth step of evaluation is to organize the data in a way that enables it to be interpreted. Evaluation analyzes the data to compare the information with the goals and standards previously established. Again the DRE may facilitate this process using staff time to interpret the study, or enabling material to be entered into the church's computer for formal evaluations of the comphensive program.

Report Findings

The summarized findings are reported to the designated groups and persons for discussion and clarification in the last step. Formal evaluations are always reported in written form. For administrative purposes, the DRE should maintain regular written summaries of informal evaluations. The people should affirm that the evaluation indeed answered the questions desired, providing objective and accurate information. When the comprehensive educational program is evaluated in a formal fashion, it is usually helpful to publish the results for the whole congregation either in complete or summary form.

Evaluation findings provide concrete feedback for the church to use to modify and improve current and future programs. The value of a specific activity or the total religious education program is now established in relationship to the overall objectives of the church. The questions of how well something was, or is being done, now leads into what shall we do to improve our religious education activities. The purpose of evaluation is never to just collect information but to enable decisions leading to action.

Curriculum Evaluation

The responsibility for the evaluation of curriculum and instructional resources is a common role requirement for the DRE. The goal is to obtain the best resources possible. The DRE must find resources that fit the goals and objectives of religious education set by the local church.

Traditionally, Protestant DREs have had a high loyalty to their own denomination's curriculum resources for the Sunday school. Today that loyalty is often challenged, reflecting the difficulty of a nationally produced curriculum to meet the pluralistic needs of a local congregation. Some denominations have a primary set of resources with some elective units for their church school. Other denominations have offered several alternative models such as the "Christian Education: Shared Approaches," which enabled the local church to choose either a series primarily for Bible study, a series on the life application of scripture, or a social-action series. Still other denominations may chose from competing publishing houses such as the Episcopalians or the Roman Catholics choosing for the CCD.

Catholic DREs, for their part, often have loyalty to one or another religion textbook series published by independent companies such as Benziger, Sadlier, or Silver-Burdett. Today, that loyalty is often challenged for many reasons. First of all, like their Protestant counterparts, these curricula are rarely if ever tested empirically so that the DRE cannot know how effective the curricula are. Second, the company "consultants" who go to various dioceses to help DREs teach the DREs and others how to use the curricula are typically untrained at a professionally adequate level in the area of teaching methodology. These "consultants" are on board to sell the company's textbooks primarily by whatever gimmick is available. Third, the curricula are not prepared with the help of first-class experts in curriculum construction or teaching methodology. Fourth, some textbook series are conservative religiously while others are liberal.

To evaluate the multitude of prepared curriculum resources for events such as the Sunday school/CCD, vacation Bible school, plus the infinite number of resources for elective educational programs, the DRE needs to have an objective criterion for a recommendation and choice of a specific instructional resource. Some components of a sample criteria might include the comparison of the written objectives in the material with the church's goals.[70] What content is shared in the resources. Does it represent the best of current theological and biblical scholarship? How is the Bible used in the curriculum? Does the theological perspective adequately reflect the theological heritage of our denomination? What doctrines are taught in the curriculum? What bias is reflected in terms of racial, sexual, age, and family life stereotypes. How are other religious perspectives treated? Is there recognition of the development of religious and moral thinking in the students? Are the recommended teaching-learning procedures appropriate to accomplish the desired goals and objectives? Are the activities varied? Are the teaching resources and materials suitable for the skills of our volunteer staff? Criteria similar to these provide a framework for a DRE to evaluate curriculum for most ongoing activities.

Staff Evaluation

A key area of evaluation is the review and evaluation of the volunteer staff. Today, many churches recognize the imperative of the annual review and evaluation with the professional staff. It is also important that the volunteer staff be involved in periodic evaluation. The volunteer staff includes the wide variety of persons involved in the parish's religious education program such as coordinators/superintendents of age-group programs, Sunday school/CCD teachers, youth counselors, mid-week group leaders, church librarians, and office volunteers. A benefit of the effective evaluation of the whole staff is increased morale.[71]

The first part of a staff evaluation is a review of the church's volunteer program.[72] The church proclaims the importance of the priesthood of all believers or the ministry of all Christians. Does the local church actually practice this? Are the laity enabled to do acts of ministry for each other, or are the only opportunities related to institutional maintenance? Are the professionals doing tasks that should be done by lay persons? Have the lay persons received the training and supplies necessary to do the activities for which they were recruited? Are the opportunities for volunteers in the church made accessible to all the members or are they known only to a few? Are job descriptions available for the volunteers as well as for the professional staff? Are the volunteers recruited for a specified time, such as one year, and given realistic opportunities to rotate into other positions? Do they complete their terms of service or is there a high drop-out rate? Is there a plan for the public recognition of volunteers throughout the church's life?

The DRE has the major role in the evaluation of the volunteers in the educational ministry. Effective evaluation of staff requires communication and human relations skills.[73] Sensitivity to feelings in addition to concerns for excellence of program is a delicate combination that must be part of the evaluation relationship. Personnel evaluations require that everyone concerned be jointly involved in setting the standards for the task to be done.

As the Apostle Paul insightfully wrote in his Letter to the Romans (12:6-7), people have different gifts and not everyone is called to be a teacher, or any other specific leader for that matter. Evaluation of the gifts volunteers bring to ministry as well as life situations should become more important in the placement of persons in the church's religious educational program. A person who does not like to talk in front of groups may be a poor teacher prospect, but a great librarian. Or a former first grade teacher who happens to be currently the mother of a one-year-old and a four-year-old may not be a good prospect for a children's Sunday school class as she may need adult relationships for a few years. The DRE needs to interview persons to make evaluations for effective placement.

In staff evaluation, clarity of the role of the DRE is essential. The primary role of the DRE is to facilitate the ministry of the volunteer. The DRE serves as a supervisor, rather than one who brings judgment for dismissal.

One area where DREs spend large blocks of supervisory time is with the Sunday school/CCD teachers. The DRE needs to provide regular feedback to teachers. Regular communication enables the DRE to develop a rapport with the teaching staff. Suggesting ideas for curriculum, lesson planning, or other resources, and then checking later to hear reports of how effective the ideas were for the teacher assists in perceiving the DRE as an expert resource person and supporter.[74] The key to evaluation of the teaching staff is "evaluating teaching, not teachers."[75]

Models for Staff Evaluation Interviews

While feedback should be part of the ongoing supervision of the religious education staff, it is desirable to have a systematic annual interview with the volunteer by the DRE or the age-group coordinator. Distribution of self-evaluation resources is one effective means in the church to begin teacher evaluations.[76] These become the background for questions on areas perceived by the teacher needing improvement or enrichment. The self-evaluation instrument is followed-up by an interview, preferably in the person's home. In classes where team teaching occurs, the whole team might be part of any annual review. However, group dynamic skills on the part of the DRE are essential for each person to fully participate.

One effective pattern for the systematic evaluation is to begin with questions on how the class is going. What is happening in the group that is exciting for this religion teacher? The evaluation should focus on the tasks and feelings related to the teaching role. How does the person feel about teaching the suggested curriculum? The next part should be to raise any problems that the teacher perceives to be part of the class experience. The concern is not to find fault but to identify real problems. Sometimes the DRE may have received information of a problem from an outside source. Through skillful, nonthreatening questions, feelings as well as problems may be opened for evaluation. What resources are needed to do a more effective job? Are there behavior problems in the class that could use some outside assistance? Even if it is an exit interview for a "retiring leader," the focus of the evaluation is on the future.[77] Using the data gathered from the interview and mutually analyzed, the evaluation should move toward specific recommendations for changes. Specific dates for meeting the recommendations should be recorded as they lead to action.

One very effective form of teacher self-evaluation is to have teachers arrange to have their teaching videotaped. Due to the volunteer nature of most of the church's regular teaching staff, each teacher must be a full participant in this decision as it may be threatening to some.

The video self-observation may be done in several ways. One simple method is to arrange for a "mni-cam" or other home video format camera and recorder to be in the teacher's regular classroom. The actual taping of the class session can be done by a class member, a parent, or a member of the church's camera crew. The video tape allows the teacher to observe interactions between class members and the teacher and between the class members. Voice tone, mannerisms, as well as teaching techniques are available for the teacher to observe first-hand without the filtering of a second party.

At the lowest level of useful evaluation, a teacher could watch the tape at home by herself or himself. To be more effective, specific behaviors to be observed and criteria of effectiveness should be designated prior to the teaching and viewing event. These criteria guide the teacher during the personal viewing.

A more effective model is for the teacher to identify some teaching behaviors to be developed, and then, following the actual taping, view the tape with the DRE or other experienced teacher professionally prepared in the area of educational methods for expert advice regarding specific concerns.[78]

Summary

A comprehensive information management design is essential for the church to meet the changing religious education needs of its congregation. Religious education requires both research into the learner and improved ways for communication of ideas and feelings. It involves knowing the values of an organization such as the church as well as the values present in a specific group. Through diagnosis the DRE must be able to discover the real religious education needs of persons and groups so that a variety of educational opportunities can be created for the benefit of the whole congregation. The DRE must be aware of the evaluations of the positive and negative features of various models of communication used for teaching-learning and be able to predict their affect on a specific group. Through ongoing evaluation, experiences can be redesigned and created to match the learner's needs as well as institutional needs and societal needs.

The DRE links the church with information based on research, diagnostic studies, and evaluation. The emphasis on the information gathered during research and diagnostic and evaluation activities is on future decisions leading to actions to improve the whole church's ministry.

The ability to conceptualize the present comprehensive goals as well as the future needs and goals of the congregation's ministry enables the DRE to gather data effectively for the religious education program. The DRE must become sensitive to books, articles, or reports relevant to the future of the church so that they may be appropriately saved, filed, and retrieved at a later date. With the overwhelming amount of information in our society, the DRE must acquire the technical skills necessary to analyze that information in terms of its general value and its relevance to the specific situation.

Much of the information gathered will be done personally by the DRE who must make it available in meaningful ways to appropriate leaders and committees. Communication skills are essential. Communication is not just telling people ideas. Rather, communication consists in enabling ideas to be heard with understanding on the part of the listener.[79] If it is not read or understood by the intended audience the most colorful or well-documented report of some research or evaluation done, is of little value. Sometimes the communication will be through oral reports and other times through elaborate written reports or simple memos. The DRE must become a skillful communicator of information both in administration and in the classroom.

NOTES

1. Helen B. Schwartzman, "Research on Work Group Effectiveness: An Anthropological Critique," in *Designing Effective Work Groups,* ed. Paul S. Goodman and Associates (San Francisco: Jossey-Bass, 1986), pp. 237-276, describes the cultural and methodological lenses that shape the questions, content, and group deemed appropriate by various researchers.

2. See John Diebold, *Managing Information: The Challenge and the Opportunity* (New York: American Management Association, 1985), pp. 25-29, for a wider description of the information manager in business settings.

3. Ibid., p. 41.

4. Pat-Anthony Federico, Kim E. Brun, and Douglas B. McCalla, *Management Information Systems and Organizational Behavior* (New York: Praeger, 1980), p. 150.

5. Gloria Durka, "Modeling Religious Education for the Future," in *The Religious Education We Need: Toward the Renewal of Christian Education,* ed. James Michael Lee (Birmingham. Ala.: Religious Education Press, 1977), p. 103.

6. Federico, Brun, and McCalla, *Management Information Systems and Organizational Behavior,* p. 96. Federico presents a summary of research on the impact and changes that information management will bring to general business organizations in the future.

7. Allen J. Moore, "Religious Education as a Discipline," in *Changing Patterns of Religious Education,* ed. Marvin J. Taylor (Nashville: Abingdon, 1983), p. 92. Moore makes a clear and positive distinction between the scholarly purpose of an academic discipline and the local professional's practice (p. 94).

8. Edward E. Lawler III et al., *Doing Research that Is Useful for Theory and Practice* (San Francisco: Jossey-Bass, 1985), p. 15.

9. George Mendenhall, "Research, Evaluation and Diagnosis: Some Basic Distinctions," *Viewpoints: Bulletin of the School of Education, Indiana University* 49:5 (September 1973), p. 18.

10. Walter R. Borg and Meredith Damien Gall, *Educational Research* (New York: Longman, 1979), p. 13.

11. The descriptions of the four types have been taken from Peter F. Oliva, *Supervision for Today's Schools,* 2nd ed. (New York: Longman, 1984), pp. 312. Eric Hoyle, "Educational Research: Dissemination, Participation, Negotiation," in *World Yearbook of Education 1985: Research, Policy and Practice,* ed. John Nisbet, Jacquetta Megarry, and Stanley Nisbet (London: Kogan Page, 1985), pp. 221-222, provides a similar typology with the addition of summative and formative evaluation to the list. Oliva also mentions that formative evaluation unfortunately is sometimes described as descriptive research. I will treat summative and formative evaluation as types of evaluation rather than

types of research as both tend to be directed toward the question of "how well something is being done?"

12. Douglas E. Mitchell, "Research Impact in Educational Policy and Practice in the USA," in *World Yearbook of Education 1985: Research, Policy and Practice*, p. 37.

13. See Howard P. Colson and Raymond M. Rigdon, *Understanding Your Church's Curriculum* (Nashville: Broadman, 1981), pp. 29-32, for a complete list of participating churches and the description of the curriculum's emphasis.

14. Jean Royer Dyer, *Understanding and Evaluating Educational Research* (Reading, Mass.: Addison-Wesley, 1979), pp. 157-193, describes the various techniques of data collecting.

15. Ernest E. McMahon, "The Needs of People and the Needs of Their Communities," in *Priorities in Adult Education*, ed. David B. Rauch (New York: Macmillan, 1972), p. 45.

16. Psychologists have referred to this as the "Hawthorn Effect" based on experiments in the Hawthorn Plant of the Western Electric Company. Borg and Gall, *Educational Research*, p. 163.

17. Charles F. Melchert, "Hope for the Profession," *Religious Education* 67 (September-October 1972), p. 361.

18. Edgar H. Schein, *Process Consultation: Its Role in Organizational Development* (Reading, Mass.: Addison-Wesley, 1969), p. 13.

19. Roger D. Evered, "Transforming Managerial and Organizational Research: Creating a Science that Works," in *Human Systems Development*, ed. Robert Tannebaum et al., (San Francisco: Jossey-Bass, 1985), p. 454.

20. Harold W. Stubblefield, "Teaching Diagnostic Skills: Procedures and Problems," *Viewpoints: Bulletin of the School of Education, Indiana University* 49:5 (September 1973), p. 64.

21. See Timothy Arthur Lines, *Systemic Religious Education* (Birmingham, Ala.: Religious Education Press, 1987), for descriptions of the various subsystems of education and religious education.

22. Don Hellrigel, John W. Slocum Jr., and Richard W. Woodman, *Organizational Behavior*, 3rd ed., (St. Paul: West, 1983), pp. 535-538, describes the key variables that are part of a systems model of change. John McKinley, "Perspectives on Diagnosis in Adult Education," *Viewpoints: Bulletin of the School of Education, Indiana University* 49:5 (September 1973), p. 76, cautions the educational diagnostician that not every problem may be addressed by an educational program.

23. Donald G. Emler, "A Program of Teacher Recognition," *Church School* (Nashville: Graded Press, November 1978), p. 14.

24. W. F. Pounds, "The Process of Problem Finding," *Industrial Management Review* (Fall 1969), pp. 1-19.

25. William H. Newman, E. Kirby Warren, and Jerome E. Schnee, *The Process of Management: Strategy, Action, Results*, 5th ed. (Englewood Cliffs, N.J.: Prentice-Hall, 1982), p. 111.

26. David A. Nadler, J. Richard Hackman, and Edward E. Lawler III,

Managing Organizational Behavior (Boston: Little Brown, 1979), p. 265.

27. Ibid., pp. 265-266.

28. Newman, Warren, and Schnee, *The Process of Management,* pp. 110-114.

29. Ibid., p. 113.

30. Hellriegel, Slocum, and Woodman, *Organizational Behavior,* pp. 538-539.

31. Action research is the diagnostic tool used by consultants in process consultation. For a full development of the process consultation model see Schein, *Process Consultation,* p. 4. Action research differs from process consultation in that the leadership for action research may be a group member or a local leader rather than an external consultant.

32. This is a modification of "Needs Assessment," a curriculum development and evaluation model described in Jon Wiles and Joseph C. Bondi, *Curriculum Development: A Guide to Practice,* 2nd ed. (Columbus, Ohio: Merrill, 1985), pp. 103-127, and Oliva, *Supervision for Today's Schools,* pp. 317-322.

33. Sara Little, *To Set One's Heart: Belief and Teaching in the Church* (Atlanta: John Knox, 1983), p. 40.

34. H. Mason Atwood and Joe Ellis, "The Concept of Need: An Analysis for Adult Education," *Adult Leadership* (January 1971), p. 210.

35. Marlene Wilson, *Survival Skills for Managers* (Boulder, Colo.: Volunteer Management Associates, 1981), p. 72.

36. This section is an application of the basic skills discussed above in Chapter 5. Additional information on these skills in the areas of research, diagnosis, and evaluation may be found in the following resources: Chris Argyris, *Intervention Theory and Method* (Reading, Mass.: Addison-Wesley, 1970); Borg and Gall, *Educational Research;* June Gallessich, *The Profession and Practice of Consultation* (San Francisco: Jossey-Bass, 1982); Paul S. Goodman and Associates, *Designing Effective Work Groups* (San Francisco: Jossey-Bass, 1986); Herman Holtz, *How to Succeed as an Independent Consultant* (New York: Wiley, 1983); Lawler et al., *Doing Research that Is Useful for Theory and Practice;* Schein, *Process Consultation;* Tannebaum et al., *Human Systems Development.*

37. Lee, *The Content of Religious Instruction,* pp. 173-177.

38. Newman, Warren, and Schnee, *The Process of Management,* pp. 121-127.

39. See many examples in Tom Peters and Nancy Austin, *A Passion for Excellence: The Leadership Difference* (New York: Random House, 1985).

40. William V. Coleman, *Planning Tomorrow's Parish: Leader's Edition* (West Mystic, Conn.: Twenty-Third Publications, 1976), p. 20.

41. Gallessich, *The Profession and Practice of Consultation,* pp. 320-321.

42. Wilson, *Survival Skills for Managers,* p. 64.

43. Mendenhall, "Research, Evaluation and Diagnosis: Some Basic Distinctions," pp. 19-20.

44. D. Campbell Wyckoff, *How To Evaluate Your Christian Education Program* (Philadelphia: Westminster, 1963), p. 9.

45. Scarvia B. Anderson et al., eds., *Encyclopedia of Educational Evaluation* (San Francisco: Jossey-Bass, 1975), pp. 178-179.

46. Richard M. Wolf, *Evaluation in Education: Foundations of Competing Assessment and Program Review,* 2nd ed. (New York: Praeger, 1984), p. 7.

47. Robert L. Browning, "The Nature of Evaluation," *The Church School* (December 1977), p. 3.

48. Borg and Gall, *Educational Research,* p. 602.

49. Arden D. Grotelueschen, "Program Evaluation," in *Developing, Administering, and Evaluating Adult Education,* ed. Alan B. Knox (San Francisco: Jossey-Bass, 1980), pp. 89-94.

50. Malcolm Knowles, *The Modern Practice of Adult Education* (New York: Association Press, 1980), p. 223.

51. Michael Scriven, "The Methodology of Evaluation," in *Perspectives of Curriculum Evaluation,* ed. Robert E. Stake (Chicago: Rand McNally, 1967), p. 40. This is the classic monograph on evaluation which introduced the terms "formative" and "summative" into the field.

52. Borg and Gall, *Educational Research,* p. 599.

53. Lee J. Cronbach, *Designing Evaluations of Educational and Social Programs* (San Francisco: Jossey-Bass, 1982), pp. 24-25.

54. Although based on public education models, many examples and ideas for evaluation models are presented in Edward F. DeRoche, *An Administrator's Guide for Evaluating Programs and Personnel* (Boston: Allyn and Bacon, 1981).

55. Borg and Gall, *Educational Research,* p. 607.

56. Malcolm Provus, *Discrepancy Evaluation* (Berkeley, Calif.: McCutchan, 1971).

57. Egon G. Guba and Daniel L. Stufflebeam, *Evaluation: The Process of Stimulating, Aiding, and Abetting Insightful Action* (Bloomington: Indiana University Press, 1970).

58. Goodman, *Designing Effective Work Groups,* p. 185.

59. Will Beal, *The Minister of Education as Educator* (Nashville: Convention, 1979), pp. 84-85.

60. Coleman, *Planning Tomorrow's Parish,* p. 62.

61. Two examples, although somewhat dated, of formal religious education evaluation models with different questionnaires which can be modified by religious education committees are: Wyckoff, *How To Evaluate Your Christian Education Program* and Coleman, *Planning Tomorrow's Parish.*

62. DeRoche, *An Administrator's Guide for Evaluating Programs and Personnel,* p. 7.

63. Thomas G. Cummings and Susan Albers Mohrman, "Assessing Innovative Organizational Designs, in *Human Systems Development,* ed. Robert Tannenbaum et al. (San Francisco: Jossey-Bass, 1985), p. 525.

64. John A. Fairbank and Donald M. Prue, "Developing Performance Feedback Systems," in *Handbook of Organizational Behavior Management,* ed. Lee W. Frederiksen (New York: Wiley, 1982), pp. 281-299.

65. Ibid., pp. 290-291.

66. Cummings and Mohrman, "Assessing Innovative Organizational Designs, p. 522.

67. Anderson et al., eds., *Encyclopedia of Educational Evaluation,* pp. 178-179.

68. Knowles, *The Modern Practice of Adult Education,* pp. 226-231, presents many sample questions that may be adapted for evaluation.

69. See Coleman, *Planning Tomorrow's Parish: A Self-evaluation and Planning Guide,* Coleman, *Planning Tomorrow's Parish: Leader's Edition,* for sample questions for the evaluation of both the total parish program and the religious educational program. Wyckoff, *How To Evaluate Your Christian Education Program,* pp. 55-102, provides model forms for a committee to use as a formal evaluation. See also DeRoche, *An Administrator's Guide for Evaluating Programs and Personnel.*

70. See Iris V. Cully, *Planning and Selecting Curriculum for Christian Education* (Valley Forge, Pa.: Judson, 1983), pp. 111-113, for an example of a criteria checklist.

71. Wilson, *The Effective Management of Volunteer Programs,* p. 88.

72. Ibid.

73. Robert A. Fellenz, Gary J. Conti, and Don F. Seaman, "Evaluate: Student, Staff, Program," in *Materials and Methods in Adult and Continuing Education,* ed. Chester Klevins (Canoga Park, Calif.: Klevins, 1982), p. 339.

74. See Oliva, *Supervision for Today's Schools,* pp. 343-575, for suggestions on ways to help educational workers to help themselves.

75. Adolph Unruh and Harold E. Turner, *Supervision for Change and Innovation* (Boston: Houghton Mifflin, 1970), p. 281.

76. Bruce P. Powers, *Christian Education Handbook* (Nashville: Broadman, 1981), p. 67. See also DeRoche, *An Administrator's Guide for Evaluating Programs and Personnel.*

77. Fellenz, Conti, and Seaman, "Evaluate: Student, Staff, Program," p. 341.

78. See James Michael Lee, *The Flow of Religious Instruction* (Birmingham, Ala.: Religious Education Press, 1973), pp. 279-284.

79. John M. Culkin, "A Schoolman's Guide to Marshall McLuhan," in *Selected Educational Heresies,* ed. William F. O'Neil (Glenview, Ill.: Scott, Foresman, 1969), p. 302.

Chapter 10

The DRE as Faith Interpreter

There is a sense in which the role of interpreter of the faith flows from the DRE's own spirituality or religious commitments. In most Christian churches, a professionally certified DRE must be a member of the community of faith.[1] Spirituality has been described by James Michael Lee as "the way in which one mobilizes oneself religiously in the total and actual living out of one's daily activities."[2]

Thomas Groome observes that "spirituality and the call to holiness include all humankind; it is not only for an elite few."[3] In the ecumenical community there is an emerging consensus on the general ministry of all Christians as the people of God.[4] In baptism-confirmation each member of the community is consecrated into the general ministry of Jesus Christ to be the people of God with ministries. One of the current emphases is that this ministry be understood to be both within and especially beyond the church in the world.[5]

Within the people of God there are many gifts and unique callings. The DRE is one who has responded to a call from God to participate in a specialized ministry of the church and has accepted the responsibility to prepare for the ministry through personal spiritual development and academic study.

As explained in previous chapters, the foundation for the profession of religious education definitely lies in education and the related social sciences. Chapter 4 described mature religious education as enabling the learner to identify, evaluate, and synthesize appropriate values that have been personally developed in dialogue with the community's story and then respond as people of God with ministries in the world.

Concomitantly, the DRE is also a person of faith. The DRE's own spiritual life begins with a personal faith commitment. These faith commitments guide consciously and unconsciously the choices and values acceptable to the DRE. The value of trusting persons to develop their own religious perspective from general resources, an essential component of religious education, leads the DRE to develop models of religious education that offer the learner the opportunity to evaluate, synthesize, and even reject ideas. Trusting people to make reasonable choices and commitments requires different models of education than those based in a commitment to a single perspective of religious understanding requiring absolute acceptance without question.

The DRE's Spiritual Development

The DRE must intentionally seek to sustain and develop his or her own spiritual life in order to serve the faith community from the conscious presence of God's love. One of the constant temptations of any professional (clergy or lay) in the church is to be so caught up in the functional tasks of the church's program that one's own spiritual nurture becomes malnourished.[6] The various spiritual disciplines such as corporate worship, personal meditation and prayer, Bible study, and participation in some form of Christian service are the basic resources of the DRE's spiritual life.

The development of the spiritual life begins by being open to the awareness of God's presence and hope. To have the resources to enable others to have a relationship with God, DREs must have "a sense of God's presence in their lives."[7] It is an awareness of the mystery of God's love that seeks the richest fulfillment of human life while sensing that God's spirit is not limited to any one understanding that provides a meaning for our lives.[8] Thus the DRE's spirituality enables the DRE to share life with God. At the same time, the DRE will live out that spirituality by faithfully preparing and serving to the best of his or her ability, knowing

that in the mystery of God's activity, it is often a small or insig-
nificant action that will be the instrument for God's love in the
lives of the people served.

Spirituality is a blend of many activities. It is nurtured through
corporate worship, prayer, and meditation. However, if the religious educator's own spirituality is only concerned with himself
or herself, then such a person is incomplete. Richard Foster describes one of the paths of spiritual growth as "the discipline of
service."[9] The spiritual discipline of service is based in the servant
ministry revealed by Jesus. To be Christ's servant is to serve
through the daily activities of life. In one sense, the servant ministry is deceptively simple while paradoxically being the most
difficult. Too often we think of service as something that involves
major projects, a lot of time, and requires us to attend community meetings. Dietrich Bonhoeffer describes the paradoxical nature of servant ministry as being helpful through "simple assistance in trifling, external matters," in addition to the ministry of
listening and sharing the life concerns of the other.[10]

However, true spirituality is also lived in the world. Spirituality
involves more than nurturing the inner life without considering
the rest of creation. Spirituality is linked with the congregation's
mission to be the people of God with ministries in the world. It
recognizes God in the midst of human life and the physical and
emotional concerns of every human being.

The Work of Religious Education
Directly Nurtures the DRE's Own Spirituality

The DRE's own spiritual life is a valuable wellspring for effective religious education leadership. Furthermore, the actual work
of religious education is a constant source for the development of
the DRE's spiritual life. Leon McKenzie suggests that the norm
for spiritual development "occurs in proportion to the degree the
religious educator fulfills his or her professional roles."[11] The
unity of spirituality and professional service is crucial for a re-
newed sense of ministry. The person who views the role of the
DRE as just another job will lack the inner vision and support of
knowing God's presence. Likewise, there is the sense of guilt that
there is little time for spiritual renewal in the active parish life
lived by most DREs. The experience of God in the center of life

must be found in the center of the DRE's ministry. Henri Nouwen declares that "prayer is not a preparation for work or an indispensable condition for effective ministry. Prayer is life; prayer and ministry are the same and can never be divorced."[12]

While all of the tasks of the DRE have potential for spiritual development, the preparation for the intentional interpreting the faith to others is one of the richest potentials for spiritual development. The DRE's spirituality according to James Michael Lee, "is organically intertwined with that individual's participation in religious instruction endeavor."[13] Judaism has long understood the relationship of study with spirituality. It is a double mitzvah or blessing for one to study scripture, even while "listening" to a sermon. One can recall that the reason Teyve, in the musical *Fiddler on the Roof*, wanted to be a rich man was to be able to study the scriptures so that he could discuss them with the wise men at the gate.

The richness of the DRE's spiritual life is correlated with the activities that nurture it. A person who regularly studies scripture and participates in activities that nurture faith will tend to develop a more meaningful spiritual life.[14] A central part of my own spiritual growth is teaching an adult Sunday school class. The discipline of the weekly preparation is a part of my spiritual formation and enrichment as many insights into the faith are discovered that would not receive my attention otherwise. A typical lesson may take over four hours to prepare as commentaries are checked, related books are skimmed, as well as the printed denominational resources guiding the preparation. Questions from the class are anticipated which require me to broadly prepare. In this way, the class challenges the teacher *before* the actual meeting.

Preparing for religious instruction causes changes in the DRE's spiritual development in at least two ways.[15] In the first place, learning changes everyone, even the teacher. As the DRE learns new ideas, additional interpretations of ideas, or refreshes previous knowledge, his or her perceptions, feelings, and maybe actions are changed. The second interaction of teaching with spiritual growth is in the teaching act itself. By using teaching-learning procedures that create interaction between teachers and students, each person in the experience is open to change.

To grow spiritually, the DRE will need to create opportunities to interpret the faith and mediate the tradition with the life situation of congregational members.[16] The ordained clergy have a Sunday sermon built into their schedule, which both creates the need for study and an opportunity for expression. However, the DRE must intentionally schedule teaching activities related to the religious faith of the community. Otherwise, the potential distractions of general administration and consulting with other leaders will fill the time.

The DRE is concerned about the spiritual growth of the members of the congregation and provides direction toward that goal. The general tasks of leading the religious education program through program planning for groups and teacher training are the common forms for the DRE to help persons develop their spiritual lives. This recognizes that the role of the DRE is different from the pastor's regarding leading some of the tasks of the congregation's spiritual life. As a spiritual facilitator, the DRE functions primarily from the educational base using the many educational opportunities of classes, meetings, and visits that already exist under the DRE's direction.[17]

Preparation of the DRE as Faith Interpreter

While most DREs accept the broad role of program developer, many are hesitant to accept their role as an interpreter of the faith held by the community. As an interpreter of the faith, the DRE links the learner's present life with the community's tradition of scripture and theological tradition with the community's present experience so that the present is transformed in the direction of God's reign.[18]

Part of the hesitancy to accept the role of faith interpreter is due to a limited background in the content areas of the faith such as biblical, theological, religious, and historical studies. Part of this hesitancy also lies in the assumption that it is the role only of the ordained clergy to interpret the faith. All Christians must accept their role as interpreter of the faith, especially those who teach. The specific authority as faith interpreter of the DRE is based in his or her call to ministry and ordination in baptism-confirmation as well as from academic training.[19]

As an interpreter of the faith, the DRE links current events with the community's tradition of scripture, history, and contemporary theological writers. Howard Grimes states that the responsibility for being theologically literate is complex as the DRE must be involved in biblical, historical, and theological scholarship, while keeping abreast of developments in general education.[20]

One way to improve the self-confidence of many DREs as interpreters of the faith would be to encourage an undergraduate major in religious education or religious studies in addition to the common two-year (sixty-hour) Master of Religious Education degree in most Protestant seminaries, or the less academically demanding thirty-hour program in Catholic universities. The professional role requirements of the DRE are very diverse. Using only the masters-level degree to develop depth in substantive content, skill in methodology, and administration limits the DRE's professional preparation.

The DRE as Mediator and Interpreter of the Faith

One role of the DRE as a spiritual facilitator or guide is that of mediating and interpreting the faith to nurture spiritual growth in others.[21] The DRE serves as a mediator between the faith's tradition and the present life of many learners, so that the faith's heritage is connected with the present vocation of ministry in the world in God's name. The model for the mediator might be illustrated in the actions of President Jimmy Carter during the Camp David Summit in the late 1970s where his role was to intercede as an equal friend of two parties, Israeli Prime Minister Menachem Begin and Egyptian President Anwar Sadat, so that they could reconcile the differences between them. Thomas Groome uses the symbol of God's reign to describe the life-relatedness of the Christian tradition. The DRE as a mediator describes a "commitment to educating with practical and life-giving intent, that people may mobilize themselves to live as if God rules in their lives and in our world."[22]

The DRE is the incarnation of the presence of God to children, youth, and adults; to teachers and leaders; to one's own family. The DRE mediates between the community's past and the present by incarnating meanings from the community's past to those they teach and lead in the present.[23] This mediation begins with the DRE's own spiritual development.

The DRE Develops Interpretation Skills in Others

The DRE combines the knowledge of the basic concepts of the faith and its historical development with the ability to assist learners in developing skills for interpreting the Bible and understanding the tradition. One major resource in this process is the DRE's skill as storyteller. Storytelling is a re-creating of the event which connects the listener with the community's living and lived past. As the community's heritage is told so that it increasingly becomes the learner's story, the learner becomes shaped to a certain extent by encountering the past history of the faith community.[24]

The DRE as spiritual facilitator encourages participation within the life of the whole church (local, regional, and national levels of the denomination as well as ecumenically) as a means of spiritual growth. The DRE's personal life, such as church attendance and the level of involvement in peace and justice ministries, can also be a source of nonverbal witnessing to the faith that is verbally and experientially taught by the community of faith. Attitudes and skills for effective participation in the church's life are part of the DRE's concerns. Understanding what happens in the congregation's worship service, knowing what ideas or doctrines are central to the identity of the faith community, and clarifying why our denomination does this practice rather than another are helpful ways to deepen the religious commitment of both children and adults.

Creating courses on using various spiritual activities, devising opportunities for participation in retreats, and setting periods of special emphasis for the congregation's spiritual enrichment create the sense that the spiritual life is important in the parish. The meaning of the spiritual life can be implied by the activities suggested during a special spiritual enrichment emphasis. For instance, during Lent some churches emphasize repentance and making sacrifices by giving up something enjoyed, while other churches use programs that emphasize intentional efforts to enrich the lives of others by caring acts such as writing letters of appreciation, phone calls, and special gifts of service. The DRE should be aware of how the methods form the understandings of the faith.

Awareness of how human growth and development are correlated to spiritual development is important in the nurture of spiritual growth.[25] At various stages of the person's life, the DRE creates a learning atmosphere that develops the spiritual life. A nursery staffed by persons who like little children and are capable of expressing joy and love with the little ones establishes the basic trust needed to feel the church is a friendly place for the infant. Training both professional and volunteer teachers on ways to let children make decisions and even pointing out places in the curriculum where children ought to be given opportunities to make decisions regarding how to act out their faith in the larger world can help mesh spirituality with the rest of life. Making sure that at least some of the worship services are genuinely inclusive where children can participate at their level is another area for the DRE to represent the spiritual needs of children. Recruiting counselors and teachers who are comfortable with those students who ask questions is a way to develop the spiritual life of youth and adults.

DRE Creates Opportunities for Participation in Peace and Justice Activities

In addition to being a mediator with the church's religious heritage, the DRE is also a bridge between the larger global village and the local community. Helping youth and adults to become involved in interfaith activities may challenge many ideas held and assist them in creating new ways to envision life. A dialogue with DREs from other denominations can force DREs to confront their own personal prejudices in ways that would never happen without such cross-denominational relationships. Mature spiritual life involves helping the congregation to be involved in the work for unity and God's shalom among the people of God as the ecumenical faith community seeks to be faithful to its mission.

The spiritual activity of servant ministry is important for lay persons just as it is for the DRE. The church's pilgrimage to the physical world is completed by return to the physical world where the concern is to share the ministries of peace and justice.[26] The special role of the DRE in developing this spiritual discipline is in bridging the church with the larger social community's concerns for peace and justice. The DRE must help teachers acquire the skills that move the ministry of members outside of the church's institutional concerns into the larger community. The DRE serves the church by identifying the variety of the community's concerns and reporting them to the congregation.

It is also essential for the DRE to train teachers on how to analyze world issues and global concerns and then how to reflect theologically on their meaning so that the teaching throughout the whole church, from children through adults, reflects the struggle of the dialogue of the faith with the particular concern. The DRE guides the church in creating opportunities to apply the message learned in the study of the faith's heritage to the personal life of the child, youth, or adult lived in the daily world of work, school, and play.

The DRE as Mentor

One opportunity related to the role of spiritual facilitator is to be a mentor for the faith pilgrimage of another person. Rather than being a duty assigned by a typical job description, which is the source for the other functioning roles, a mentor is chosen by another as the need for spiritual guidance is experienced. Because of the visibility of the DRE in the life of the church, a DRE who reflects the lifestyle of faith respected by youth and other adults may be invited to serve as a spiritual guide by one or several members.

There are many models of spirituality and thus many different styles of mentoring are described.[27] The formal forms of spirituality typically come from Roman Catholic and Orthodox Christianity and from non-Christian Eastern religion sources. For its part, Protestantism has typically used informal models such as when a youth asks the DRE a question of meaning following a youth fellowship program or an informal prayer group that meets weekly.

Anyone to whom another turns for spiritual guidance becomes a potential mentor.[28] In the mentoring relationship God is experienced through the mutual sharing of the guide and the pilgrim. Maria Harris describes the centrality of the spiritual life as the rediscovery of the life lived in the recognized presence of God who comes to us in "the touching and being touched of human incarnate persons."[29] The mentor is one who becomes the incarnation of God to another who also relates to the mentor as the presence of God.

Another description of the role of mentor comes from the Jewish tradition of being a *mensch*, a German word which when used in Yiddish, describes a person of integrity. "To be a *mensch* is to be the kind of person God had in mind when he arranged for human beings to evolve, someone who is honest, reliable, wise enough to be no longer naive, but not yet cynical, a person you can trust to give you advice for your benefit rather than his or her own."[30] A mentor does not have to incorporate a perfect spiritual life. However, a mentor should be capable of openly sharing the struggles of her or his own faith journey that include both the meaningful experiences and the difficulties.

Mentors Facilitate Spiritual Growth

The DRE may be a mentor in a structured relationship in the style of a spritual facilitator. This role generally calls for direct guidance and the raising of questions with the pilgrim.[31] For example, there might be a journaling process in which questions are raised by the mentor or in reflection using a resource such as the "Intensive Journal" program by Ira Progoff.[32] Bible study and praying together are often part of the mentor-mentee spiritual relationship. Due to its formal nature, a regular time is set aside for meeting such as weekly or twice a month.

As a spiritual guide, the DRE may serve as a mentor in less structured fashion. In the evening hours of most youth retreats the questions of faith flow from the students seeking a trusting relationship. Many DREs find it helpful to make a call in the home following a family member's death to specifically visit with the children. The clergy's time is typically dominated by adults. The DRE can be more free to focus on the child of the family. Later, the child may seek out another conversation with the sensitive DRE. Sitting beside an older adult on the bus as the "senior adult fellowship" travels to some conference may be the ideal time to talk about feelings related to placing an elderly parent in a nursing home and the meaning of life.

The spiritual guide or mentor provides structure to the experiences that enable growth in spirituality. The spiritual guide is sensitive to the life situations of the various members of the group.[33] Central to the growth in spirituality is being part of a loving and accepting atmosphere. The development of trust that each person's ideas are valued and that they are important is an initial requirement for people to feel free to probe their spiritual existence. Knowing the interests of the many individuals, the significant persons in their lives, the commitments they fulfill helps to understand the issues that creates their personal story.

A spiritual guide is also sensitive to the fears and loneliness of the persons around them. The actions of many people often are the unconscious result of these anxieties. Identifying and bringing these anxieties to the conscious level often allows persons to accept the feelings and to control them in acceptable ways. The mentor intentionally links the faith tradition in ways that are meaningful to the people, seeking to connect the feelings of the experiences of the modern person with the feelings expressed in one's faith tradition. It is essential that the pilgrim be encouraged to make the connection between the historical faith tradition and his or her own life rather than depend on the spiritual guide.

Contrasting Examples of Spirituality

Roman Catholics and Eastern Orthodox have traditionally placed spirituality at the center of their ministries and the religious education activities.[34] Thanks to the worldwide Christian ecumenical movement which began with vigor in the mid-1960s, Protestants have discovered anew the crucialness of holistic spiritual living as the axis of both ministry and religious education. Matthew Fox points out that there have been two major streams of spirituality.[35] The first stream is the traditionally popular spirituality based in fall/redemption theology which emphasizes withdrawal from life. Another style of spirituality is based in creation/incarnation theology which is concerned about justice-making, grace, and affirmation of a holistic relationship to the global community and our earth. Fox challenges Protestants to lead the whole church into renewal of Christianity based on creation spirituality.[36] All religious educators who affirm the value of persons in learning can identify with the spirituality proposed by Fox.

The DRE as Counselor for Church-related Occupations

One aspect of spiritual development that has not heretofore been emphasized in spiritual facilitation is counseling and inviting persons to enter church-related occupations. Certainly it is true that not everyone who develops a vital spiritual life should enter the professional ministry as clergy, DRE or lay missionary, and so forth. However, it is from being in a deep relationship with God that one is most likely to hear the call of God to serve in that fashion. This is especially true if we accept the idea that the DRE's spirituality is confluent with the DRE's professional roles.[37]

It should be emphasized that a call to serve God is not restricted to the ordained clergy. A divine call to full-time religious service can and is given to lay persons to serve God as lay persons in one or another professional position within the church. The DRE is just as much a religious calling from God as is a minister, priest, or nun.

Church-related Career Opportunities

As a spiritual guide, the DRE brings the resources of being familiar with the variety of options for service through the church. The ordained clergy, the lay DRE, the church musician, and the church business administrator are common professional vocations related to the local church. Chaplains may be assigned to a hospital, the military, a children's home, or a college campus. Lay missionaries are needed in rural and urban areas, through the church or in a variety of social agencies.

Sometimes misconceptions of requirements either for educational preparation or for service prevent a person from exploring a church-related career. Several college students have told the author that they enjoyed working in the church but chose to major in public education because they thought the only way to be a DRE was to attend a seminary and take courses in preaching. Even when the scope of the potential leadership role of the public school teacher being limited to the classroom was compared to the broad multiple leadership roles of the DRE in planning and structuring a wide variety of religious education programs, these students were still hesitant. Some of the misconceptions harbored by these students came from ordained clergy who discouraged them from considering professional areas of church service other than as ordained clergy. In a counseling/advising situation the DRE has the opportunity and the obligation to guide potential candidates for all available forms of church-related occupations.

The "Call to the Ministry"

Unique to church-related occupations has been the traditional "call to the ministry." This deeply personal experience is confusing to many people, and the DRE is one resource, along with the ordained clergy, to share the pilgrimage of persons who believe they have received such a call. It is important for the DRE to help clarify the nature of a vocational call of a person before actually preparing a person professionally who has received the call.

There is an old story of a farmer who saw a vision in the clouds one day that told him to, "Go preach Christ." The farmer then began to preach Christ. But alas, the farmer's vision was not supported by the quality of his sermons. An old timer asked him to state exactly what his vision was. The new preacher reported he has seen the letters "G.P.C." in the sky. "Oh!" declared the old-timer, "you misunderstood. It meant, "Go plow corn!" This anecdote indicates that while every Christian is called to general service by virtue of baptism, only some are called to specialized service as a DRE, a lay missionary, or an ordained cleric.

Sometimes a person will seek out the DRE or pastor for counseling about entering a church-related occupation. At other times, the DRE needs to invite persons who seem to possess the gifts and graces for the religious educational ministry as a DRE to consider entering preparation for this career. A sense of pride in being a DRE and what that represents for the church should be part of the self-identity of a DRE. It is essential to value what one does professionally for others to believe that the role is vital and is worthy of consideration as a career.

Counseling with Candidates
for Church-related Careers

A significant concern when counseling a person about any career decision is whether the person has the required skills for the intended occupation. Does the person have the competencies needed to perform basic tasks of the occupation, the temperament and personality skills that are relevant to environmental and interpersonal job conditions, and the knowledge required for specific job performance or the ability to acquire it through additional educational preparation?[38] Guidance from the DRE to assist the candidate to honestly assess personal skills in relationship to potential goals can focus talents and opportunities into a realistic picture.

In advising anyone who is considering entering a church-related occupation, especially those who seek out the DRE, the counselor should follow several basic principles.[39] First there should be a realistic sharing of job opportunities relating to the proposed career and the necessary support systems the person will need. In some denominations there are many vacancies for a DRE who is able to move from region to region; however, the support systems may be difficult to cultivate. The future trends indicate that large churches will continue to grow. That means that there will be opportunities for employment as a DRE in many urban/suburban areas. However, the DRE must be able to develop a personal support system in each location and must be capable of finding his or her own employment opportunities.

When counseling about church-related occupations the DRE needs to look for different signals given by the prospective candidate in terms of why this person wishes to enter church service. Are the reasons healthy or are they avoiding some situation in the person's life? What personal problems would limit the potential for service as a DRE or another area of church service such as the ordained clergy? This may be a spouse who would resent a different profession or unrealistic expectations on the person's part. Does the person have the academic ability and the motivation to do the graduate work that is necessary in many denominations for certification or ordination? If a prospective candidate says he or she wants to be a foreign missionary or work with inner-city missions does the person have the necessary foreign language and other skills? What is the background involvement in the local church? Have they been active in the church's youth fellowship or are their religious experiences all from a group operating outside of the local church and denominational structures? One resource the DRE has when career counseling with young adults is to provide them an opportunity to work as an "intern" in the local church's religious education activities with the DRE. The DRE is a role model and provides life-testing opportunities.

It is essential to remember that the candidate will serve the whole church. Asking difficult questions concerning the gifts and graces of the person may be the most loving thing the DRE can do for the candidate. It is possible for a person to mature and certainly to learn biblical and theological knowledge, but emotional problems may be cause for discouragement.

Counseling for Persons
Exiting from Church-related Careers

Finally, it is important for the DRE when serving as a career counselor to assist the person to cease being a candidate for full-time church-related occupations without any guilt for that decision. There is often a great deal of expectation placed on a young person who has indicated a desire to pursue preparation to enter a church-related career. Then when alternative choices are made the person may feel guilty because they "let someone down."

Related to this change of plans is helping colleagues exit the career after several years of service. It has been suggested that adults should not ask children what are you going to be when you grow up; rather the question is more accurately stated, what do you want to be first when you grow up. There seems to be an increasing number of middle-aged persons entering seminaries. If we are recruiting people for the ministry in mid-life as a second career, we should also expect people to leave the ministry for new careers at mid-life. This may become the new area of vocational/career counseling for the whole church.

The DRE as Counselor

Most of a DRE's ministry is providing opportunities for people to be in relationship with God and others, or to discover a meaning in life that makes living significant beyond the accumulation of wealth, happiness, and knowledge. Sometimes, however, the DRE is invited to share as a counselor in the life of a parishioner.

The role of the nonprofessional counselor is different from a mental-health psychotherapist or clinical psychologist. "Counseling" and "counselor" will be used in this section for the nonprofessional role in contrast to psychotherapy or the social/mental-health professional. Few if any DREs have the academic background or clinical training to do long-term psychotherapy. Most of the personal counseling done by a DRE will be very short-term and should focus on a specific crisis or emergency in the life of the person. By definition, a crisis is something that needs immediate attention and has a maximum duration of four to six weeks. The opportunities for counseling are usually spontaneous and seldom are the result of a formal appointment.

The DRE Counsels Through Relationships

Counseling often happens within the context of other activities. Counseling may take place through the relationships shared by the DRE with teachers, youth, students in classes taught, and parents. Personal relationships are the key to the invitation to be a counselor. Counseling is often done at the level of a friend who listens briefly to a person who needs to verbally sort out some options. Sometimes it is a simple answer to a direct question. Some of the most common times for counseling to occur are immediately following a youth fellowship meeting, a church business meeting, or class when the individual stops to visit with the DRE and to ask a question or two. Sometimes the DRE may not even be aware that counseling is occurring, but if the DRE is sensitive and oriented toward the personal affirmation of the one seeking counsel, these informal moments may have great value to the seeker.

By virtue of office, the DRE is a representative of the community's faith. Many times a question of faith is directed to the DRE which is actually a request for an interpretation from the perspective of the church by one of its servants. The spirituality of the DRE is a quality that may cause church members to seek her or him out as a religious resource person. James Michael Lee challenges the DRE to remember that the religious educator is not a social or mental health counselor, nor a vocational counselor, nor a scholastic counselor. In the counseling role, the DRE functions from within the context of religious education and the religious community.[40] As a counselor, the DRE seeks to help persons develop an understanding and appreciation of who they are so as to come to a realistic sense of self-worth.

There are several assets that a DRE brings to a counseling relationship which may be more important than knowledge.

Common sense is always a valued asset along with maturity and experience.[41] Maria Harris describes two other key assets of the DRE as being able to "listen well and to treat other people with care."[42]

Preparation as a Crisis Counselor

The primary identity of the DRE is that of a religious educator. It is out of this identity and this context that the DRE responds to persons in need of counseling. As a member of a service profession, the DRE needs to develop some basic skills as a nonprofessional counselor. Due to the nature of a crisis, i.e., a critical situation that is limited in its duration, the DRE must, like a good scout, "be prepared" in advance. In addition to some basic preparation at the graduate level through a couple of foundational counseling courses, the DRE can supplement this preparation through professional reading and through attending workshops on how to be an effective nonprofessional counselor.

It is also necessary for the DRE to reflect on personal feelings and beliefs concerning the "normal" or commonly predicted crisis areas such as death, suicide, teen-pregnancy, drugs, illness, unemployment, divorce, family conflict, rape, and child abuse. Then an analysis of the teachings of the church or the social principles of the denomination should be made so that the DRE knows how personal feelings reflect and differ from the church's official position. In counseling, the counselor must be able to separate personal feelings and beliefs from the needs of the person in crisis, although the counselor still functions from personal values and beliefs.

The purpose of this minimal preparation is to free the DRE to respond in sensitivity to the person, rather than having to deal with personal issues first. In addition, basic counseling skills enable the DRE to be more effective in reducing the intensity of the crisis so that the person can cope with alternatives. In a crisis, efficiency of action is important.

Cautions for the DRE as a Counselor

Several points of caution need to be stated. The DRE should be careful of accepting too much responsibility as a counselor. The DRE is not a professionally trained counselor and should never attempt to be such. If a person cannot return to a balanced life quickly, then the DRE should recognize his or her own professional limitations and make a professional referral as quickly as possible.

Another area of caution is confidentiality. The DRE should be aware of attempts of the person to trap the counselor into promises of not telling a parent or spouse some bit of information that may need to be revealed for follow-up action. It is a wise counselor who does not reveal information without permission, but a "trapped secrecy" is not beneficial for a counseling relationship.

In terms of legal confidentiality, since the DRE is not a professional counselor or one who hears confessions, the DRE does not have "privileged communication" legal status by which information shared during a counseling session would be protected from a court of law. In addition, most states now require professional persons, including day care workers who work with children and youth, to report suspected child abuse situations for investigation. This often creates conflict for the DRE, but a central issue is the protection of the child.

Common Areas for DRE to Serve as Counselor

The DRE tends to engage in certain activities which invite him or her to be a counselor because of the DRE's regular presence in the program. Counseling with youth and children and with parents concerning family situations typically are primary concerns for a DRE. Sadly, in many churches the DRE represents the only church professional who will relate to children. Some male pastors may not see working with children as masculine, and some female ministers are also blocked by the "sexist" stereotype that "caring for children" is woman's work and in an effort to avoid appearing weak, avoid the children.[43] This is in addition to the fact that most seminary education does not prepare future pastors to care for children. The DRE, as well, must seek skills in this area in addition to religious education courses of the general sort since skill in working with children constitutes a major part of the DRE's religious education activity.

When working with children and youth the DRE can initiate many personal contacts. Public school teachers know that when the behavior of a student changes suddenly there is usually something happening in the family setting or in the personal life of the young person. A change in the family situation such as marital separation, death, or plans to move also means a potential need in the lives of children.

Divorce Crisis Counseling. The DRE may be helpful to children and youth when a family faces a divorce or other major conflict. Assuring elementary children that they are not the cause of a marital conflict is essential. Children in a family involved in divorce face a major crisis. Pain of loss, anger against parents with concurrent feelings of guilt that the child caused the divorce, and anxiety about the future in a new home structure threaten the coping abilities of children.[44] Youth may perceive a parent who becomes socially active as immature, or the young person may be fearful of entering into relationships with others. Sometimes there is a sense of relief that the fighting has stopped in some families, and this may cause guilt. The DRE may perform a major role in helping the children to articulate feelings about their situation and to reduce feelings of personal guilt, while the minister/priest may be serving as a marriage counselor for the parents.

Hospital Visits. Many DREs make hospital visits to children and youth of their parish. Encouraging children to share concerns about being ill is helpful for their healing, just as it is for adults. The DRE can assist children and youth struggle with their feelings about their own death and the death of a significant other person in a home visit following the death of a family member. Most adults in these times of crisis are so caught up in their own issues that they have limited energy to work with the children. By focusing on the younger members of the home, the DRE ministers to the whole family.

Suicide Crisis Counseling. Suicide and its threat creates an emergency crisis situation for any family, and often for the whole community. The suicide of a parent brings questions of guilt as well as despair for the other family members. Teenage suicides create a double crisis. First family members must receive attention. In addition, the church's youth fellowship generally needs to spend time struggling with the issues.

Sex Education Counseling

Counseling in the area of sex education is common for the DRE. When working in this area, the DRE must go beyond personal embarrassment and be willing to sensitively ask explicit

questions about meanings held by the youth.[45] While youth typically do not respond to adults who set down moral restrictions as
a price for acceptance, the youth are usually interested in how
adults have come to their convictions or thought through issues.
Be sure that the sexual information shared with the youth is
accurate both in terms of biological concerns and in terms of the
church's position about the topics discussed.

One does not serve in a church with youth long before being
confronted with the issues of teenage pregnancy. Feelings about
abortion, adoption, and teenage marriage and parenting flood
the situation. This is why the DRE must have a grasp of his or
her personal feelings as well as resources for referral. The DRE
should be aware of any official denominational statements regarding these issues. The counselor will want to work with the
teens to explore feelings about causes of the pregnancy, feelings
related to alternatives at this point in the situation, as well as
providing information about resource groups.

Rape Crisis Counseling. A special counseling area for the
woman DRE is rape crisis counseling. This need is often found in
churches located in smaller cities rather than in the large metro-
politan regions where women's crisis centers may be present. The
DRE will need to receive special training as a rape crisis counsel-
or, usually from a women's center that ministers to the special
needs of women in crisis. Unfortunately, in some settings, the
church needs to educate the courts that rape is an act of violent
hostility against the victim rather than the work of the attacker
seeking sexual gratification.[46]

Crisis counseling in this situation calls for one who is able to
hear the victim's struggle to resolve issues of pregnancy, venereal
disease, guilt, shame, and fear of a second attack. Even when law
enforcement officers are sympathetic, they must be concerned
about the legal situation and do not have the time nor duty to
relate to the woman's emotional concerns. The DRE would also
assist in referring the woman to emergency medical help for the
physical trauma as well as long-term legal resources. This is another area where the feelings related to the various issues of
sexuality must be clear in the counselor's mind before the event.
Rape crisis counseling is a special type of counseling, but when a
DRE is prepared in the area it is a significant resource for the
congregation.

Summary

The DRE will be sought for guidance and counseling in both formal and informal ways. As a nonprofessinal counselor functioning primarily from the perspective of education, the DRE will generally serve persons involved in the religious education program of the church in informal opportunities. People will seek advice both inside and outside regular class and group activities. The most important aspect of the counselor role is the ability to care. As the DRE is sensitive to the needs of persons in the congregation, opportunities to empathetically listen and to enable the person to consider appropriate alternatives will constantly cry out for the DRE's attention. Caring is part of every Christian's ministry. Through the ministry of caring, God's love is incarnated to the people needing the touch of grace in the person of the DRE.

NOTES

1. This is true in terms of specific guidelines for certification in most Christian denominations. Many of these denominations also emphasize the moral obligation to be able to authentically witness to the faith professed by the community.

2. James Michael Lee, "Lifework Spirituality and the Religious Educator," in *The Spirituality of the Religious Educator*, ed. James Michael Lee (Birmingham, Ala.: Religious Education Press, 1985), p. 7.

3. Thomas H. Groome, "The Spirituality of the Religious Educator," *Religious Education* 83 (Winter 1988), p. 11.

4. Robert L. Browning and Roy A. Reed, "The Sacraments of Vocation: The Ordination of Clergy and the Consecration of the Laity for Ministry, in *The Sacraments in Religious Education and Liturgy* (Birmingham, Ala.: Religious Education Press, 1985), p. 220.

5. Ibid., p. 222.

6. Charles Healey, "The Spirituality of the Religious Educator," in *Emerging Issues in Religious Education*, ed. Gloria Durka and Joanmarie Smith (New York: Paulist, 1976), pp. 128-129.

7. Donald G. Emler, "Your Personal Communion with God," *Church School* (Nashville: Graded Press, August, 1981), p. 12.

8. Iris V. Cully, *Education for Spiritual Growth* (New York: Harper & Row, 1984), p. 36.

9. Richard Foster, *Celebration of Discipline: The Path to Spiritual Growth* (New York: Harper & Row, 1978), pp. 110-122.

10. Dietrich Bonhoeffer, *Life Together* (New York: Harper & Row, 1954), p. 99.

11. Leon McKenzie, "Developmental Spirituality and the Religious Educator," in *The Spirituality of the Religious Educator*, p. 59.

12. Henri J.M. Nouwen, *Creative Ministry* (New York: Doubleday, 1971), pp. xx-xxi.

13. James Michael Lee, "Lifework Spirituality and the Religious Educator," in *The Spirituality of the Religious Educator*, p. 19.

14. Ibid., p. 26.

15. Ibid., p. 37.

16. INSTROTEACH Board, *The Role of the Teacher in the Church: Five Areas of Competence* (Wichita, Kans.: Instroteach, 1973), pp. 17-19. The terms "Interpreter" and "Mediator" of the faith are borrowed from my participation in an Instroteach Lab in 1976.

17. Maria Harris, "The Religious Educator as Spiritual Director," in *The DRE Reader: A Source Book in Education and Ministry*, ed., Maria Harris (Winona, Minn.: Saint Mary's Press, 1980), p. 113.

18. Mary Elizabeth Moore, *Education for Continuity and Change*, (Nashville: Abingdon, 1983), p. 85.

19. Browning and Reed, *The Sacraments in Religious Education and Liturgy*, p. 221.

20. Howard Grimes, "Theological Foundations for Christian Education," in *An Introduction to Christian Education*, ed. Marvin J. Taylor (Nashville: Abingdon, 1966), p. 40.

21. Frank E. Dunn, *The Ministering Teacher* (Valley Forge, Pa.: Judson, 1982), p. 57. It is recognized that for Christians, Jesus the Christ is the Mediator between God and humanity in terms of salvation, but the DRE is a mediator in human terms.

22. Groome, "The Spirituality of the Religious Educator," p. 19.

23. Charles R. Foster, *Teaching in the Community of Faith* (Nashville: Abingdon, 1982), p. 121.

24. David S. Steward and Margaret S. Steward, "Action-Reflection-Action: Our Embedment in the World," in *Parish Religious Education*, ed. Maria Harris (New York: Paulist, 1978), p. 90.

25. Cully, *Education for Spiritual Growth*, pp. 145-165. Iris Cully provides many ideas for nurturing activities that any church would be well advised to consult.

26. Rodney R. Romney, "Nurturing a Church's Spirituality," *The Christian Ministry* (November 1986), p. 8.

27. Lee, *The Spirituality of the Religious Educator*, pp. 109-189, describes four major among many organized forms.

28. Cully, *Education for Spiritual Growth*, p. 159.

29. Harris, "The Religious Educator As Spiritual Director," p. 111.

30. Harold S. Kushner, *When All You've Ever Wanted Isn't Enough* (New York: Summit, 1986), p. 135.

31. Katherine DeGrow, "Finding a Spiritual Friend," *Youth* (Nashville: Graded Press, April 1987), p. 34.

32. Ira Progoff, *At a Journal Workshop* (New York: Dialogue House, 1975).

33. Susan D. Detterman. "Teacher as Spiritual Guide," *Church School Today* (Nashville: Graded Press, Fall 1986), pp. 3-5.

34. See Cheslyn Jones, Geoffrey Wainwright, and Edward Yarnold, eds., *The Study of Spirituality*, (New York: Oxford University Press, 1986), for an exhaustive survey of the history of spirituality.

35. Matthew Fox, *On Becoming a Musical, Mystical Bear: Spirituality American Style* (New York: Paulist, 1976), pp. ix, xxiv.

36. Matthew Fox, *Original Blessing: A Primer in Creation Spirituality Presented in Four Paths, Twenty-Six Themes, and Two Questions* (Santa Fe: Bear & Company, 1983), pp. 20-21.

37. Lee, *The Spirituality of the Religious Educator*, p. 19.

38. Peter A. Manzi, "Skills Assessment in Career Counseling: A Developmental Approach," *The Career Development Quarterly* 36:1 (September 1987), pp. 45-53.

39. Charles F. Kemp, *The Pastor and Vocational Counseling* (St. Louis: Bethany, 1961), pp. 129-133. Many of the examples in the book are dated, but generally the principles given are still valid and it represents one of the last efforts to guide pastors (and DREs) in this area.

40. James Michael Lee, *The Religious Education We Need: Toward the Renewal of Christian Education* (Birmingham, Ala.: Religious Education Press, 1976), p. 152.

41. Eugene Kennedy, *Crisis Counseling: An Essential Guide for Nonprofessional Counselors* (New York: Continuum, 1981), p. 1.

42. Maria Harris, *The D.R.E. Book* (New York: Paulist, 1976), p. 184.

43. Andrew D. Lester, *Pastoral Care with Children in Crisis* (Philadelphia: Westminster, 1986), p. 33.

44. William Van Ornum and John B. Mordock, *Crisis Counseling with Children and Adolescents: A Guide for Nonprofessional Counselors* (New York: Continuum, 1984), pp. 86-101

45. Eugene Kennedy, *Sexual Counseling: A Practical Guide for Nonprofessional Counselors* (New York: Continuum, 1980), p. 117.

46. Kennedy, *Crisis Counseling*, p. 61.

Chapter 11

Conclusion

The vision of the early pioneers who responded to William Rainey Harper's call to establish the Religious Education Association was to improve instruction in the Sunday school integrating the best theories of educational psychology and social science, including the best of the liberal biblical and theological scholarship. As the field matured, the focus changed from the Sunday school to the broader concept of church school. Eventually, the multifacets of church education were included. Currently, religious education relates to the diversity of educational opportunities found in the church from leadership training, parent enrichment, and RCIA/adult confirmation studies, to preparation for a child's first communion and the basic CCD or Sunday school programs.

The New Vision for Religious Education

It is important to remember the distinction between the specific field of religious education and the profession of the DRE. The academic field of religious education in most seminaries has been based in practical theology. The emphasis tends to be on the content of theology, Bible, and general religion subjects.

One is reminded of the radical commentary on public education written in 1939, *The Saber-Tooth Curriculum.*[1] Even after the tigers had died, the tribal education leaders sought to continue the original curriculum of tiger-scaring. "They claimed that a practical education based in real-life needs, such as protecting the camp from bears was not timeless, not able to stand like a solid rock in the middle of a raging torrent. The purpose of the saber-tooth curriculum was not to scare tigers, but its purpose was to give that noble courage which carries over into all the affairs of life and which can never come from so base an activity as bear-killing."[2]

The appropriate vision for the academic field of religious education is to be grounded in education. However, the choice of the theory base of education is as critical as the decision to ground it in education. Those theories of education which are primarily transmissive,[3] such as those typically derived from theology or devised by theologians, are incapable of meeting the needs of current religious education. Religious education is more than the learning of certain essential facts or ideas.[4] Even those progressive educational models which are primarily concerned with cognitive problem solving or praxis knowing fail to provide a base for the education of the whole person.

Religious education needs a framework based in transformation models of education. Personal and cultural transformation is considered in religious education. The learner is not passive but interacts with the community's heritage so that both the learner and the tradition are transformed. The invitation is to create intersections in which human life becomes transformed in the direction of creative-responsive love. Education that challenges traditional stereotypes and invites commitment to a style of discipleship lived in the world, leading to love and justice for all in the global community is central to this new vision of religious education.

The challenge is to communicate with children and youth whose vision of creation consists of multiple universes rather than a single universe, black holes, and expectation of hyperspace travel within their lifetime. Interaction and transformation of the learner with the community's tradition (subject-matter content), with the global world, and with God are components of an educational theory base that will meet the conceptual, emotional, and religious needs of the highly educated persons who are going to be part of our churches in the coming years.

The Vision for the Profession

Professional practice should inform the educational preparation of the DRE. Based on the functional roles, in addition to a basic knowledge of general religious subjects, the DRE needs to be grounded in religious education, communication theory, and the social sciences of administration, organizational development, psychology, and sociology.

The profession of director of religious education should begin to claim its rightful role as a professional specialization. The fact does not diminish the need for general lay ministries in the area of education, nor does it detract from the role of a pastor who serves multiple roles in small churches. As a professional specialist in education, the DRE is not in competition with the senior clergy who serve as generalists. To be a professional is to be competent in the content of the religious faith, in the means to communicate that faith, and in ways to enable the congregational members to respond to the faith as people of God with ministries in the world.

The professional DRE is capable of envisioning the whole church's work and understanding how the educational program with its various age-level ministries, special events, evolving organizational life fit into a comprehensive whole. In addition, skills in working with groups, as well as working individually with persons at the feeling level are needed.

The DRE is also professionally prepared to lead and administer a comprehensive education program, making decisions based on theoretical understandings rather than hunches. Religious education is comprehensive in its concern for the whole person, ministering to the spiritual and general-life needs of individuals of every age level and circumstance. It brings concerns that any theological interpretation expressed in the church today be relevant to a culture that uses science as a mode of thinking so that individuals and the social fabric of humanity are transformed by the living interaction with the God of the Bible and the God of our present lives. Religious education is primarily built upon the contributions of the social sciences including education, organizational development, sociology, and psychology.

The functional roles of the DRE, such as program administrator and developer, teacher, and spiritual mentor are relevant to the professional serving the church in a narrowly defined educator's position or in the broader program director's job description. Although the DRE brings the professional skills of working with organizations in terms of educational research, planning, and evaluation, the DRE also shares in the task of interpreting the faith for the community by teaching in organized settings and witnessing to the faith by living out personal faith commitments.

As a professional, the DRE can and indeed must be flexible. Because of a commitment to continuing education, the DRE does not have to be anxious about changes either in procedures, curriculum design, or theological perspectives. Emerging technologies of computers and videos can be integrated into a professional's technical skill area so that the resources from the broad ecumenical church will be available for the local church's ministry.

Education and theology are not enemies, nor are education and ministry. To be professionally grounded in education does not deny the importance of theology as an area for content expertise. It is a goal of religious education to enable persons to have a personal relationship with God. It is never the transmission of facts for their own sake. To enable persons to achieve to the highest level of faith development appropriate for their age level becomes a way to express that relationship. Religious education understands that ministry does not end in the institutional church but begins as the people of God serve in the world as the incarnation of God. The professional DRE offers the church planning skills and content opportunities that will enable the laity to be in ministry as the people of God in the world.

NOTES

1. Harold Benjamin, *The Saber-Tooth Curriculum* (New York: McGraw-Hill, 1939).

2. Ibid., p. 43.

3. The models of transmission, transaction, and transformation are described in Chapter 8 above as they are adapted to religious education. See John P. Miller and Wayne Seller, *Curriculum Perspectives and Practice* (New York: Longman, 1985), for descriptions in public education.

4. This philosophy is represented in Allan Bloom, *The Closing of the American Mind* (New York: Simon and Schuster, 1987) and E. D. Hirsch Jr., *Cultural Literacy: What Every American Needs to Know* (Boston: Houghton Mifflin, 1987).

Index of Names

243

Subject Index